THE SCHOOL
OF
JESUS
CRUCIFIED

THE SCHOOL
OF
JESUS
CRUCIFIED

From the Italian of

Fr. Ignatius of the Side of Jesus,
Passionist

TAN BOOKS AND PUBLISHERS, INC.
Rockford, Illinois 61105

Nihil Obstat: Alphonse of the Blessed Virgin Mary
                  Provincial of the Passionist
                      Congregation in England and Ireland

Imprimatur: ✛ Henry Edward [Manning]
                  Cardinal Archbishop of Westminster

ISBN: 0-89555-732-0

Illustrations of the Stations of the Cross are from *Way of the Cross: Liguorian Method*, Benziger Brothers, 1908.

Printed and bound in the United States of America.

TAN BOOKS AND PUBLISHERS, INC.
P.O. Box 424
Rockford, Illinois 61105
2002

"Nihil tam salutiferum nobis, quam quoti-die cogitare quanto pro nobis pertulit Deus et homo."

"There is nothing so salutary for us as to meditate every day on what Jesus, God and man, has endured for our sakes."

—St. Augustine
Serm. 33 ad Fratres in eremo

About the Author

FR. IGNATIUS (Carsidoni) of the Side of Jesus (1801-1844) was one of the behind-the-scenes influences on the rebirth of the Catholic Faith in England. Fr. Ignatius taught theology in Rome. There he became fired with the zeal of his fellow Passionist, Blessed Dominic Barberi (1792-1849), for the conversion of England. Bl. Dominic had "inherited" this supernatural passion from St. Paul of the Cross, the founder of the Passionists.

In 1831, an English Catholic lady named Mrs. Louisa (Spencer) Canning met Fr. Ignatius in Rome and from him "caught" the Passionist zeal for the conversion of her homeland. Mrs. Canning became part of a little network of Catholics who prayed ardently and worked valiantly to bring the Passionists—and the Catholic Faith—to England. After many trials, Bl. Dominic finally succeeded in planting the Passionist Order there in 1842. His work coincided with "The Oxford Movement" in the Church of England; Bl. Dominic was God's instrument in inaugurating the "second spring" of the Catholic Faith in England, the most famous element of which was John Henry Newman's reception into the Catholic Church by Bl. Dominic Barberi on October 9, 1845. Fr. Ignatius had played his providential part in these crucial first steps of the return of England to the Catholic Faith.

Information from *Shepherd of the Second Spring: The Life of Blessed Dominic Barberi, C.P.*, by Jude Mead, C.P., St. Anthony's Guild, Paterson, NJ, 1968, and The Passionist Historical Archives, Union City, NJ.

Preface to the 1895 Edition

IN PRESENTING this valuable little book to the Catholic public, it may be well to say a few words on the nature and advantages of such a work. It is a translation from the Italian of Father Ignatius of the Side of Jesus, a member of the Passionist Order, and may be recommended as one of the best books that has yet appeared in any language on the sufferings and death of Our Divine Lord, presenting at the same time a simple and easy method of uniting our lives and actions, our sufferings, our mortal toil and the weariness of spirit that follows us our whole life through, with the sufferings of Our Crucified Lord. The plan of the book is so clearly laid down in the author's *Address to the Devout Reader* that it is unnecessary to say more on that head. But the advantages to be derived from the habitual use of such a book cannot be too highly estimated, and to that we would call the reader's attention.

"The School of Jesus Crucified!" What Christian would not wish to study therein, to learn wisdom and patience and resignation to the Divine Will from the example of the God-man, who came on earth and assumed our frail mortality to be to us a model, as well as a Redeemer? This is the school in which all the Saints of God obtained their honors. There doctors and schoolmen, popes and prelates learned wisdom, virgins purity, martyrs and confessors strength and fortitude; there all the faithful learned faith and piety. The whole world united could not teach one lesson of the heavenly science whose treasures are all contained in this small volume. Whosoever would gain eternal life must become as a little child, and apply himself with humble, docile heart to study in "The School of Jesus Crucified," the manual of which is here presented to the Catholics of America. It has been prepared expressly to spread devotion to the Passion of Our Lord by a distinguished member of the Passionist Order. The present translation will be found a very good one. The work is henceforward to be used by the Passionist Fathers in their missions and has received all the additions necessary to adapt it to the purpose of a mission book. It contains Devotions for Mass, also Prayers for Confession and Communion, and the Holy Way of the Cross. With these few remarks, we commend it to all devout Christians as a book calculated to increase their fervor and unite them more closely to Jesus Crucified.

Passionist Monastery, West Hoboken
Feast of All Saints, November 1, 1895
With the approbation of F. Ignatius
    of the Infant Jesus (*Paoli*),
    Passionist G. V.

Contents

Exercises of Devotion

THE SCHOOL
OF
JESUS
CRUCIFIED

Address to the Devout Reader

THE principal object I have had in view in publishing this little book has been to awaken in the hearts of all Christians a devout remembrance of the Passion of Jesus Christ. I have attempted to lay down some simple rules, by the observance of which, in the principal actions of the day, we may never lose sight of our Divine Model, and of His bitter sufferings. I have arranged a short meditation on some mystery of the Passion of Jesus Christ, for each day of the month, in order to facilitate the practice of spending some small portion of every day in meditating on the sufferings of our Crucified Redeemer. And in order that the most sacred actions of the Christian's day, such as the reception of the Sacraments, and assistance at Mass, may be performed with more piety by means of a devout remembrance of the Passion, I have attempted to arrange an easy method for that purpose. I have endeavored, as far as possible, to adapt my method to the requirements of all classes of persons, so that everyone may find therein a practical means of continually dwelling in spirit in the wounds of Jesus Crucified; and thence deriving

1

those innumerable spiritual blessings which are the fruits of our Saviour's Passion.

It will be utterly useless for anyone to read this book solely for the sake of novelty, as it contains nothing but what may be found scattered over the pages of many other books of piety. Read it, on the contrary, O devout Christian, in a spirit of devotion, and with a sincere desire for the sanctification of your soul. Faithfully and perseveringly practice what you read, and you may be sure of experiencing the most blessed effects in your soul. A great change would take place in the lives of many Christians, if such were the spirit in which they read all the good books which are in their possession. I hope that the brevity of this little work, as well as the importance and sublimity of the subject treated of, will induce many persons to profit by these observations.

To each meditation is added some particular fruit to be drawn from it, at least for that one day, and some devout practice, in honor of Jesus Crucified. If you are desirous of meditating to some purpose, you will neglect neither the one nor the other. You will also every day find an example applicable to the preceding meditation, which I have carefully selected from the Lives of the Saints and Servants of God, and which I propose to your consideration as an additional and efficacious inducement to the practice of some particular virtue, and to confirm you more and more in the holy resolution of frequently meditating on the sufferings of Our Redeemer, from whom the saints were quite unable to distract their minds and hearts, and who was to them the source of all consolation and spiritual happiness.

Jesus Crucified to the Heart of the Christian

"SON, for thy sake I have sacrificed My life on a cross, amidst the most fearful sufferings and tortures; can I then be requiring too much when I ask thee sometimes to remember all I have done for thee; sometimes to call to mind My Passion? Can a Father ask less of thee, O son, a Father who for love of thee has suffered and died, was most cruelly transfixed with nails, and breathed His last, plunged in a sea of sorrows? I ask thee not for thy blood, although I shed every drop of Mine for the love of thee. I ask thee not to endure the scourge, to which also I submitted for thy sake. I ask thee not for the sacrifice of thy life, although I laid down My own with infinite love, for the salvation of thy soul. No, My son. I ask thee but to pause for a moment, to contemplate Me suffering, covered with wounds, and dying on the Cross; to contemplate Me in the state to which I am reduced by My ardent desire for thy salvation. I ask of thee a thought, a feeling of love, a sigh, a tear of compassion at the sight of My countless sufferings; can thy heart, O My son, be so hardened and unfeeling as to refuse thy tender Father, thy loving Redeemer, this slight tribute of

5

gratitude—the occasional recollection of My Passion? Canst thou so liberally bestow thy thoughts and affections upon the world, upon creatures, and upon thy own interests, and yet refuse Me even a sigh, or a feeling of love and sympathy? Ah, son! I beseech thee to satisfy My desires, and not to refuse what I ask of thee. Remember all My sufferings, My wounds, and My death, compassionate and love Me. At least, let thy first thoughts each day be devoted to the remembrance of some one of My bitter sufferings; let at least one sigh be given to thy Crucified Saviour as the hours speed on their course; and let the last emotion of thy heart, after all the cares of the day are over, be a feeling of compassion for thy Redeemer expiring on a Cross.

"Ah, My son, forget not how much thy salvation has cost Me; forget not at how dear a rate I have ransomed thy soul, how much blood I have shed, and how many sufferings I have endured in order to atone for thy sins! If thy mind is continually occupied with such thoughts, and if thou dost often meditate upon My Passion, never, never more wilt thou so barbarously crucify Me again by willful sins."

A Practical Rule of Christian Life for Daily Observance

NOTHING can be begun well unless begun in God, the sole Fountain of all real good; begin, therefore, each day by raising your mind and heart to God.

1. On awaking in the morning, let your first thoughts be devoted to this great truth: *God is here present;* and make an act of lively faith in His Divine Presence. Let your first action be the Sign of the Cross, according to the custom of the early Christians; your first words the holy Names of Jesus and Mary; and the first impulse of your heart an offering of yourself to God, by saying with the deepest feelings of respect: *I adore Thee, O my God; I love Thee with my whole heart; I thank Thee for all the blessings Thou hast bestowed upon me, and especially for dying for me on the Cross, shedding all Thy blood for the salvation of my soul, and preserving me in life up to the present moment; to Thee I consecrate my heart and my whole self.*

2. Nothing can be more thoroughly in opposition to a well-regulated Christian life than late rising;

for which reason never allow sloth to get the better of you, but rise early, and dress yourself diligently and modestly, remembering the presence of God. While dressing, devoutly reflect upon the sufferings which Jesus Christ endured in His most sacred Body to save you from the torments of Hell. Offer your heart to Jesus Crucified, and promise to spend the day granted you by His goodness, in loving and serving Him, and in reflecting, as often as possible, upon His bitter Passion. Remember that the day you are now entering upon may be your last, and let your mind be deeply impressed with this truth. Thus, death will never find you unprepared, and you will pass each day in a manner worthy of a Christian.

3. As soon as you are dressed, kneel down and say your prayers with the greatest possible devotion. You will be wanting in religious duty if you omit this practice, and such negligence is the fatal source of many misfortunes, and the cause of the loss of innumerable souls. If you defer the payment of this tribute to God, other occupations will intervene, and you will not be able to find time for fulfilling so important a duty.

Prayer containing the Principal Acts Which a Christian Ought to Make

I BELIEVE, O Lord; but do Thou increase my faith. All my hopes are in Thee; do Thou secure them. I love Thee with my whole heart; teach me to love Thee daily more and more. I am sorry for having offended Thee; do Thou increase my sorrow.

O my God, grant that my will may be ever conformable to Thine, so that I may will whatever Thou willest, because it is Thy Will, and in the manner Thou willest. Grant that I may in everything seek to please Thee, and to promote Thy greater glory.

Grant that I may strenuously labor to serve Thee faithfully, to observe the greatest modesty in my deportment, preserve my purity unsullied, overcome every temptation, avoid all occasions of sin, and persevere in Thy grace.

To Thee, O my God, do I offer all my thoughts, that they may ever be wholly Thine; my words, that they may always be conformable to Thy Will; my actions, that they may all be in accordance with Thy law; and my sufferings, that they may be made acceptable in Thy sight.

I offer every breath I draw, every step I take, and all my labors, cares, anxieties, sorrows, weaknesses, and feelings of repugnance to suffering, in union with the infinite merits of Jesus Christ, and the Dolors of the most Blessed Virgin Mary. I offer them all to Thee in honor of the Passion and Death of my Redeemer, in satisfaction for my sins, to obtain the eternal salvation of poor sinners, and by way of suffrage for the holy souls in Purgatory. (Often renew these intentions, and you will thus sanctify all the actions of the day.)

O my God, bestow upon me the gift of Thy love, a sincere hatred for every kind of sin, love for my neighbor, and a contempt of the world. Make me prudent in my undertakings, constant in good works, patient in affliction, humble in prosperity, and resigned to Thy holy Will in whatever may befall me.

Enlighten my understanding, in order that I may know Thee, O my God, to love Thee, the vanities of the world to abhor them, the deceits of the devil to avoid them, and the malice of sin to detest it. Impart strength and fervor to my will, so that it may never yield to any of the fatal insinuations of the devil, but may courageously resist all temptations. Purify my body, and sanctify my soul.

Grant that I may spend this day in preparing for a good death, that I may fear Thy judgments, endeavor to escape Hell, never fall into sin, and gain Heaven through Thy great mercy. Amen.

4. Then dedicate yourself to the most blessed Virgin Mary, to be her servant and child, and thus place yourself under her especial protection. Be very exact in daily offering this little tribute of respect to Mary, your loving Patroness and Mother, and you will not fail to experience the blessed effects of her powerful patronage. Devoutly recite three *Hail Marys* before her image or picture, together with the following.

Prayer by which a Devout Christian May Dedicate Himself to The Blessed Virgin

O MOST holy Virgin Mary, Mother of God, although most unworthy of being thy servant yet inspired with confidence in thy extreme goodness, and filled with an earnest desire of serving thee, I, N_____ N_____, this day choose thee, in the presence of thy Son, of my Angel Guardian, and of the whole Court of Heaven, for my especial Advocate, Mother, and Queen, and I firmly purpose, with the assistance of thy prayers, to serve thee constantly, and to do all that lies in my power to cause thee to be served by all men. I therefore humbly beseech thee, O most compassionate Mother, through the Precious Blood of thy holy Son, to receive me as thy devout client and thy servant forever, assist me in all my actions, and obtain grace for me, that I may so regulate all my thoughts, words, and deeds, as never to offend thy Son Jesus. Forget me not, and never forsake me, either now or at the hour of my death. Amen.

5. Regularly every day, as soon as you have finished your prayers, make half, or at least a quarter of an hour's meditation, for which you may prepare your mind by the preparatory acts given on page 28; then read slowly and attentively the Meditation on the Passion of Jesus Christ, as marked for that day in this little book. If you are desirous of leading a devout life, you will never omit this meditation. Be not of the number of those who say they have not time to meditate when they can find plenty of time to dissipate it in useless amusements. Once seriously desire your salvation, and you will not be at a loss for time to meditate.

6. Your meditation being finished, you should then resolve that in all your actions you will seek to imitate Jesus suffering and dying for your sake. Resolve that during the whole course of the day, you will most lovingly remain in spirit by the side of your Divine suffering Redeemer, calling to mind as often as possible that portion of His Passion on which you have been meditating in the morning. Nothing can be more efficacious in affording us consolation under the trials of this life than the remembrance of the sufferings of Jesus.

7. Reflect that you are traveling through a hostile country, where at every step you are liable to meet with dangerous snares; therefore, in order that you may always have some place of security in which to take refuge, select one of the most holy Wounds of Jesus for your abode that day; often retire there to pour forth the feelings of your heart in acts of love and compassion for Jesus who endured those wounds for your salvation, and ask Him to bestow upon you the gift of some virtue, which you may endeavor to practice in a particular manner during the day.

For Sunday

The loving Heart of Jesus—Ask Him to bestow upon you the gift of His holy love and of a spirit of detachment from all earthly affections.

For Monday

The Wound of the Left Foot—Ask for Holy perseverance.

For Tuesday

The Wound of the Right Foot—Ask for true contrition for your sins.

For Wednesday

The Wound of the Left Hand—Ask for humility.

For Thursday

The Wound of the Right Hand—Ask for resignation in all things to the Will of God.

For Friday

The Sacred Wound of the Side—Ask for grace to maintain a continual remembrance of the Passion and Death of Jesus.

For Saturday

The suffering heart of the Blessed Virgin Mary—Ask for sincere devotion and tender love towards her.

8. Never let a day pass without hearing Mass; and that you may more easily do so with devotion and benefit to yourself, go in spirit to Calvary, and remain there by the side of Jesus, who for your sake offers the sacrifice of His life to His Eternal Father, and for your sake renews it on the Altar. If you cannot assist at the holy Sacrifice in person, be there at least in desire, and offer this pious desire to Our Lord; unite yourself in spirit with all the faithful who this day hear Mass, and, above all, with the priests who are celebrating, and in union with them offer Jesus Christ, and His Passion, His Blood, and His Death, to the Eternal Father in satisfaction for your sins, for the conversion of poor sinners, and for the salvation of your soul; and beseech Him, through the merits of His adorable, Crucified Son, to give you grace never to fall into mortal sin.

Daily attendance at Mass is a source of many graces, both spiritual and temporal; endeavor, therefore, never to deprive yourself of them.

9. Begin your daily occupations with the intention of fulfilling the Will of God. Be careful at the commencement of each action to offer it to Our Lord in union with all His labors, fatigues and sufferings; and to have a pure intention of pleasing God, of promoting His glory, and of fulfilling His holy Will in all things. You will not suffer thereby more fatigue, but, on the contrary, far less, and your actions will all be meritorious. Great is the fatigue, frequent are the failures, and numerous are the annoyances experienced through the want of such pious intentions.

10. Make it a rule to employ all your time in a Christian manner, punctually to fulfill all the obligations of your state of life, and carefully to avoid everything that can offend God and be hurtful to your soul. What bitter grief, agony, and despair is felt at the hour of death by those who have not led a Christian life, and who have made a bad use of that time which was given them solely to gain Heaven!

11. Amidst your occupations, forget not sometimes to raise your heart to God by pious ejaculations. If you are suffering from weariness and fatigue, think of Jesus crucified, and say to Him with all the affection of your heart: *O my sweet Jesus, how much more didst Thou suffer for my sake! How much pain and sorrow and how many sufferings didst Thou endure for the salvation of my soul! O my loving Redeemer, how much has my soul cost Thee! I thank Thee for dying on a Cross for the love of me.* Thus you will labor as becomes a Christian, and the devout remembrance of Jesus Crucified will lighten every burden and relieve you under any fatigue.

12. Fly idleness as the mother of all evil. Avoid those amusements which pander to the passions. Enter not into any society which may be prejudicial to your innocence. You are to be a Christian in your recreations as well as in your occupations. Recreate your mind by some innocent amusements, but remember that the early Christians would have considered it a crime to appear in the Circus, or at public profane spectacles.

13. In anxieties, sorrows, and afflictions, have recourse in spirit to Jesus Crucified; make known to Him your sufferings with entire confidence, offer them to Him, and take courage in the thought that if you suffer something for the love of Jesus, you therefore resemble Him, and bear Him company in His sufferings, and are meriting the glory of Heaven. Remember that Jesus has suffered more than you do, and that He suffered for your sake.

14. In time of temptation, and when in danger of offending God, instantly call to mind the Wounds of Jesus, invoke His name with perfect confidence, and imagine that you behold Him on the Cross, lovingly saying to you, *"Son, do not offend Me; do not renew My Passion and Death. Son, I have always loved thee, why wilt thou now grieve My heart by thy hateful sins?"* Prostrate at His feet, renew your determination rather to die than offend so dear a Father, so loving a Redeemer. There can be no thought more efficacious in preventing us from committing sin than that of the sufferings and wounds of Jesus Crucified.

15. If your neighbor offend you in word or deed, or if he weary or contradict you, remember the outrages, contempt, and injuries suffered by Jesus during the course of His Passion, and say to yourself: *My soul, see with what humility and meekness Jesus the Son of God keeps silence in the midst of all the evil treatment He has to endure; and wilt thou nourish feelings of resentment? Ah, no, my sweetest Jesus, for Thy sake I will suffer in silence.*

16. When you feel sad, sorrowful, or disturbed in mind, think of Jesus agonizing in the garden, and overwhelmed with the deepest sorrow at the sight of your sins, and the prospect of His own most bitter Passion. Unite yourself in spirit to Him, and say with Him: *Beloved Heavenly Father, Thy will be done!* For want of Christian reflections like these, men often give way to feelings of impatience most unworthy of a follower of Jesus Christ Crucified.

17. When you see the poor, the sick, the unfortunate, and the imprisoned, entertain charitable feelings of pity for them, and relieve them if it be in your power, remembering that it was for love of you that Jesus Christ became poor, endured so

many sufferings, and did not refuse to be igno-
miniously bound in order to liberate your soul
from the chains of sin. To a lover of Jesus Crucified, there is nothing which may not frequently
suggest thoughts of Him, and of His sufferings.

18. When you take your meals, remember that
Jesus Crucified had not even a drop of water
wherewith to assuage His thirst during the last
hours of His bitter agony. Never sit down to your
meals without first saying some short prayer; nor
rise from them without lifting up your mind and
heart with feelings of sincere gratitude for His
goodness, and conclude by making the Sign of the
Cross. Such has ever been the pious custom of all
the Faithful from the earliest ages of the Church.
To do otherwise would show a great want of piety,
and be an imitation of the pagans and infidels.

19. In time of prosperity, or when everything succeeds according to your desires, and your heart is
overflowing with joy and happiness, do not lose
sight of Jesus Crucified, or forget how He endured
the most painful sufferings and agonizing dereliction of spirit, without the slightest consolation or
relief. Say to Him: *In Thee, and in Thy wounds, O
my suffering Jesus, and not in creatures, will I
ever seek consolation.* The joys and merriment of
the world are nought but vanity. The service of
God and sincere love of Jesus are, on the contrary,
an unfailing source of pure happiness to the true
Christian.

20. When you have had the misfortune to fall into any sin, hasten to cast yourself at the feet of Jesus Crucified, implore His pardon for the offense you have committed, and beseech Him, through His Passion and Death, to forgive you, and to bestow upon you grace never to offend Him more. If your sin was a mortal one, endeavor to go to Confession as soon as possible. Beware of living for any length of time with your soul defiled by sin, that enemy of God and crucifier of Jesus Christ. Remember that you might be surprised by death, and precipitated headlong into Hell.

21. Conclude the day by saying your prayers with great devotion. Fail not every evening to spend a short time in reflecting upon some point of the Passion of Christ. Remember, at least, to thank Him most gratefully for the love which induced Him to die for your sake. Say to Him, with lively feelings of gratitude: *My sweet Lord, I thank Thee for having suffered so much, and having died on the Cross for love of me. Most amiable Redeemer, through the merits of Thy Passion, save my soul;* together with three *Our Fathers* in memory of His bitter Passion, and three *Hail Marys* in honor of our Lady of Dolors, to place yourself under her protection.

22. Before going to bed, examine your conscience, and make an act of contrition, never daring to fall asleep with your soul defiled by mortal sin, but cancel every stain by sincere repentance, when you have not been able to approach the Sacrament of Penance. It would be the very height of imprudence to close your eyes quietly in a sleep which may be followed by death, without having discovered and bewailed all your sins at the foot of the Crucifix.

23. Undress yourself with modesty and decency, commending your soul to God, and begging your Angel Guardian to bestow his assistance upon you, by saying an *Our Father* in his honor. As you lie down to rest, think of Jesus stretched on the hard bed of the Cross, and fastened down to it by sharp nails. Say to Him: *Ah, my sweet Jesus, Thou art nailed to the Cross, and enduring unspeakable tortures, and I am lying on this bed! I compassionate Thee, and love Thee with my whole heart.*

24. Fall asleep in the midst of pious thoughts, such as these, and thus you will sanctify even your sleep. When you wake in the night, raise your heart to your suffering Jesus, who should be the beloved object of all your thoughts and affections. Say to Him: *My Jesus, I am Thine, do Thou save me. My Jesus, dying on the Cross for my salvation, grant that I may ever love Thee. My beloved Jesus, I thank Thee for all Thy love. I compassionate Thee in all Thy sufferings.*

25. You might also, when in bed, imagine yourself to have reached the last hour of your life, and to be lying with the holy Crucifix in your hand,

and you might ask yourself the following questions: *"If I were now about to die, what should I wish to have done? Would this Crucifix afford me consolation and comfort, because I always loved Him who was Crucified, or would it be a reproach and terror because I offended Him and abused His love and mercy?"* No words can express how useful such reflections, if seriously made, would be to induce a Christian to resolve on leading a more holy life.

In this manner you will pass your day in a holy manner, gain a great deal of merit with little comparative fatigue, sanctify all your actions, and give satisfaction to the loving Heart of your suffering Jesus.

A Practical Method of Meditating on the Most Sacred Passion of Jesus Christ

PERHAPS there is no subject for meditation more suitable to every class of persons than the most sacred Passion of our Lord Jesus Christ. In it may sinners find the encouragement and graces necessary for their conversion; from it may beginners derive strength and fervor wherewith to subdue their passions; in it may the good discover fresh incentives to advance in the paths of virtue. In short, there are none who will not find it an inexhaustible mine of hidden treasures, and an endless source of graces and spiritual blessings. In all ages it has been a favorite exercise of the Saints, who greatly to their spiritual consolation have been in the habit of spending hours, day and night, in meditation on the bitter sufferings of their Saviour. So much is not required of you, O devout Christian, but only that you should daily spend half, or at least a quarter of an hour, in attentive consideration of some point of the Passion of Jesus. The man who is desirous of ascertaining the degree of pungency possessed by a grain of mustard seed, chews it leisurely, tastes it deliberately, keeps it in his mouth, and is careful

23

not to swallow it whole, by which means its heat is fully communicated to his palate so as to bring tears to his eyes. Similar are the mysteries of the Passion of Jesus Christ; swallowed, as it were, in one mouthful, they touch not the heart; superficially run over by a single passing thought, their virtue is not experienced in the soul; but when slowly digested by attentive consideration, they give rise to holy affections and wonderful resolutions. Only make the attempt, apply your mind diligently to this holy exercise, and you will be convinced, by your own experience, how great a change of heart, reformation of life, hatred of sin, and love of God it will produce in your soul. Make the attempt, and you will behold all the difficulties foolishly apprehended in meditation by foolish worldings vanish before your eyes, and you will feel how sweet it is to the soul to remain in silence, contemplating Jesus Crucified.

In order to facilitate the practice of this holy exercise, I have arranged a Meditation, divided into three points, upon the principal mysteries of the Sacred Passion of Christ, for every day of the month. Do not be satisfied with merely glancing your eye down it and reading its contents in a hasty cursory manner, but read it very slowly, and pause frequently, in order to reflect attentively upon what you are reading.

Whatever mystery of the Passion you take for the subject of your meditation, you may always bestow attentive consideration on the following five points:

1. The infinite greatness of Him who suffers.

2. The excess of suffering and ignominy which He endures.

3. How great is the love with which He suffers.

4. The infinite unworthiness and vileness of those for whom He suffers.

5. That His principal aim in all His sufferings is to be loved by men.

Let these reflections sink deep into your mind, and if one of them, or any other point of the meditation which you are reading, should make a lively impression upon your heart, dwell awhile on it without caring to go on any further. You may even make your prayer upon the same point for several days, and even weeks, in succession, if you find it productive of good thoughts, reserving the other points for the following days, and you will soon perceive how useful such repetitions will be to your soul. After your mind has been employed in attentively considering and reflecting upon the mystery and its attendant circumstances, it will not be difficult for your will to be excited and touched by different holy affections, which you ought to pass some short time in exercising with great calmness of spirit, giving free vent to the emotions of your heart, and following the sweet impulses of God's grace.

The principal affections to which you may excite your mind during your meditation upon the sufferings of Jesus are as follows:

1. Admiration—*How is it possible,* you may say, *that a God can suffer so much for the love of me, a vile creature? Oh, what excessive love and charity!*

2. Gratitude—By exciting yourself to interior emotions of gratitude and appreciation of the greatness of the benefits bestowed upon you by Jesus in His Passion, feeling how much you are indebted to your dear Redeemer, and resolving constantly to praise and thank Him for His infinite love toward you.

3. Compassion—By compassionating your Crucified Jesus overwhelmed with sorrow and suffering, and by earnestly desiring that you had been present to have afforded some relief to your most afflicted Lord.

4. Contrition for your sins—By considering all that those guilty pleasures in which you have indulged contrary to the law of God have cost Jesus Christ, and how large a share you have had in His Passion and Death. Bewail your sins at His feet, and firmly resolve to die rather than ever more to offend a father so worthy of your love.

5. Love—By protesting that you will bestow all the affections of your heart upon Him who has so much loved you, and by desiring to have, if possible, a thousand hearts solely occupied in loving Him, and corresponding in some measure with His infinite charity. Offer and consecrate yourself entirely to the love of Jesus Crucified. Desire that He may be known and loved by all men.

6. Prayer—By asking of Our Lord grace to love Him, to imitate Him, and never to offend Him. Endeavor to inspire your heart with lively feelings of confidence that God will grant all your requests through the merits of the Passion of Jesus Christ. Your most fervent request ought to be for grace to correct some habitual fault, to overcome your predominant passion, and to practice that virtue in which you are most deficient, and which has occupied a prominent place in the subject of your meditation, thereby to imitate Jesus Christ; for the imitation of Christ should be the principal object of every meditation on His Passion. Having made the affections, you should proceed to resolutions. Promise Our Lord that you will never more displease Him by mortal or even deliberate venial sin. Determine to avoid such or such a fault (*name it*), and to make use of such or such means (*specify which*). For example, to fly from such or such a house, to avoid such and such a companion, instantly to dismiss this or that thought, immediately to curb those bursts of passion, to place a guard over your eyes, to keep silence on such and such occasions, etc., etc.

Remember that the principal fruit of your prayer consists in these resolutions, and far more in keeping them faithfully. Place them in the sacred Wounds of Jesus, and in the hands of Mary, and implore grace to put them in practice. Keep them in view during the whole course of the day, and an occasional examination as to the manner in which you are practicing them will be a most efficacious means of ensuring your fidelity.

Whoever follows the instructions here given will discover by experience how easy a practice is meditation on the Passion of Jesus Christ, and will clearly perceive how greatly those are deceived who say that it is a practice suitable only to religious and too difficult for seculars. Meditation, as I have already said, is in fact nothing more than the exercise of the memory, understanding and will, upon some mystery or truth of our holy Faith. Now, if we are accustomed to exercise those powers from morning till night on sensible objects which are often sinful, why should we not be able, with the assistance of God's grace, to exercise them in the consideration of the bitter Passion of Jesus Christ, our most loving Redeemer?

ACTS OF PREPARATION FOR MEDITATION

An Act of Faith

I BELIEVE, O my God, that Thou art here present. Wherever I direct the eyes of my mind, there do I find Thee. O how wonderful and incomprehensible is the omnipresence of my God! Thou dost deign to converse with me during this hour, and to communicate Thyself to my poor soul with so much love and condescension. O how great is the goodness of my God!

An Act of Adoration

O MY God, from out of the deep abyss of my nothingness, I humbly adore Thy infinite Majesty and Greatness with my whole heart and soul. I acknowledge Thee for my First Beginning, and my most blessed Last End, for my great and only Good, and for my All in time and eternity. I would willingly adore Thee as Thou dost deserve, and as my own heart desires to adore Thee, but since I never could succeed in so doing, I offer Thee all the acts of adoration which have been, or will be offered to Thee for eternity by the Saints and Angels in Heaven, and by the blessed Virgin, as also those made by the most holy Soul of Jesus Christ now and during all eternity. Accept them, O my God, in the place of those which I am unable to offer Thy Sovereign Majesty.

An Act of Humility

WHO am I, O my God, that I should dare to present myself before Thy infinite Majesty? I am a most wretched creature, or rather, an abyss of nothingness, an abominable sinner immersed in a sink of uncleanness. I am an abyss of sin and misery, deserving of nothing but Hell, where I should long ago have dwelt, had not Thy mercy so lovingly delivered me. I acknowledge, O my God, my great unworthiness, and I confess that I deserve to be forever banished from Thee; nevertheless in Thy infinite condescension Thou dost call, invite, and command me to come to Thee, to address Thee, and to converse with Thee. How great must be Thy goodness, O my God, who disdaineth not to admit me to familiar intercourse with Thee! I most profoundly humble myself before Thy Divine Majesty, and from out of the abyss of my sins and nothingness do I raise my voice in suppliant accents to implore Thy mercy.

An Act of Contrition

HAVE mercy on me, O my God; I repent of having so often offended Thee, and I am deeply grieved at having by my sins outraged Thy infinite goodness, O Thou who hast loved and still lovest me to such a degree. Would that my grief were such as might break this heart which has dared to be unfaithful to Thee. I promise Thee, with the help of Thy grace, never more to return to my hateful sins, and rather to forfeit life itself than Thy love.

An Act of Petition

BEHOLD me then, my God, prostrate at Thy feet, for the purpose of beginning my meditation; O do Thou assist me by Thy grace that my soul may be benefited by it; do Thou enlighten my mind that I may know how much Thou hast loved me, and give an impulse to my will that I may form an efficacious resolution of loving Thee. Give me courage to devote myself without delay to the fulfillment of Thy Will, whatever it may be, and grace faithfully to correspond with all Thy holy inspirations. Most holy Virgin Mary, my dear Mother, and thou, my blessed Angel Guardian, obtain for me the assistance necessary to make this meditation in a manner profitable to me.

31 DAYS IN
THE SCHOOL OF JESUS
CRUCIFIED

∽ DAY 1 ∽

Jesus Christ Takes Leave of His Blessed Mother

Meditation

DURING the whole course of His life, Jesus had in an especial manner respected and obeyed His blessed Mother, and had never in the slightest degree been wanting in filial duty; it is, therefore, natural to suppose that, before delivering Himself up to death, He should give a last proof of His love, by taking leave of so tender a Mother.

1. Consider the indescribable sorrow experienced by Jesus and Mary at the mournful moment of separation.

Jesus, the most affectionate of the sons of men, takes a last farewell of His beloved Mother, before parting from her to go, not to live in a distant land, but to die amidst unspeakable sufferings. What bitter sorrow do they both experience! Mary knows that she is soon to behold her Son agonizing on a Cross, His sacred Body mangled, bleeding, and covered with wounds. O how her maternal heart throbs with anguish! "My beloved Mother," saith Jesus to her, "thou must submit to my delivering Myself up unto death. Such is the Will of My Father; and the redemption of mankind can be accomplished only at the expense of every drop of the Blood of Thy Son." At these painful tidings, what tongue can describe the martyrdom suffered by the Virginal heart of Mary! She would fain have made some answer to these words of her beloved Son, but the intensity of her grief deprives her of the power. Jesus sighs, and the sorrow He inflicts on Mary's heart is a source of the deepest anguish to His own. Mary laments, and the necessity of parting from Jesus is the sword that inflicts the deepest wound on her soul. David wept at being separated from his beloved friend Jonathan, and oh, what tears of bitter anguish and lively sorrow must Mary have shed on embracing for the last time her only and innocent Son about to deliver Himself up to death! What affliction must Jesus have felt on parting from, and bidding a last farewell to, the tenderest of Mothers! O Sacred Hearts of Jesus and Mary! I dare not ask to fathom the depth of your sorrow at this separation, but I presume to implore grace to compassionate and love you, and to weep over my sins by which I have so many times expelled Jesus from my heart, renounced His love, and rejected His graces.

2. Consider the generous offering which Mary makes of her Son to suffer death, and of herself to participate in His sufferings:

Mary is a mother, and the heart of a mother cannot naturally nerve itself to dismiss a son to death amidst a thousand tortures for the salvation of guilty man. But the heart of Mary is a generous heart—a heart ready to make the most painful sacrifices for the love of God, and for the benefit of us, her children. She feels her soul pierced through with a sharp sword of grief at being under the necessity of consenting that her beloved Son should deliver Himself up to death. She sees that in losing Jesus she loses a Son who is at once her Father, her God, her All. She comprehends how deep is the sea of sorrow into which her maternal heart is to be plunged at the sight of the innumerable wounds and the barbarous death which await her Son, and of which she is to be a mournful witness. And yet Mary, filled with love for me, and a desire for my salvation, and burning with charity toward God, who requires this painful sacrifice from her, rises superior to herself, offers generously to suffer everything; and although the Passion and Death of Jesus will be to her a source of infinite grief, she willingly, and with her whole heart, gives her consent, and, with more than a martyr's strength of mind, makes the sacrifice of her beloved Son. "Go, my Son!" she says, "Go, to suffer on the Cross; go, even to death; such is the Will of Thy Heavenly Father; and such, also, is mine. Would only that I were permitted to die with Thee!"

What charity is displayed toward me by this

tender Mother in her submission to the loss of her
innocent Son, that I may be saved from eternal
death! What strength of mind does she show in
willingly offering to endure the most painful martyrdom that I may be saved! Oh, how greatly am I
indebted to thy love, my dear Mother! But, oh, how
widely does my conduct differ from thine, as
regards the acceptation of sufferings, and the sacrifice of anything for the love of my God and for
the eternal salvation of my soul! I know well that
to be a Christian and a follower of Jesus implies
an obligation to suffer. I know that unless I make
an offering of my heart and of my affections I shall
not save my soul; and yet there is nothing I am
more anxious to avoid than the occasions of suffering with Jesus, and of sacrificing my corrupt
inclinations for the love of them. O, my dear
Mother, obtain for me a share in the strength and
generosity of thy most holy heart on all those occasions when I may have to do or suffer anything to
please God, and to obtain eternal happiness.

3. Consider the resignation of Jesus and Mary to
the Divine Will:

When a son is about to die, the mournful news
is communicated to the mother by her friends and
relations; but here, the Son who is about to endure
death—the death of the Cross—Himself makes
the painful fact known to Mary, and requires,
moreover, that Mary herself should give consent
and permission. Maternal affection suggests that
she should dissuade Jesus from taking such a

step, but resignation to the Will of the Eternal Father prevails in her suffering heart, and causes her to exclaim, with heroic submission, though tears are flowing fast from her eyes, "I submit to the Divine Will; I consent that Jesus should suffer death." Mary consents to be deprived of her beloved Son, and to pass the remainder of her days overwhelmed with affliction, because it is the Will of God that she should cooperate, by her tears, and by the pangs of her sorrowing heart, in the great work of our redemption. When shall we also learn to sacrifice everything to the Will of God?

Jesus now leaves Mary, and departs to deliver Himself up to His bitter Passion and ignominious Death. But He goes willingly; because it is the Will of His Father that he should suffer and die for our salvation. Oh, how great is the love of Jesus for me! and in what manner do I resign myself to the Divine Will for the love of Jesus? How many are my complaints, and how frequent my bursts of impatience, in being forced to submit and resign myself to the dispositions of Providence? Mary parts from the dearest object of her affections— her beloved Son—with the most heroic resigna- tion, and you have not yet detached your heart from the world! You are desirous, perhaps, of tak- ing leave of it, as Jesus did of Mary; but there is no similarity between your position and His, and the world will continue forever answering that you must delay a little longer and enjoy a few more of its pleasures. If you once seek to come to terms with the world, you will never detach yourself from it. God calls you to Himself. God makes known to you His Will. It is not His will that you should love the world, but that you should detach yourself from it; make, then, a firm resolution to do so, and—in imitation of Jesus and Mary—hasten to execute the Will of God.

The Fruit

Compassionate Jesus and Mary in their painful trials. Weep over your sins, which were the cause of so much sorrow to their sacred Hearts! Imitate the generous sacrifice of Mary by sacrificing your whole self to Jesus—ready to suffer whatever He may require of you, for love of Him and in expiation of your sins. In every trial be conformed to the Will of God, like Jesus and Mary—often exclaiming to Our Lord, in submission and humility of heart, *Fiat voluntas tua!*—Thy Will be done!

Example

The lovers of Jesus Christ Crucified manifest their devotion and reverence for Him by tenderly kissing the Crucifix, willingly hearing discourses on His sufferings, and attentively reading about them. Sister Mary Minima, of Jesus of Nazareth, a Carmelite nun, who died in the odor of sanctity, at Vetralla, about the year 1831, was accustomed, while yet a child, frequently to spend some little time in reading accounts of the Passion of Jesus Christ; and so great, even then, was her compassion for her suffering Lord, that she would shed tears in abundance over what she read. After she became a nun, she could not even look at a book upon the Passion, or at any picture or image of Jesus Crucified, without being touched to the heart, and bursting into a flood of tears. She would most tenderly kiss the Crucifix, and was in the habit of spending much time with great compunction of heart in beholding and embracing her Redeemer nailed to the Cross. (See her *Life*.) I exhort you also to begin and imitate her, and perform similar devout practices in honor of Christ Crucified, and by degrees you will find your love and devotion towards them sensibly increase.

∽ DAY 2 ∽

Jesus Is Sold by
Judas Iscariot

Meditation

JUDAS having resolved to execute the unholy scheme which he had long been forming in his heart, of betraying his Master, goes secretly to the high priests and elders of the people, and makes them the impious proposal of selling Jesus, and of delivering Him up into their hands.

1. Consider who the man is who sells Jesus.

Not a stranger, not disliked by, nor an enemy of Our blessed Lord. No, one of His disciples, one of the dearest objects of His love, one of His intimate friends, one of the select band most favored by the Divine Master! How can we, in any degree, comprehend the deep grief, the bitter sorrow, experienced by Jesus at such a return from Judas, whom He has always treated with such love and mild forbearance, and on whom He has unsparingly bestowed the most signal favors? Ah, most bitterly does He deplore this enormous crime, of which He has perfect foreknowledge! "Oh!" says

Our Lord, in His Heart, "I am not grieved that a cruel Caiphas should wish my death; I feel no resentment at being persecuted by an excited and infuriated mob; that a council of the iniquitous scribes and Pharisees is plotting against My life, this does not grieve Me so much; that a heathen judge should unjustly pronounce upon Me the sentence of death on the Cross, this I suffer in peace; but how can I endure that thou—My disciple, My companion, one of My household, and eating at My own table, My intimate friend and apostle, thirsting for My blood—shouldst betray Me and sell Me? Ah, this is too deep a wound for My heart!"

But do you correspond any better with the goodness and love of God when you commit sin? Has He less cause to complain of your ingratitude? Remember all the singular favors which Our Lord has bestowed upon you. He has called you to be His disciple and follower, so that you have had an especial share in His confidence, and in the benefits which He has showered down upon the world. He has bestowed upon you the tender care of a Father. He has admitted you many times to His table, and fed you with His own most precious Body and Blood. He has loaded you with gifts and graces, besides having prepared for you a kingdom of everlasting beatitude, and you most perfidiously and ungratefully have by sin betrayed your Benefactor, renounced His friendship, bartered away the precious treasure of His grace, and given infinite pain to His loving Heart.

Judas sold his Master once only, but can you even remember how many times you have been guilty of the same dark treason? Ah, at least detest your wickedness and, prostrate at the feet of Jesus, weep over the enormity of your crimes, and return, by sincere repentance, to regain your place in His tender Heart, which is still burning with love for you.

2. To whom is Jesus Christ sold by Judas?

The perfidious disciple, to increase the suffering which his Divine Master will experience from the frightful treason he is about to accomplish against His sacred Person, goes to the high priests and heads of the Synagogue, to arrange the terms of the betrayal. And what description of men are these, O Lord, into whose hands one of Thy disciples is meditating and scheming to deliver Thee? They are Thy most cruel enemies, inflamed with rage and hatred against Thee. They have many times sought Thy life. They will rejoice and triumph at having Thee in their power; and they will subject Thee to the most ignominious treatment. This is what in effect came to pass, O my soul, but in the meantime, as Jesus sees and knows all things, how deep is the affliction with which His Heart is overwhelmed at beholding so atrocious an insult offered to His Divine Majesty by one of His Apostles, now an apostate and betrayer of his Lord! And moreover, how must His loving Heart grieve at beholding you so entirely under the dominion of your passions, as to be occupied, day after day, only in finding out new means of satisfying them, and in thinking of committing sin, deserting Jesus, and delivering up your soul into the hands of the devil, His most cruel and implacable enemy! Jesus bewailed the perfidy of Judas, but far more does He bewail yours, because it has been so often repeated, and repeated in defiance of so many interior inspirations, of so much remorse of conscience, of so many internal lights, which have reminded and made known to you at how dear a rate Jesus has purchased that soul which you sell to His infernal enemy when you fall into sin. O my Jesus! O my sweet Saviour! I acknowledge and confess my excessive malice. I detest and deplore my past infidelities. Thou didst give me this soul; endow it with Thy grace, sanctify it by Thy Blood, enrich it by Thy merits, and save it from Hell by Thy death; and I, ungrateful for all Thy love, have torn it from Thy arms to sell over and over again to the devil! I implore and beseech Thee to receive my repentant soul which now returns to Thee, and grant, that since it is Thine by right of conquest, it may be Thine for all eternity, and never more have the misfortune to be separated from Thee.

3. The reason for which Judas sells Jesus.

Has any man urged or besought the wicked Apostle to become a traitor, and sell his Divine Master? Has anyone suggested the shameful thought? No. He himself, of his own free will, has offered his services. Oh, how great is the malice and depravity of the human heart! Has he been induced to commit this foul deed through a motive of jealousy or desire of revenge? But how could this have been, since his good Master has neglected no means of gaining his affections, and deterring him from the execution of his design? Again, how could this have been the case, when Jesus, not satisfied with having received him among His disciples, and raised him to the dignity of an Apostle, had bestowed upon him particular marks of love and singular favors? What wrong, or what ill-treatment, can he have received from his adorable Master to stimulate him to take such atrocious vengeance? None whatever. He betrays Him for the sole purpose of satisfying a most depraved passion, which has long tyrannized over his heart, and made him callous and insensible to inspirations, graces, and remorse of conscience. He betrays Him for the sake of a paltry gain, for the sake of obtaining a few pieces of money, with which to gratify his avarice. *"What will you give me,"* says the traitor to the high priests, *"and I will deliver my Master to you?"* Such is the language held by Judas, as though he were speaking of selling the commonest merchandise! What a degradation for the Person of the Son of God to be thus offered by one of His disciples at the low valuation which His enemies shall please to put upon Him! How painful to His Heart, to behold His precious life sacrificed to the brutal passions of His disciple! The scribes rejoice that one favored by Christ should offer to be His betrayer, and promise the perfidious wretch thirty pieces of silver as the price of his iniquity. Judas, being quite satisfied with his sacrilegious bargain, closes it at once, and thinks of nothing further than the execution of his agreement. See here into what excesses we may be hurried, if we allow even one single passion to take entire possession of our hearts. Judas was a Prince of the Church, and is thus transformed into a son of perdition. He was in the school of Christ, *His familiar friend,* and had *sat at His table,* and is changed in one moment into a demon. Who will not fear? Who can feel secure of standing at beholding such a fall?

You regard Judas with horror, and yet feel none at so often renewing his foul treason by your sins. "What will you give me, and I will deliver unto you Christ, and His grace, and His love, and His friendship," is the language of your heart, when for some vile interest, deceitful hope, or forbidden pleasure, you betray Christ, your duty, and your own conscience. O unhappy merchant, you are indeed at once bereft of sense and of faith! Can the possession of anything in this world compensate for the loss of your soul, and of your God? But, oh, what detestable perfidy is yours! to sell your faithful Friend, your priceless Good, for a mere nothing! Now, at least, expiate your sins by tears of true repentance, and fall prostrate at the feet of Jesus, with the determination henceforth to love and esteem Him above every created object.

The Fruit

Examine your heart to see whether you really love God with a love of preference, and value His grace above everything besides. Lose no time in purging your heart of all that can in any way be prejudicial to the love of God. Endeavor to overcome that passion to which you are most addicted, and from which so many of your faults derive their source. Frequently during the course of the day renew your act of contrition at the foot of the Crucifix, for the innumerable faults which you have committed, and which have been so many betrayals of Jesus.

Example

The man who is devout to the most holy Passion of Jesus Christ is certain to grasp eagerly at every opportunity of inspiring others with a similar devotion. St. Paul of the Cross, a great lover of Jesus Crucified, was accustomed, while yet a child in his father's house, to make frequent little discourses on the Passion of Jesus Christ, to his brothers and sisters, in order deeply to impress upon their minds the remembrance of the sufferings of their Redeemer. He was accustomed, on these occasions, to take them into his own room, and very devoutly read to them some book on the subject, that so they might be early inspired with sentiments of devotion toward those mysteries which are the fountains of grace. He used to exhort them in the most persuasive terms to reflect often on the sufferings and death of Jesus Christ; and when he left home to found that Order to which he gave the name of *The Passion,* [the Passionist Order] and to preach Jesus Crucified to the people, in which holy employment he passed his whole life, he left them as a legacy these important words: "Constantly bear in mind the sufferings of our Crucified Love." Let these, his last words, be also impressed on your heart. (See his *Life*).

∽ DAY 3 ∽

Prayer of Jesus
In the Garden

Meditation

THE Last Supper being over, the discourse finished, and the hymn of thanksgiving said, Jesus leaves the supper-room with His eleven Apostles, and enters the Garden of Gethsemani. Consider:

1. Jesus is in the habit of retiring after the fatigues of the day, to pass the night in solitude and prayer; and even on this last evening of His life He does not depart from His pious custom. Learn hence the great importance of prayer, and never neglect it, particularly in spiritual sufferings and trials. Jesus Christ knows that it is in the Garden His Passion is to commence; that in a short time His betrayer is to appear with a body of armed men to arrest Him. He foresees that in a few hours He will have to return by the same road, bound with cords, and dragged along by His enemies, and yet He does not flinch. His ardent charity leads Him onward, and urges Him to

enter the Garden without delay, and begin at once to pray and to suffer. Be confounded at the sight of such an example. The slightest trouble, or the most unimportant business, distracts you from prayer, and the consequences of neglecting to strengthen your soul with that Heavenly food is, that you become weak and languid, sink down, and fall into sin. Ah, my sweet Jesus, through the merits of Thy Passion bestow upon me a spirit of prayer like unto Thine!

2. Jesus prays with the most profound humility. He falls prostrate on the ground before the Majesty of His Divine Father, almost as though He were unworthy to raise His face and eyes to Heaven; and yet He is the Son of God! With what humility should you pray, you, who are but a wretched sinner. Jesus prays with the utmost fervor of spirit, accompanying His prayer with tears, groans, and sighs. In our name, He asks for the graces which we require to save our souls, appeases Divine Justice, and implores pardon for our sins. Cold and languid prayers, such as yours, are not pleasing to God. Jesus prays in the most lively and tender spirit of confidence, and invokes His Eternal Father, calling Him many times *My Father.* God is our Father, and He loves us like a Father. Can any thought be more efficacious to excite the firmest sentiments of hope in our hearts when we pray to this most loving Father? Jesus prays with the most perfect conformity to the Divine Will. He recommends this afflicted human nature to His Father; He represents to Him all His sorrow and sufferings, to excite His compassion; He implores to be dispensed from drinking the bitter chalice of His Passion, and yet He prays that what His Father pleases may come to pass—that the Will of His Father, and not His own, may be done. Learn to pray in the language and spirit of Jesus Christ, and to will nothing but what God wills. Finally, Jesus prays with perseverance, continuing in prayer for the space of several hours. His most holy soul is overwhelmed with mortal anguish, and yet He is neither disturbed nor impatient, but perseveres constantly in prayer. You may here discover the real secret of obtaining consolation in affliction; to have recourse to God, the true Comforter, and never to grow weary in prayer.

3. After our loving Jesus has three times, with uplifted eyes, besought His Divine Father that if the salvation of the world can be accomplished without His delivering Himself up to death, He may be dispensed from it, finding that His prayer is not to be granted, but that, on the contrary, the hour of His bitter Passion and ignominious death is near at hand, He permits His suffering humanity to tremble, and to shudder, and to be overwhelmed with fear and anguish. Behold how our sorrowing Jesus, pale, trembling, and anguishstricken, now groans, sighs, and seeks to give vent to the profound internal sorrow oppressing His heart. Oh, how great is the charity of Jesus! When suffering for me is in question, His eager love anticipates all the torments of His Passion. At least compassionate your Redeemer in this His mortal anguish and make an offering of yourself to suffer something for love of Him. Our most afflicted Lord turns in His agony to His Apostles, to obtain from them some consolation in His sorrow, and He finds them sleeping. Once again He has recourse to His Eternal Father, and receives an inward intimation that it is His Will that He should die for the salvation of men. Jesus bows down His sacred head, accepts death, and exclaims with perfect resignation, "Father, Thy will be done!" Behold at how dear a rate your salvation is purchased by Jesus! Can you any more grieve at having to suffer something to save your soul, after all that Jesus has endured for you?

The Fruit

Never neglect your accustomed prayer, and when prevented from making it, supply the deficiency by desires, and by frequent aspirations to Jesus suffering. Let your prayer rest solely on the merits of Jesus Christ, unite it with His prayer in the Garden, and offer it up in a true spirit of humility and confidence. Let the prayer *Fiat voluntas tua, Thy will be done,* become familiar to you. In dejection of spirit, in sorrow of heart, and in all your sufferings, remember the internal anguish and affliction endured by Jesus in His prayer in the Garden, and they will be rendered sweet to you.

Example

A true lover is always anxious to keep up in his mind a remembrance of the object of his affections, hence souls enamored of Jesus have ever discovered a thousand ingenious ways of keeping alive in their hearts the remembrance of His sufferings. St. Philip Neri always kept near him a figure of Jesus, unfastened from the cross, in order that he might be able the more freely to give vent to the affections of his heart. At night he would place it by his bedside, so that the moment he awoke, he might concentrate all his thoughts upon the sweet Object of his love (see his *Life*). St. Paul of the Cross, when alone in his room always had a very devotional image of Jesus Crucified by his side, and when he went out, he wore it on his breast, so that the sufferings of his Redeemer might be constantly in his thoughts; and in order that so sweet a remembrance might never be effaced from his mind, he wore on his breast, next to the skin, a wooden cross garnished with 186 sharp iron points, which continually pricked him, and thus recalled to his memory the sufferings of Jesus Crucified, and excited his heart to lively feelings of compassion.

The Agony and Bloody Sweat of Jesus in the Garden of Olives

Meditation

1. SCARCELY has the Angel who appeared from Heaven to comfort Jesus presented Him with the bitter chalice of His Passion, when, by His own Will, death displays itself to His mind under the most frightful form, to overwhelm Him with terror. He beholds how in a brief space of time He will be bound like a criminal, scourged as a malefactor, and crucified as a notorious thief. He is fully aware of the inestimable value of His Life, and yet He sees that He must abandon that life to the mercy of His enemies, and lose it by the ignominious death of the Cross. He sees that He is going to die for sins not His own, and the knowledge of His unspotted innocence renders His horror of death more painful still, so that truly no sorrow is like unto His sorrow. But the most painful wound of His tender Heart is inflicted by the thought that there is no one to pity Him. Jesus is about to suffer and die because it is His own Will, and on that very account He suffers

55

more in His agony, because it is at His own command that such painful apprehensions assail Him. Oh, if you could but enter into the Heart of Jesus, how you would now behold Him overwhelmed beneath so indescribable a load of sorrow, as to be in fact reduced to the painful position of the agonizing. Learn now, O my soul, how dear thou art to Jesus. Thy salvation is dearer to Him than His own life. He consents to lose His most precious life to save thine. What then ought to be thy love and gratitude to Jesus?

2. Jesus having excited in Himself the liveliest apprehensions of His approaching death, allows His heart to be oppressed with fear, terror, and horror. Nature would willingly avoid so much suffering, but reason would rather obey God, and accept the chalice of suffering and death, and it is during the course of this painful struggle that Jesus, making a violent effort to vanquish the repugnance of nature, grows pale, faints, and sweats large drops of blood from every part of His sacred Body.

Behold, O my soul, behold thy Redeemer sinking to the earth, overpowered with inward anguish, and bathed in His own Blood! At such a sight, what are thy sentiments? This Blood is not forced from His veins by the fury of His enemies, but wrung from His Heart at His own express desire, that so we may understand the excess of His love for us. Have thy struggles with thy natural inclinations, restraint of thy passions, and submission to the holy Will of God, ever cost thee a drop of blood? But the acceptance of death for thy salvation costs Jesus a bloody sweat!

3. Jesus sweats blood to prove how excessive is His hatred for sin. He beholds Himself laden with the sins of the whole world, and His heart is thereby filled with unspeakable horror, so that blood issues from every pore, as though He would wish to shed even tears of blood over our sins! Oh, how great an evil must sin be, since the Son of God enters into an agony, and sweats blood on account of it. How wretched am I if these streams of blood, drawn forth by such excessive love, do not soften my heart! Jesus sweats blood to prove how great is His sorrow for the loss of so many souls infinitely dear to Him, for which He is about to die, and which nevertheless He foresees will be lost through their sins. Ah, who can understand the anguish of His tender Heart at this thought! Finally, Jesus sweats blood to prove how tenderly He compassionates the elect, and particularly His most holy Mother, in their afflictions and sufferings. Oh, how tender is the love of Jesus, for it seems as though the sufferings of His beloved ones, are more painful to Him than His own! Then, if you have anything to suffer for the love of Jesus, remember that in Him you have a Father who knows how to compassionate, and a God who knows how to reward you.

The Fruit

Examine and see what will be your sentiments in your last agony, and live so that the remembrance of your past life may then be a source of consolation to you. In imitation of Jesus, refuse nature everything that is contrary to the Will of God. Do violence to yourself if you wish to be saved. Such efforts for the salvation of your soul will not cost you blood, and even if they do, remember that it has cost Jesus yet more. Frequently make an offering to the Eternal Father of the Blood of His Beloved Son in satisfaction for your sins.

Example

It is impossible to love Jesus suffering, and not desire to suffer for His sake. St. Philip Neri being moved by meditation on the sufferings of Jesus, and inflamed with love for Him, earnestly desired to go to the Indies and shed his blood for love of Christ, and being unable to follow up his wish, he besought Our Lord to grant that whenever blood should flow from his nose or mouth, it might flow in such abundance as in a degree to correspond with the blood shed by Jesus for the love of him. It was the Will of God in some measure to grant his request, for one day he lost so much blood that his eyesight failed, and he fell fainting on the ground (see his *Life*). If you cannot make an offering to Jesus of your blood, you can at least sacrifice to Him one of your passions.

❧ DAY 5 ❧

Jesus Is Betrayed
With a Kiss by Judas

Meditation

1. OUR Blessed Jesus, after the bloody sweat, by which He was greatly exhausted, rises from prayer, and with admirable courage advances to meet Judas, who at the head of a band of armed men is already approaching the Garden, to betray his Master, and deliver Him up into the hands of His cruel enemies: "Arise," He says to His disciples, "let us go; behold the traitor is at hand. There is no time for sleeping." My soul, what is the source of this courage in Jesus? Prayer. Prayer it is that has filled His soul with heavenly fortitude, and imbued Him with strength to triumph over every difficulty in the obeying of His Father's Will. Behold the example which you have to follow. Do you feel any repugnance in overcoming yourself? Do you fear suffering? Do you tremble at the thought of penance? Have recourse to prayer, and then say to your timid shrinking heart, "Arise, let us go to combat our enemies. Let us mortify this passion, let us pardon that injury. Jesus resisted even unto blood in overcoming His difficulties, it is right that we should follow His example." The more constant you are in the practice of virtue, the more easily will you resist temptation, and very speedily all your sadness and sorrow of heart will be dispelled, if you fortify your soul by prayer.

2. Judas had said to the soldiers, *"Whomsoever I shall kiss, that is He, hold Him fast."* Conformably to his agreement, the traitor draws nigh to Jesus, for the purpose of embracing Him, salutes Him, throws his arms round His neck, calls Him Master, and imprints a kiss upon His sacred face. My soul, give one glance at Judas. Of how many crimes is he not guilty in this single kiss! What execrable perfidy, to make use of the sweetest mark of peace and friendship as a signal of betrayal! What hatred of the blackest die, affectionately to salute Jesus at the very instant of delivering Him up into the hands of His enemies! How atrocious an insult! To call Him *Master* for whose blood and for whose death he is thirsting! Good God! By what means can Judas have fallen so low? Judas the Apostle, the familiar friend of Christ, the witness of His miracles, His disciple, His companion at the same board! Ah, into what excesses may not, and does not a ruling passion lead us! It blinds our eyes, hardens our hearts, perverts our reason, and finally conducts us even to the depth of iniquity. If you do not early restrain your passions, you will surely fall very speedily into the most fearful crimes.

3. There is no trial more painful to a feeling heart than to be betrayed, and there never has been more frightful treachery than that of Judas, and yet observe with what meekness and patience Jesus submits to what is a source of such acute sorrow to His tender Heart. He repels not that unnatural monster of ingratitude, but receives him with humility and sweetness, and embraces him with every demonstration of the most ardent charity. He selects this last moment to bestow upon His betrayer the tenderest additional proofs of unbounded love, and by the interior movements of His grace and exterior demonstrations of friendship, He calls, invites, and urges him to repent and be converted. Oh, charity of my Jesus! When will you also learn not to resent an offense, and not to be so unforgiving toward those who offend you? When will you learn from the example of Jesus to bear patiently any trifling injury?

Jesus answers the traitor who is making such an assault upon His sacred Person, calls him His *friend,* assures him of His love by His encouraging language, and offers him His pardon and friendship. *"Friend,"* He says, with ineffable sweetness, *"whereto art thou come? Dost thou betray the Son of Man with a kiss?* But Judas is as a deaf man, and persists in his crime. How many times, when you have been on the point of committing sin, has Jesus most lovingly called you by name, and said to your heart, *"Son dost thou betray Me thus? What harm have I done thee that thou shouldst thus offend Me?"* But you were as a deaf man, and continued in sin. Weep over your ingratitude, and return to Jesus.

The Fruit

Do not flatter yourself that you love God, if you allow any passion to predominate in your soul. Examine this day what your predominant passion is; resolve to overcome it at any cost, and to resist all its unjust pretensions. Ask God's pardon for the ingratitude with which you have frequently corresponded so ill with His loving inspirations, and in time of temptation; or when in danger of committing sin, imagine that you hear Jesus saying to you, *"Wilt thou betray Me thus?"* and you will never have heart to offend so good a Father.

Example

In the midst of your occupations, and even of your amusements, you may keep up in your heart a lively remembrance of the sufferings of Jesus Christ. St. Philip Neri used frequently to take several youths to an open spot, where they could recreate their minds with some innocent amusements, which he himself would set on foot; and then he would retire aside to read or meditate on some point of the Passion out of a little book which contained the whole history, and which he was accustomed to carry about with him. (See his *Life*). What is there to prevent you also from retiring at least into the recesses of your heart from time to time, to bestow one look of love and compassion upon your suffering Jesus?

∽ DAY 6 ∽

Jesus Is Taken and
Bound by the Soldiers

Meditation

1. THE Jews would never have succeeded in taking and binding Jesus, if He had not so willed; and having fallen to the ground at the mere sound of His voice, they never could have risen again, if Jesus had not first given them permission. But the love of Jesus cannot endure that the Passion, which He has so earnestly desired, should be longer deferred. His enemies are burning with impatience to lay hands upon His sacred Person, and bear Him away a prisoner, and equally does Jesus burn with impatience to be deprived of liberty and life for love of us. Oh, how great is the charity of Jesus! If I really loved Jesus, I should not so carefully avoid even the shadow of suffering for His sake, while He goes forth eagerly to endure torments and death for mine. Jesus might fly, or escape in some other way out of the hands of His enemies, or He might command the assistance of many legions of Angels. But He does nothing of the sort, because He

desires to die. He allows Himself to be taken and bound, and it is for this very purpose that He goes forth to meet His enemies, and draws nigh to them with a sweet, mild, and loving countenance, like a victim that is led to sacrifice for the salvation of mankind. Jesus allows Himself to be bound, because His bonds are to break the chains of our sins. Jesus becomes a slave for our sakes, through the excess of His charity alone, to free our souls from the slavery of the devil. Offer yourself to Him now, to be entirely His, beseeching Him to bind you fast with the sweet chains of His love.

2. While Jesus Christ, with tranquil heart and serene countenance, permits Himself to be taken by His enemies, they, on their side, fall upon Him with diabolical fury, and bind Him fast lest He should again escape them, while each man rejoices and triumphs at the grand capture that has been made. Full of rage and hatred, they smite Him with their hands, throw Him on the ground, strike Him with their feet, drag Him along with violence, and illtreat His sacred Person in every possible way. What but love for you has reduced Jesus to so lamentable a condition? There is none to defend, none to console Him. All His disciples have deserted Him. And yet all protested but a few hours previously that they would die with Him.

How many times have you also protested that you would follow and imitate Jesus, and yet, when occasion has offered, you have abandoned Him! O thoughtlessness of an ungrateful soul! Jesus makes no resistance to His cruel enemies; Jesus shows no resentment; but, on the contrary, with a heart burning with love for His Heavenly Father, He rejoices that the long sighed-for hour of suffering is come at last, and that He is to make satisfaction for our sins by His Passion and Death. When will you learn from the example of Jesus to submit patiently to affronts and injuries?

3. Indescribable is the barbarity manifested by the furious enemies of Jesus Christ in their treatment of His sacred Person, but equally wonderful is His unalterable patience. They bind His neck, hands, and waist together, with cords and chains, as though He were the most wicked of malefactors, and Jesus refuses not to wear these chains, but accepts them with joy and offers them up to His Eternal Father, thereby to merit for us the liberty of the children of God. Contemplate Jesus in the hands of sinners, loaded with chains, and bound with cords; enter in thought with all possible reverence into His sacred Heart, and see how He suffers not so much from those chains and cords as from the sight of the sins of the whole world, with which He is loaded, and which form a chain so oppressive and painful as to overwhelm and bow Him down to the ground. Yet He submits to its weight with the most heroic fortitude through His earnest desire of breaking it asunder, and liberating our souls. O infinite mercy of my

Jesus! Thou art intent solely upon delivering and saving me, while I, instead of compassionating Thee thus bound, and breaking asunder those chains which torture and oppress Thee, increase their weight by adding to the number of my sins. I beseech Thee, my sweet Jesus, that now, once for all, I may put a stop to such malice. May I now at least begin to return Thee love for love.

The Fruit

Jesus, when ill-treated, beaten, and bound, is silent and complains not; learn from his example to restrain your feelings, to bridle your tongue, and to accept in peace and bear with meekness whatever may befall you that is trying to self-love. Carefully examine whether you are enslaved to any bad habit or evil passion, promise Jesus that you will at any cost burst all such hateful bands, and beseech Him to bind your soul closely to Himself by the chains of holy love.

Example

The remembrance of the sufferings of Jesus renders all pains and sorrows sweet and light. A friend of St. Paul of the Cross being astonished at his austere and penitential mode of life, and unable to understand how so weak and sickly a man could endure such continual, excessive sufferings, questioned him one day on the subject. "Tell me, Father Paul," he said, "how you contrive to lead such a life?" The servant of God replied with deep emotion, "Jesus Christ has suffered so much for love of me, therefore it is not wonderful that I should do and suffer something for love of Him." (See his *Life*). When you feel any repugnance to suffering, say the same to yourself, and you will soon feel the beneficial effects of such a reflection.

∽ DAY 7 ∽

Jesus Is Led before the
Tribunal of Annas

Meditation

1. JESUS being taken and bound by the Jews, is violently dragged from the Garden to Jerusalem, to be presented before the tribunal of Annas, the High Priest. Never has any culprit, or even any notorious malefactor, been treated with such barbarous cruelty as is the most innocent Son of God upon this occasion. One man drags Him forward, another smites, another insults, another blasphemes, another maltreats His sacred Person in divers ways. And what is the demeanor of Jesus under such an accumulation of outrages and sufferings? Without uttering one word of complaint, without making the slightest demonstration of anger, or desire of revenge, He advances like a meek lamb led to the slaughter. Jesus, with one single word, might have struck terror into His enemies, and yet He submits to everything in patient silence. He might in one moment have delivered Himself from their fury, and yet willingly subjects Himself to it, and

regards all their insults and outrages as so many outbursts of the anger of God punishing the sins of the world in His sacred humanity, and He implores mercy for us, offering them all to His Eternal Father. Behold our blessed Jesus walking in the midst of this insolent band of soldiers, His head bowed down, His eyes bent on the ground, His hands bound, His face disfigured with blows, His whole frame exhausted and trembling, and with scarcely the strength to proceed further. Can it be possible that a Christian with such a spectacle before his eyes, should continue to be proud, should give way to anger, should be unable to preserve a moment's silence under affronts, or be unwilling to bear the slightest injury. Ah, shame, shame upon your own self, for you have truly deserved all the outrages and affronts which are heaped upon your innocent Jesus!

2. As soon as the Jews arrive at Jerusalem, they conduct Jesus to the house of Annas, enter the great hall without delay, and present the Holy of Holies before the High Priest, as a malefactor. Jesus remains standing, bound like a criminal, before His proud judge, who examines Him concerning His disciples and His doctrine. What a sight to behold! The Son of God, the Eternal High Priest, the universal Judge of all mankind, presented before an earthly tribunal to be judged by a sinful, proud, hypocritical man! What must the Angels have thought on beholding their Lord in a state of such deep humiliation? But what do you say to so wonderful an example of humility and patience, you who seek applause and the esteem of men—you who cannot endure to see an equal preferred before you—you who so greatly fear the judgments of men, and who, although but a sinner, yet shrink from being thought such? Observe your most patient Jesus standing before the tribunal of Annas, and with what serenity of countenance, intrepidity of heart, and modesty of speech, He who is innocence itself, submits to be judged by a sinner. Oh, what will be your fate when you shall appear before Jesus Christ, your judge, and be convicted of having so little profited by His example, and of having led a life directly in opposition to His teaching?

3. Consider how painful it must be to Jesus to behold His character defamed, while His disciples utter not a word in His defense. He looks round to see whether there are any of His friends or followers to interest themselves in His behalf, but there is not one man to come forward in His defense. Every day do not you also inflict this wound anew upon His Divine Heart, when you remain cold and insensible, and take no pains to defend the honor of God attacked by sinners, or the sanctity of religion blasphemed by the impious. Our most afflicted Redeemer beholds also brought forward a number of false witnesses, who by their accusations conspire to hasten His condemnation. By the slightest bid of His omnipotence He might have silenced all these wretches, who have been formerly the witnesses of His miracles, or benefited by His loving charity. But Jesus is silent, and endures their execrable ingratitude with indescribable patience. How long has Jesus patiently borne with you, who, after having received so many benefits from His liberal hand, never cease most ungratefully to offend and outrage Him? Ah, my sweet Saviour, grant through Thy great mercy that I may from this moment cease to be ungrateful to Thy love.

The Fruit

God is greatly glorified when we humbly accept those mortifications and humiliations which daily fall to our lot. Reflect on what may happen to you in particular, and resolve that such shall be your conduct. Fear not the judgments of men, and far less allow yourself to be persuaded to neglect virtuous actions and works of piety for fear of what the world will say. Love to be considered imperfect, and to appear a sinner before men, but strive with all the energy of your soul not to be such before God.

Example

The remembrance of the sufferings of Jesus inspires a man with long enduring patience under injuries. It once happened that St. Paul of the Cross was making a voyage in the same ship with some individuals who, forgetting the sanctity of their character, seasoned their discourse rather freely with indecent expressions. The good Father mildly reproved them, and sought in the most charitable manner to bring them to a sense of their fault, but they, burning with anger against their benefactor, overwhelmed him with such a torrent of abuse and scornful words as to horrify all who listened to them. The humble servant of God, calling to mind the outrages offered to Jesus in His Passion, remained perfectly silent, without being in the slightest degree discomposed, and with the most serene and peaceful expression of countenance. Are you desirous of gaining a similar victory over yourself? Adopt the same means.

∽ DAY 8 ∽

Jesus Receives a Blow

Meditation

IT appeared to the Evangelist that so great a wrong was done to Jesus when he received a blow, that it deserved particular mention as a subject worthy of our meditation. Consider:

1. This insult is of a most degrading character.

Jesus is a King of infinite Majesty, the Eternal Son of God, and yet receives a blow from the hand of a servant. Can any affront bear comparison with this? Jesus receives a blow on His face, in the presence of a large multitude, and of the high priest and heads of the people. Thus, then, is the Majesty of God outraged by a presumptuous slave! The Heavens themselves must have recoiled with horror at such a sight! Jesus receives a blow, which is so great an outrage to His dignity that the mere thought causes you to burn with zeal and indignation against the brutal wretch who gave it: yet Jesus bears it patiently, makes not a gesture of anger, and indulges not in the slightest desire of revenge. You regard an opprobrious word as a dreadful offense, and magnify a slight act of discourtesy into a grievous insult, to which you imagine you cannot possibly submit. Do you call such slight grievances as these equal to the blow received by Jesus? Are you more noble, more worthy of veneration than Jesus? Can it be possible that you are nourishing thoughts of resentment and revenge, when your God endures the ignominy of being struck on the face with such admirable patience?

2. The blow is given most unjustly.

The person who gives it possesses no authority, but, in order to please the high priest, smites Jesus heavily on the face, at the same time reproving Him with arrogant boldness for having offended the judge. How many times have you imitated the example of this wretch? To please such or such a friend, or to satisfy such or such an unworthy passion, have you outraged Jesus. Jesus receives this blow for no reason whatever, solely on account of a pretended fault against the High Priest, as though our most humble Redeemer were bold and insolent in His demeanor. He had spoken, it is true, but with the greatest modesty, prudence and Divine wisdom, and for this is He punished by a blow. Could there be more manifest injustice? And yet no one reproves the daring servant—no one condemns such an unjust proceeding—no one compassionates our innocent Lord, but on the contrary, all rejoice at this outrage, while Heaven itself is silent, and does not strike dead the man who dares to be guilty of such an atrocity. But far more reason have you to wonder that Heaven and earth have not united to exterminate a being like yourself, who have so many times had the boldness to offend your God and Creator by sin. Can anyone be more daring and insolent than you, who have offended God, notwithstanding all the obligations you are under of loving Him?

3. This blow is given in a cruel manner, and therefore inflicts severe pain upon Jesus Christ.

It is given with all the energy of anger, with all the force of a strong arm, and perhaps even with a hand covered with an iron gauntlet. What pain must our patient Jesus have endured! The sacred face of Jesus is peculiarly delicate and susceptible to pain: what suffering then must a merciless blow on it cause! Behold how the Divine countenance, which ravisheth all hearts, is discolored and bruised by that cruel blow! See how the blood flows from eyes, nostrils, and mouth! Can we look upon that sacred Face thus disfigured, without being moved to compassion? Oh, if we could but behold the interior of the heart of our amiable Saviour at this moment! What burning charity toward him who gave the blow, what tender love toward me, for whose sake He suffers, and desires to suffer still more, should we there behold! How far am I from imitating Thee, O my Jesus! I cannot bear a sharp word, I cannot submit to even a just reproof, and I feel a secret aversion for those whom I ought to love. I beseech Thee to impress upon my mind and heart the remembrance of Thy admirable patience.

The Fruit

You are impatient because you are proud. Pride makes you think the slightest wrong done you a real injury, although in fact no wrong can ever be done you, as you deserve, by reason of your sins, far more than you can possibly receive. Let the remembrance of all that Jesus has suffered for them be ever present to your mind, and you will speedily learn humility and patience. Seek for occasions of public humiliation, imposed either by yourself or by others, thus to repair the scandal you have given by your pride.

Example

The man who maintains a lively recollection of the sufferings of Jesus Christ, esteems all trials light. St. Paul of the Cross one day entered a church to assist at Benediction of the Blessed Sacrament, when some boys knocked over a heavy bench which fell on his foot, bruising and hurting it exceedingly. The servant of God without displaying any emotion, raised up the bench, kissed it, and then continued his prayer. His companion, observing that blood was flowing from the wounded foot, told the good Father of it, but he still remained perfectly quiet. When they left the church, his companion again begged him to look at his foot and have the wound dressed, but the servant of God replied: "These slight sufferings are roses to me, for Jesus Christ has endured much more, and I deserve infinitely more, on account of my sins." And he would not even look at his wound. (See his *Life*).

∽ DAY 9 ∽

Jesus before Caiphas

Meditation

ANNAS being unable to discover any grounds for condemning Jesus Christ, and yet being desirous that He should be condemned, sends Him to the High Priest Caiphas, and leaves the decision of the case to him. Contemplate Jesus thus taken before a second tribunal.

1. Our Blessed Lord, bound like a thief, is conducted through the public streets of Jerusalem accompanied by a large body of soldiers who indulge their rage and hatred by illtreating Him in every possible way, and surrounded by a multitude of people who overwhelm Him with insults and maledictions, and rejoice over His misfortunes. Jesus advances, His feet bare, and His strength utterly exhausted by all His mental and bodily sufferings, offering up the ignominy and tortures He is now enduring, to His Eternal Father, for the salvation of my soul. The soldiers render His position still more painful, by inviting people to approach and see their renowned prisoner, while

79

Jesus proceeds on His way in the midst of them, with a humble demeanor and with downcast eyes, to teach us what value we should set on the esteem and honor of the world, and the applause of men. But a few days previously Jesus had passed through these same streets, applauded and honored by the crowd as the Messias, and now, abandoned even by His disciples, He is followed only by perfidious enemies who seek His death, and unite in deriding and insulting Him as a malefactor, and the last of men. Such is the duration of the honors and praises of the world! Learn hence to seek the good pleasure of God alone, to labor for the acquisition of a right to the immortal honors of Paradise, and to practice patience under humiliation, from the example of Jesus.

2. The Doctors and Ancients of the Synagogue are all assembled in the house of Caiphas, awaiting the arrival of Christ, and as soon as they perceive Him approaching, they begin to consult together concerning the best way of condemning Him. They are thirsting for His blood, they are eager for His death, but it is not sufficient for their purpose that He should die, He must also die as a criminal, and with the disgrace of having merited death. Witnesses are summoned from all parts, and liberty is given to every one to accuse the innocent Saviour of the world. The hall of the Great Council is filled with people, and in front of all stands Jesus, as a criminal, with His hands bound, and in an attitude of profound humility and meekness. Every one invents at will accusations, brings forward all that rage and jealousy can dictate, to stain the fair fame of our sweet Jesus, and utter the most atrocious calumnies against Him who is innocence itself. Jesus listens in silence, and His Heart is oppressed with sorrow that such horrible lies should be uttered, nevertheless His patience never wavers, and He prays for His calumniators with the tenderest charity. Jesus holds His peace, not because He is unable to justify Himself, but to teach you by His mysterious silence that whenever your own innocence alone is concerned there is no better weapon than humble silence for the refutation of calumny.

3. Caiphas, seeing that none of the witnesses can bring forward sufficient proof of any of their accusations for Jesus to be condemned, and that He, notwithstanding every provocation, still remains silent, gives the rein to his fierce passions, and adjures our Saviour, in the name of God, to tell him whether He is the Son of the Most High. Jesus is perfectly conscious that the Jews will make any acknowledgment of His Divinity serve as a specious pretext for condemning Him to death; and yet, so great is His love of truth, and respect for the adorable name of God, that He replies with angelic modesty of demeanor, "*I am.*"

No sooner has the wicked High Priest heard the humble answer of Jesus Christ, than he rends his sacerdotal garment as if through horror of an execrable blasphemy, hypocritically exaggerates the enormity of the supposed crime, and draws from thence the conclusion that Jesus must be condemned to death as a blasphemer. The whole Council concur in this sentence, and tumultuously raising their voices, exclaim: "He is worthy of death!"

Compassionate our suffering Redeemer in this painful situation. He is forced to speak when He prefers silence; and, when at length He utters a word, that word is construed into a crime deserving of death. The detractions and calumnies of the wicked have always threatened the lives of the just, but the just have always found in the example of their Saviour ample consolation for all outrages. Jesus is treated as a blasphemer, and He bears the ineffable wrong done Him with the most patient meekness. If you keep His example before your eyes, you will no longer have any difficulty in supporting the most disgraceful calumnies.

The Fruit

It is not sufficient to submit to humiliations and calumnies; you must, moreover, submit to them with the intention of imitating Jesus, and for the love of Him. Make a firm resolution that you will remember the humble and patient demeanor of Jesus Christ amidst the outrages and false accusations of His enemies, in order to encourage yourself to follow His example. Carefully repress your natural inclination to speak in your own defense, and offer up your silence to Jesus.

Example

Meditation on the sufferings of Jesus teaches us patience under the most painful trials. Blessed Osanna of Cataro, being one day oppressed with a burning fever, besought the Almighty to grant her some relief, when Jesus Christ appeared to her, covered with wounds and streaming with blood, and said, "Daughter, why dost thou grieve so much over thy sufferings, and not rather over the bitter tortures which I have endured for love of thee?" So deep was the impression made upon the mind and heart of the servant of God by the words and appearance of Jesus, that henceforward, far from complaining, she would exclaim, "Oh, what agony has Jesus endured in His Passion! How can we have the heart to complain?" (See her *Life*). Accustom yourself to compare your sufferings with those of Jesus, and you will soon cease to be impatient.

∽ DAY 10 ∽

Jesus Christ Is
Denied by St. Peter

Meditation

THREE times did St. Peter deny his Divine
Master; let us, therefore, meditate upon the
causes of those denials, which were at once so
insulting and so painful to our blessed Jesus.

1. He denies Jesus through the tepidity of his love
for Him.

The love of Peter for his Master had greatly
cooled. He had slept when he should have prayed.
He had followed Jesus *afar off,* and more through
curiosity than affection, *to see the end.* Instead of
compassionating his Lord in His Passion, he was
listening to idle conversation. In short, idleness,
listlessness, curiosity, and neglect of prayer—all
fatal marks of tepidity—prepared the soul of
Peter for his unhappy fall. A soul cannot remain
long in a state of tepidity, without falling into seri-
ous faults. The passions grow stronger as the love
of God becomes weaker. The devil assaults the
soul with a degree of violence increased in pro-

portion to her neglect of prayer. God withdraws His special graces from the tepid soul, to punish her criminal languor. In this state, she is, as it were, on the very edge of a deep, perhaps even bottomless, abyss and the slightest push is sufficient to cast her down headlong. If you have grown cold in the practice of virtue, negligent in prayer, forgetful of the presence of God, and indulgent in your passions, delay not for a moment to return to your first fervor, otherwise you will end by committing great sins, and perhaps at last incur eternal damnation.

2. Peter denies Jesus through presumption and self-confidence.

It almost always happens that interior sentiments of pride precede the commission of grievous sins. Peter was not aware of his own weakness. He preferred himself before others; he trusted in himself as though he were incapable of sinning, boasting that no temptation would separate him from Jesus. He would not even believe the assurance of his Divine Master, that he would deny Him thrice. Deceived by this vain confidence in his own strength, he neglects to pray, and to have recourse to God; and God, in His justice, permits him to fall, in punishment of his pride. There is nothing more dangerous than to confide in our own strength, and trust to feelings of fervor. We are full of malice, and capable of committing the most enormous crimes, unless God supports us. Who can now yield to temptations of pride? The

Saints have fallen. Peter, the most fervent of all the Apostles, falls after having passed three years in the school of Christ, and been taught by His Divine lips, and been so favored by Him, and after having protested so many times that he would rather die than offend Him! Peter denies all knowledge of Him, even with oaths and imprecations. Good God! how low may we fall in one moment! Be on your guard against yourself and your own weakness, and continually implore the help of Divine Grace.

3. St. Peter denies Jesus, because he rashly exposes himself to the occasions of sin.

He remains in the company of the soldiers—a licentious and dissolute set of men—and becomes on such intimate terms with them as to warm himself at the same fire. Evil company is a most dangerous occasion of sin. If you do not avoid the society of the wicked, you will end by becoming like them. St. Peter, alarmed at the voice of a servant, denies Jesus, and thus commits one sin; but still he does not avoid the dangerous occasion, or fly from that place and company which have already been fatal to him. Consequently, he sins a second and a third time, and would never have entered into himself, nor risen from the deep abyss into which he had fallen, had not Jesus Christ, by a loving look of mercy enlightened and raised him up. Every time you have fallen into mortal sin, you have denied Jesus. As often as you have exposed yourself to the danger of committing sin, so often have you declared by your actions that you know not Jesus, who has commanded you to fly from the occasions of denying Him. Ah, by the love you bear your own soul, always tremble with horror at the thought of returning to those occasions where you have at other times fallen into sin! Tremble, and fly, if you do not wish to offend God.

The Fruit

St. Peter fell into sin for one brief hour, and bewailed his fall during the whole remainder of his life. Never did he forget that he had sinned and displeased his beloved Master. By how many enormous faults have you displeased your good God, your amiable Redeemer? Repeatedly renew your acts of contrition. St. Peter did not for one moment delay his repentance and conversion. How long has God called and invited you to repentance? Resolve this very day to be converted to God. Do not wait till tomorrow, as perhaps tomorrow, time for you may be no more.

Example

The thought of Jesus suffering is a remedy against all the assaults of the devil. Blessed Christina of Cologne, being tormented by devils, interiorly with horrible temptations and exteriorly with blows and other tortures, was accustomed to repel their assaults and preserve her soul in patience amidst so many trials, by the remembrance of the sufferings of Jesus. "If I look at Jesus dying on the Cross for my sake," she would say, "I do not fear to endure all that Hell can inflict on me for His love." "When I remember how my innocent Jesus was transfixed by cruel nails," she would exclaim to the demons, "I offer myself willingly to suffer any tortures from your hands, that so I may have a share in His dolorous Passion." The utterance of these few words either freed her from the evil spirits, or enabled her to preserve unalterable serenity of mind. (Bollandists, June 22).

∽ **DAY 11** ∽

Jesus Is Derided and Treated Most Ignominiously in the House of Caiphas

Meditation

THE iniquitous sentence having been pronounced by Caiphas, Jesus remains for the whole concluding portion of that night in the power of His enemies, who keep Him bound in chains, and cruelly maltreat His sacred Person. Consider all that Jesus suffers during this night.

1. He suffers in His sacred Body.

The first outrage offered to the meek Redeemer of the world is that His enemies spit in His face. No greater insult or more decided mark of contempt can be shown to a man of honor than to spit in his face. Not once only is the face of Jesus, the only Son of God, defiled with spittle, but over and over again is He outraged in that manner by the whole band of insolent soldiers and servants, who seem to vie with each other in insulting Him, and in defiling His adorable countenance with their filthiness. What an ignominious outrage, what a

shameful degradation, is this for our most patient
Jesus! And yet He turns not away His face, but
suffers, and is silent. Such are the humiliations
caused to Jesus by our vanity! By the endurance
of such grievous insults does Jesus expiate my
pride! The second torture inflicted on Jesus is
that of being struck with the hands and feet of
His enemies, who at the same time maltreat Him
in various other ways. Contemplate our sweet
Saviour thus abandoned to the mercy of these
cruel wretches, who joyfully take advantage of
this opportunity of satiating their rage by smiting
Him with barbarous energy. See how the whole of
the sacred Body of our dear Lord is, in the course
of a few moments, bruised and disfigured by a
shower of heavy blows! Ah, to what sufferings, to
what torturing insults, is our blessed Jesus subjected for the love of you, an ungrateful creature!
And you remain unmoved by so mournful a spectacle? Do you not compassionate Jesus? Do you
not at least desire to imitate His patience, humility, and silence?

2. He suffers in His honor.

The patience and unalterable mildness of Jesus
serve but to excite the fury of His enemies, who
continue with diabolical perseverance to invent
new modes of torturing Him. Not satisfied with
the more common insults and scornful expressions with which they have hitherto accompanied
their blows, they now treat Him as a false
prophet. They cover His face with a filthy rag, and

deride Him as though He were a fool or a madman. They blindfold Him, to be able to maltreat
His sacred Person more unrestrainedly, and display increased fury and insolence in their outrages. They blaspheme, they smite, they curse
Him, without remorse or restraint. Behold to
what an excess sinners have carried their outrages against Jesus! But behold also to what an
excess Jesus has carried His heroic patience! He
is the God of wisdom, the Lord of prophets, and
the Searcher of hearts, yet He permits Himself to
be dishonored so far as even to be treated as a fool
or maniac, and the scorn of men! He might in one
moment have taken ample vengeance on those
who outrage Him, but it is His Will to teach you
by His example not to be so sensitive to all that
affects your reputation and honor, to submit to a
slight insult for His sake, to overcome human
respect, and to make a sacrifice to Him of your
anxious desire for honor and esteem.

3. He suffers in His soul.

It is impossible to describe all that Jesus suffers in His most holy Soul during this night of
agony. He has a clear knowledge of the heinous-
ness of the insults offered to Him, because He is
well aware of the excellence of His Divine Person,
thus loaded with contumely; He comprehends
that the Majesty of God is therein most shamefully outraged, and that by those very men to
whom He had been most untiringly liberal of His
favors; hence how deep is the affliction which

overwhelms His tender Heart! He hears the obscene language, the curses and calumnies, of those brutal soldiers, and they are so many wounds lacerating His pure Soul. He beholds Himself loaded with ignominy and opprobrium, defiled with spittle, and reduced so as to be *a worm, and no man.* He who is the God of Majesty and Glory—what confusion, what agony, must have been His! And yet Jesus, even when His interior anguish is at its height, rejoices in submitting to every species of outrage, thus to make satisfaction for my sins, and to apply to my soul the infinite merit of all His sufferings. Admire the boundless charity of Jesus, and never cease thanking Him for all He has vouchsafed to endure for your salvation.

The Fruit

When you contemplate the spectacle of the Jews defiling the adorable face of Jesus with spittle, remember that you also have done like them every time that you have offended God by impure and immodest words. Excite yourself to sentiments of contrition for your sins, and make a firm determination to place a guard upon your tongue, and exert the most watchful vigilance. During the day, whenever your patience is tried, contemplate Jesus in the hands of His enemies, who inflict the most disgraceful tortures upon Him, while He utters not one word of complaint.

Example

Blessed Serafino of Ascoli, a Capuchin friar, was frequently tried, while yet a young man in the world, by the reproofs and sneers of his companions, and the unjust severity of one of his brothers, who was so cruel as sometimes even to refuse him a dry crust of bread. The pious youth submitted to everything with admirable patience, all his sufferings being rendered sweet to him by the remembrance of those of Christ. Meditation on the Passion of his Lord was his sole consolation amid the numerous trials he had to endure. A like comfort will it be to you, if you follow his example. (See his *Life*).

⊸ DAY 12 ⊷

Jesus Is Led before Pilate, The Roman Governor

Meditation

EARLY in the morning, the high priests and ancients of the people again assemble and resolve to deliver Jesus up to the secular power, by consigning Him to Pontius Pilate, a Gentile, and the Governor of Judea, Consider:

1. The exterior of Jesus during this His third most painful journey.

He is bound anew with cords and chains by order of the high priests, that Pilate may at once regard Him as a man guilty of death, and unworthy of being treated with clemency. Thus bound, our sweet Saviour is dragged by the inhuman Jews, who overwhelm Him with every species of insult, as the very worst of malefactors, before the tribunal of the governor. The streets are crowded, and new spectators throng in from every side to feast their eyes upon the prisoner. All rejoice, and all endeavor by bitter insults to share in the torture of the innocent malefactor. And among all this crowd watching and deriding Him, there is scarcely one man to be found who pities Him. My soul, contemplate this Man-God bound with heavy chains, His sacred face discolored and defiled with spittle, His head uncovered and bruised by the blows He has received, and His whole Divine Person outraged at every step by the most degrading insults. Contemplate the modesty and gravity of His demeanor, and behold how His sacred countenance is expressive of the most serene patience and meek humility. Thou canst not perceive there the slightest trace of vexation, sorrow, or anger.

His strength is exhausted, He is sinking with fatigue, and bowed down beneath the ignominy of His situation, yet He hastens onward joyfully and serenely to deliver Himself up into the hands of Pilate, to be condemned to death. Oh, what charity, what mercy, what condescension, is Thine, my Jesus! And all for my sake! But oh, what lessons of virtue may I not draw from thy outward deportment on this occasion!

2. The interior of Jesus.

He is thoroughly aware of all the evil intentions of His enemies, who are resolved to have Him put to death as a public malefactor; therefore we might naturally suppose that He would be thereby afflicted and filled with indignation; but, on the contrary, the calmness of His Heart remains undisturbed, and His appearance is that of a meek Lamb led to the slaughter. He sees that the Jews have unanimously conspired against Him through motives of malice and hatred, that there is not one man to stand by Him, and that all are afraid of speaking in His favor—still, our innocent Redeemer humbles Himself amid all His sufferings, as though He were really guilty. He hears the insulting words, the sharp sarcasms, and the atrocious calumnies with which every one of His enemies delights in assailing Him, and He offers all with fervent acts of charity to His Eternal Father in expiation of my sins. He permits His senses to feel the whole bitterness of His sufferings, but, at the same time, His soul is overflowing with joy that the day for which He has long sighed, and for which he has been waiting during the space of thirty-three years, to accomplish the work of my Redemption, is come at last. Compare your interior dispositions for one moment with those of Jesus. How great a difference do we behold between them! You can bear nothing willingly, like Jesus. You grieve, lament, are disturbed in spirit, and have not even sufficient fortitude to offer your slight trials to Jesus, who has suffered so much for love of you. When will you profit by the example of Jesus?

3. Jesus before Pilate.

The Jews might have put Jesus to death secretly, and thus satiated their feelings of hatred and envy, but they are desirous of appearing innocent of His death: they wish that He should die, but not that the odium of His death should be imputed to them. They therefore conduct Him to Pilate, that he may pronounce the sentence of condemnation, and, without entering into his palace, they loudly call upon him to condemn to death the malefactor whom they have brought loaded with chains before his tribunal. Pilate, from his house, beholds our blessed Jesus advancing toward Him with the utmost meekness and humility of demeanor, and he perceives how He is almost visibly surrounded by a halo of innocence. The Jews well know the perfect innocence of Jesus, and still, with senseless fury, clamorously demand His death. A hundred times have they received proofs of His goodness; over and over again has He been to them a loving benefactor, and now they are seeking only to have Him put to death as the worst of malefactors. Let not your anger be kindled against the Jews, but against yourself, for whenever you have committed sin your crime has been far greater than theirs, in outraging your Benefactor, your Father, and your God. You knew what you were doing; you believed in Jesus, and yet sinned!

Meanwhile, Jesus stands before the governor in humble silence, surrounded by His enemies, and is desirous of giving an example of patience rather than of proving His innocence. Oh, how instructive is His silence!

The Fruit

When tempted to commit sin, and to offend Jesus, answer the devil, the world, and your own passions, in the words of Pilate to the Jews when they presented Christ before his tribunal: *"What accusation bring you against this man?* What evil has Jesus done to me that I should offend Him? Has He deserved to be offended? Ought I to hate Him who has so much loved me?" If you direct all your efforts to the acquisition of the interior virtues of meekness, mildness, and humility of heart, you will find no difficulty in the practice of other, exterior virtues.

Example

The remembrance of the Passion of Jesus detaches the soul from worldly vanities. St. Elizabeth of Hungary, having entered a church one festival day to assist at the Divine office, dressed in her royal robes, and attended by a large retinue of servants, cast her eyes upon a Crucifix, and at that sight her heart immediately smote her. "Behold thy Creator," said an inward voice, "thy Redeemer, thy God, who for love of thee hangs naked on a Cross, and suffers the most disgraceful of deaths, and thou, a wretched creature, art clothed in vain attire and costly ornaments. The head of Jesus is crowned with thorns, and thine with flowers and jewels. Thus, then, dost thou imitate thy Master, thus dost thou follow His example!" So deeply was she touched and over-come by these reflections that she turned pale, and fell trembling and fainting to the ground, where she remained for some time, until revived by the care of her attendants. (See her *Life*).

∽ DAY 13 ∽

Jesus before the Tribunal of Pilate

Meditation

PILATE being well aware of the malice of the Jews, and that they are seeking the death of Jesus solely to satiate their hatred and envy, asks them what accusations they bring against Him to form the subject of examination. Consider:

1. The falsity of the accusations brought against Jesus.

He is accused of being a seditious, turbulent man; and yet on no subject has He preached with so much zeal as on those relating to subordination, obedience and humility. In all His discourses He has inculcated no virtues with more ardor than meekness, submission and love of enemies. He is accused of having forbidden tribute to be paid to Caesar. But what dark malice must have suggested so odious a calumny to oppress His innocence, for His enemies are well aware that Christ paid the tribute for Himself and for St. Peter! Be consoled, O you who are disciples of

Jesus, whenever you are treated as was your Divine Master. You will resemble Him, if your enemies resemble His in their calumnies. The third accusation produced against Jesus, as involving a most heinous crime, is that He sought to make Himself king, and yet he never affected the outward appearance, or bore the insignia of one! His deportment has always been humble, submissive and simple, and whenever the people attempted to proclaim Him king, He always fled and concealed Himself. Oh, how many calumnies are invented by the perfidious Jews for the sake of depriving our most innocent Saviour of His honor and life! In the meantime, what is the demeanor of Jesus on beholding Himself thus falsely accused? He humbles Himself, and is silent. He loves these humiliations, and willingly embraces them to satisfy for our pride. Can anyone contemplate a Man-God thus unjustly calumniated before a public tribunal, and not willingly submit to a slight aspersion upon his own reputation and innocence?

2. The humility of Jesus throughout His examination.

The governor, having returned into his audience-chamber, summons Jesus into his presence, that he may examine His case in private, and with proper gravity, apart from any tumult. He takes his seat as judge in his tribunal, and questions Him, urging Him over and over again to answer and declare who and what He is. Represent to yourself Jesus Christ standing as a criminal, with His hands bound, and head bent downwards, before a profane idolater, to be judged by him. So profoundly does Jesus, the Son of God, the King of Glory, the Judge of the Universe, humble Himself! For three years He has been preaching humility, and on this occasion, He preaches it more loudly and efficaciously still, by His own example. Jesus Christ, having replied to Pilate in a few words full of heavenly wisdom, so as to refute all the accusations brought against Him, maintains a profound mysterious silence. The high priests grow warm in the repetition of their exaggerated calumnies, and the governor urges Him to prove His innocence. The preservation of His good name, and even of life, seems now to call for self-defense. Nothing could be more easy than for Jesus to prove His innocence, and confound His enemies, and yet He is silent. He holds His peace because His enemies are not worthy again to hear His voice. He holds His peace, to teach us by His own example how to be silent and humble in adversity. He holds His peace, because He is not desirous of being set at liberty—because He is only sighing for the moment when He is to die for me. Oh, charity of my Jesus! Can I ever sufficiently praise Thee or worthily love Thee?

3. The innocence of Jesus proclaimed by the judge.

Pilate, having examined the cause of Jesus, finds Him innocent, and publicly declares that there is no guilt in Him. Our blessed Lord has been presented before three different tribunals, and in each His innocence has been found unsullied. And yet He is treated as a criminal and sentenced to punishment. Jesus is perfectly innocent, even by sentence of His judges; Jesus has done nought but good, and nevertheless He vouchsafes to subject Himself to punishment, as though He were the worst of malefactors, and I who am guilty of so many sins, will not accept the slight penance of some little shame or suffering which Divine Justice inflicts upon me by the instrumentality of others. I have so many times deserved Hell on account of the innumerable sins which I have committed against my God. I am perfectly convinced and persuaded of this truth, and yet I cannot bear any trial sent me by Our Lord in expiation of my sins! How different is my conduct from Thine, O my Jesus! In Thy Passion Thou dost expiate faults not Thy own, and in all Thy sufferings I am ever present to Thy mind; while I have not courage to punish myself for my own sins, which have cost Thee so much, because I do not keep Thee, the Great Example of patience and penance, before my eyes.

The Fruit

Determine to love sincerely all those who calumniate or speak ill of you, making a sacrifice of all desires of vengeance to Jesus Christ. Learn from the example of Jesus to be silent on those occasions when it would be lawful or advantageous for you to speak in your own defense, and do this for the love of Him. Offer to God as a penance for your sins all the trials of this life, declaring your readiness to accept anything from the hands of God.

Example

Saint Peter Martyr, a friar of the order of Preachers, being falsely accused to his superior of a heinous crime, and on that account severely rebuked and penanced, preserved an humble silence, and submitted with heroic resignation to the punishment inflicted on him. Now it happened one night while he was praying before his Crucifix that he began to reflect upon his innocence, and how he had been unjustly accused and penanced, so that his heart heaved with sorrow, and he sighed deeply, exclaiming to Jesus Crucified, with a view to give vent to his grief, "O Lord, Thou knowest my innocence, and why hast Thou permitted that calumny should prevail against me, and that I should be so unjustly treated?" Then Jesus answered from the Crucifix, *"And what have I done, O Peter, to deserve to be thus nailed to a Cross? Learn from my example, to suffer with patience."* These sweet words made the heart of the sorrowing Saint bound with joy, and inspired him with constancy and courage in suffering any tribulation for the love of his Crucified Jesus. (See his *Life*).

∽ DAY 14 ∾

Jesus Is Presented before Herod

Meditation

PILATE, having heard that Jesus was from Galilee, which belonged to the jurisdiction of Herod, to escape judging His cause, sent Him to that monarch, who was then dwelling in Jerusalem, that he might dispose of His sacred Person, as best suited him. Consider:

1. In what manner Herod receives Jesus.

The Jews are eager to conduct our blessed Lord to the house of Herod, because they hope that this barbarous king will pronounce sentence of death upon Him, and they likewise exercise their ingenuity in finding out new modes of afflicting Him with inhuman tortures during this His fourth most painful journey. Compassionate the Son of God under the new outrages, insults, and degradations to which He is exposed as He passes through the streets of Jerusalem. Herod, hearing of the approach of Jesus, rejoices, and receives Him on His arrival with feelings of hope, joy and desire. But his joy is vain, for he rejoices solely at beholding a wonderful Man, and satisfying his curiosity, while he thinks but little of profiting by the presence of Christ for his soul's salvation. Thus it is that he sees Him, speaks to Him, and knows Him not, but remains in his sins. Rejoice when God visits and speaks to you in prayer, but be attentive for your soul to profit by the visits of your Lord. The desires of Herod are barren and unproductive. He had long desired to see Jesus, and yet he had never sought Him. He had already heard of the wonders wrought by His hand. He knew that the whole world was running after Him, and yet he would not go a step to see Jesus and profit by His preaching. Many there are who resemble Herod, who desire to do penance, to be converted and to save their souls, but who never make a firm resolution, and die before having begun the work of their conversion. The hope of Herod is impious. He hopes to see Jesus Christ work some miracle; he hopes to hear His teaching, and to be gratified by His eloquence, not for his soul's sake but to feed vanity and satisfy curiosity. Hence he is deceived in his expectations, and Jesus does not vouchsafe him a single word. Are you waiting for some miracle to be worked before you will resolve to love and serve God? God will not work one, and you will remain in sin.

2. The deportment of Jesus toward Herod.

Herod makes every effort to obtain some answer from Jesus. He questions Him in various ways, urging, and eagerly tempting Him to speak;

but Jesus is silent, and although He perceives that His silence will expose Him to be treated as a fool or madman, and that if He speaks He will, on the contrary, be regarded as a wise man and please the prince, still He opens not His mouth and utters not a single word. He hears the high priests and scribes furiously maintaining their accusations against Him, and still He is silent. Oh, how admirable, how instructive is this silence of Jesus! Herod is filled with pride and malice, and God holds converse only with the humble, the meek, and the simple. Herod is defiled with the sin of adultery, and God speaks not to sullied and impure souls. Seek then to be humble, and preserve the greatest purity of heart, if you wish to be in a state to hear the voice of God. Herod has never made any effort to see Jesus, although he might easily have done so, and now Jesus refuses to speak to him. Such is the fate of all who despise the grace of God—by a just judgment it is refused them.

Oh, how terrible a misfortune is the silence of God for a soul! How unhappy is that heart to which the Lord no longer speaks by His holy inspirations! Beware of rendering yourself unworthy of them, by turning a deaf ear to them, and by indulging your evil passions.

3. Jesus is treated with scorn in the court of Herod.

Herod being offended at the silence of Jesus, and enraged at finding himself deceived in his expectations, begins to deride Him by word and gesture, and to treat Him with scorn as a senseless, mad, deluded man. Behold, my soul the depth of humiliation to which the almighty Son of God is subjected, even to that of being publicly treated as a fool and madman. Understand now at least how great an evil thy pride must be, since, to effect its cure, a God has been obliged thus to humble Himself! The high priests, soldiers, and people, following the example of Herod, emulate each other in despising Jesus Christ, in laughing and scoffing at His ignominious position, and insulting and deriding the degradation of His sacred Person. But in the meantime, our afflicted Redeemer, thus shamefully insulted by vile creatures, is silent and complains not. Truly this is a miracle of patience worthy of a God. A like miracle has God so frequently wrought in your regard, when He has with infinite patience and mercy borne with your sins. Herod, who had so eagerly desired to behold Christ, now despises Him, clothes Him in a white robe, that so He may be openly recognized as a fool, and sends Him back to Pilate. Accompany your blessed Lord with love and compassion through the crowded streets of the city. Everywhere, and by everyone is He shamefully outraged. There is not one to defend or assist Him amid so many insults and sufferings. He is the author of wisdom, and yet rejoices in being treated as a fool, to teach me that true wisdom consists in despising the judgments of the world, and in imitating His humility.

The Fruit

Begin at length in real earnest to love and serve God; you have lost time enough in offending Him. Place the greatest value on the graces and inspirations of Our Lord; your eternal salvation may depend upon your correspondence with or rejection of, one single grace. Take for your rule of life, not the maxims and opinions of the world, but the truths of the Gospel, and the example of Jesus Christ. The wisdom of the world is as folly before God, and the truly wise are those who are reputed as fools of the world.

Example

The lovers of Christ Crucified are always most anxious to awaken a spirit of devotion to His sufferings in the hearts of men. Such, from earliest youth, was the fervent desire of Saint Paul of the Cross, and having bound himself by vow to promote devotion to Christ Crucified by every means in his power, he made it the principal object of all his thoughts, actions, journeys, spiritual exercises, missions, discourses and writings. The very day of his death, being unable to speak, he took a little Crucifix into his hand, and with his eyes fervently expressed the feelings of his heart, so as to make known to a gentleman who had come to visit him, how the Passion of Jesus Christ should be ever present to his mind, and to impress this still more strongly upon him, he gave him the little Crucifix. You also may sometimes promote this devotion by a few pious words. (See his *Life*).

Barabbas Preferred
Before Jesus

Meditation

PILATE *finding no cause in Jesus,* and being willing to save Him from His enemies, has recourse to the expedient of offering the people their choice between Him and Barabbas, who is a man so hateful to all on account of his crimes, that it does not seem possible they can for a moment hesitate to ask the favor for Jesus Christ. Consider:

1. The insult Pilate offers Jesus by comparing Him with Barabbas.

Who is Jesus, and who is Barabbas? Jesus is the Eternal Son of God, the King of Majesty, the Lord of Glory, the Creator of Heaven and Earth and the Holy of Holies. It would be a grievous insult to compare Him with the highest of the Angels, what then must it be to compare Him with Barabbas, a rebel, a thief, a murderer, and a notorious criminal? How keenly must the Heart of Jesus feel so ignominious a comparison! What

anguish must His Soul suffer on hearing Pilate
say to the people: *"Which of the two will you have?
Whom do you prefer? Whom do you love best, Jesus
or Barabbas?"* And yet He joyfully submits even to
this disgraceful outrage. How often have you
renewed this shameful comparison? Whenever the
devil has tempted you to indulge in some sensual
pleasure, or the world has instigated you to take
vengeance, and you have been careless and lukewarm in rejecting the temptation, being undecided
as to whether it were better to please God and
obey His laws, or indulge your evil passions, so
often have you compared God, the Sovereign Infinite Good, to a miserable gratification and vile
pleasure. What an outrage to God! What an insult
to His Majesty! Be ashamed of your rash presumption, and weep over your sin.

2. The unjust preference given by the Jews to
Barabbas.

The Jews having heard the proposal of Pilate,
and being inflamed with rage against our innocent Saviour, exclaim as one man, *"Not Jesus, but
Barabbas!"* They are well aware of the unsullied
innocence of Jesus—they have been witnesses of
the sanctity of His life—they have received infinite benefits from His hand, nay, many out of that
numerous crowd have been miraculously healed
by Him. And yet, though a prodigy of injustice,
there is not one man in all that multitude who
will ask for His liberation! And the most generous
of benefactors is set aside for the sake of a wicked

seditious man! The God of Majesty and Holiness is treated as nought in comparison with a murderer! Words can never describe how deep a wound is inflicted on the loving Heart of Jesus by the intolerable injustice done Him on this occasion by His chosen people. Compassionate Him in this His painful humiliation, but pause and reflect also upon your own conduct. The Jews are guilty in preferring Barabbas before Jesus, but they committed this enormous crime upon one occasion only, whereas how many times have you exclaimed in your heart, by consenting to sin, "Away with God from my soul, give unto me the devil with that wicked pleasure, or illicit gain, or that gratification of my evil passions!" You have preferred the devil to Jesus whenever you have renounced the service of God. You knew that Jesus was your King, you believed Him to be your God, you adored Him as your Saviour, and yet you thus preferred an unclean and degrading sensual pleasure before Him! What more frightful injustice than this? Detest your malice, force your perverse will to retract its shameful determinations, and resolve ever to prefer God before all created objects.

3. The Jews having asked for the liberation of Barabbas—thus proving that they set more value on the life of a public thief, than on that of the Saviour of the world, now demand with loud cries that Jesus should be condemned, that He should be put to death, that He should be crucified.

Who could have thought that this ungrateful

people would have reached such a height of iniquity as to desire the crucifixion of their King, their Messias, and their Deliverer—the Expectation of Nations, whose presence they had so long sighed for, and whom, but a few days before, they had welcomed with acclamations as the Son of God? But who would ever believe that a Christian, so liberally loaded with favors, so tenderly loved by Jesus, could commit so atrocious a crime as to exclaim in his heart, *"Let Jesus die!"* And yet such is your daily cry by the commission of mortal sin. You say, not with your voice, but by your deeds: *"Let sin triumph, but let Jesus die! The loss of God I consent to, but not the loss of this shameful pleasure. Let Jesus be crucified, and sin reign in my soul."* Can any impiety or ingratitude surpass this? Pilate says to the furious Jews: *"But what evil hath Jesus done,* that you wish Him to die?" And they persist in crying, *"Let Him be crucified!"* "What evil hath Jesus done you," was the cry also of your conscience, "that you are determined to offend Him?" And yet you obstinately persisted in sin, and in crucifying Jesus. The only crime of Jesus is that of too much love for us, His charity has induced Him willingly to accept death for our sakes. His love for you, and desire for your salvation, cause Him to wait for you with such infinite patience, even after all the outrages you have committed against Him. Love so loving a God, thank so merciful a God, and displease not so good a God any more.

The Fruit

Determine to avoid sin above every other evil. Be careful and prompt in banishing bad thoughts and the wicked suggestions of the devil, declaring your firm determination of serving God alone. Conceive a holy hatred against your flesh, your passions, and your self-love, which have so frequently caused you to offend God. Often say of these enemies, *"Let them be crucified!"* and endeavor to crucify them by mortification.

Example

There is nothing which may not serve to remind the lovers of Christ Crucified of the sufferings and death of their beloved Redeemer. The servant of God, Sister Mary Minima, of Jesus of Nazareth, a Carmelite nun, was one Friday in March sitting down to table, when she saw a little lamb come into the Refectory, run towards her and take refuge in her arms. More was not required to make her think of Jesus, the Lamb without spot, delivered up by the furious Jews to the bitterest torments and most ignominious death. She was so much overcome by this reflection, and so many tears flowed from her eyes, that she was quite unable to take any food for the remainder of the day.

Accustom yourself in like manner to take occasion from everything to remember the sufferings of Jesus. (See her *Life*).

➳ DAY 16 ➳

Jesus Scourged at the Pillar

Meditation

PILATE, perceiving the obstinacy of the people in requiring that Jesus should be crucified, sentenced Him, in the first place, to the shameful punishment of scourging, and consigned Him to the hands of the soldiers, that his orders might be executed. Consider:

1. Jesus before the scourging.

The soldiers having received orders to scourge Jesus Christ, fall furiously upon Him, and lead Him to the public place where it is customary to flagellate the lowest criminals. The Jews rejoice at seeing their hated Saviour at length condemned to so dreadful a punishment, but Jesus rejoices even more at beholding the long sighed for hour arrived at last, in which He is to shed His Blood for my salvation through the instrumentality of the scourges. He is consumed with an ardent desire of suffering for my sake, and therefore it is that He allows Himself to be led by His executioners wherever they will, and offers not the slightest resistance. Learn to accept with patience all the sufferings God sends you in expiation of your sins. Jesus being arrived at the spot appointed, His enemies fall upon Him with the fury of wild beasts, unbind His chains, strip off His clothes, and, binding Him tightly to a pillar, expose Him in this state of nakedness and humiliation to the sight and undisguised scorn of the insolent rabble. Oh, what ignominy, what shame, what painful confusion must our blessed Jesus have experienced on beholding His virginal purity thus exposed to the derision and insults of a large crowd of people! And yet He endures everything in silence, and offers all with infinite charity to His Eternal Father, in satisfaction for my sins of immodesty and pride. The force of love alone is sufficient to bind Him to that pillar, ready and willing to submit to the scourges, and to shed every drop of His Blood. O beloved Son of God! I thank Thee for such infinite charity.

2. Jesus during the time of scourging.

The executioners having prepared instruments proper for the purpose of inflicting intense suffering on Jesus, now strike that virginal and immaculate flesh with unparalleled fierceness and cruelty. That most Holy Body is soon all wounds. From the top of His head down to the soles of the feet, it is so lacerated that at length all the bones may be counted. And yet out of all the vast number of persons who behold this heart-rending sight, there is not one to compassionate our suffering Jesus. Hard indeed must your heart be if it be not moved to compassion at the sight of your blessed Lord enduring such a martyrdom. The executioners continue to strike Him, encouraging one another in their cruel labor. Wound succeeds wound, the suffering thus inflicted becomes more and more acute, and the Body of Jesus is one entire wound. The scourges fall heavily upon His tender limbs, tearing, rending, and even carrying away portions of the flesh, which fall on all sides. The blood flows in streams, blood bathes the whole person of our blessed Redeemer, blood trickles down the pillar, blood soaks the earth, and blood is sprinkled on the executioners, who feel no emotions of pity even at such a sight. The cruelty of the executioners is at length exhausted, but the patience of Jesus wearies not; He suffers excruciating torments, it is true, and each blow inflicts fresh torture, alone sufficient to cause His death, but yet He rejoices to shed so much blood, to suffer agony so unspeakable, to give us incontestable proofs of the greatness of His love for us, and to show us the enormity of sin. Jesus is scourged, for no crime of His own, but to expiate, in His innocent flesh, those sins of impurity with which you have so often defiled your body. Contemplate Jesus at the pillar, bleeding and lacerated from head to foot, and learn hence all that your sins of impurity have cost Him. Beseech Him to cleanse all the stains of your soul with His divine Blood.

3. Jesus after the scourging.

The executioners, weary of inflicting further torture upon Jesus, unbind Him from the pillar, and He, unable from exhaustion and excess of suffering to support Himself on His feet, falls to the ground bathed in His own Precious Blood. Ah, who would not have been touched at so mournful a sight? The Jews alone feel no compassion for Jesus. Behold, my soul, behold thy loving Redeemer lying prostrate and almost powerless, on the ground, and recognize in His Wounds the effect of thy sins, and of the excess of His charity, which has thus opened to thee new sources of grace. Compassionate Him who has suffered so much for thy sake, and love Him who has so much loved thee. Draw near to Jesus as He lies bleeding on the ground, with no one to assist Him to rise, and do thou afford His afflicted Heart some relief by the affections of thine. See with what meekness He endures the derision and contempt of His enemies in this His state of humiliation and suffering. Acknowledge how deeply thou art indebted to Jesus, who has bestowed on thee a bath of His own most precious Blood in which thou mayest cleanse thy corrupted sores, and who, by so plentiful a Redemption, has delivered thee from the eternal maledictions thy sins deserved.

The Fruit

Resolve to endure any inconvenience which may befall you, and to deprive yourself of some lawful gratification, in punishment of your sins, which have cost Jesus so dear. Determine upon what particular points you will mortify yourself, and take great care to mortify those senses by which you have so often offended God. And offer to Jesus tears of sincere repentance for your sins, and of loving compassion for His sufferings, as some slight testimony of gratitude for all the Blood which He has shed for you.

Example

Blessed Serafino d'Ascoli, a Capuchin Friar, not satisfied with spending whole nights in meditating on the Passion of Christ, passing entire weeks almost without food for love of Him, and paying his suffering Lord the tribute of plentiful tears and sighs, offered Him, moreover, the sacrifice of his own blood. When meditating on Jesus scourged at the pillar, he would enter into so holy an indignation against himself, scourge his body so severely, and draw forth such streams of blood, through his love of Christ, and through his great desire of resembling Him, that he seemed bent on rendering his body one wound, like that of Jesus in His scourging. Jesus Christ asks not so much of you, but at least do not refuse to endure some slight penance for love of Him.

∽ DAY 17 ∽

Jesus Is Crowned with Thorns

Meditation

THE soldiers, having scourged Jesus, are inspired by the devil with a new method of torturing Him. They take a bundle of long, sharp, strong thorns, and having woven them into a crown, place it on His head, thus constituting Him the King of ignominy and suffering. Consider:

1. The inexpressible agony inflicted by this torture.

If a single thorn were to pierce your head, what exquisite pain would it not cause? But if it were ever so slightly pressed, the anguish would become quite insupportable. The sacred Head of Jesus is encircled with a whole wreath of long sharp thorns which pierce it on every side. Oh, what torture must our suffering Redeemer now experience. Behold what your impure thoughts, guilty pleasures, and sinful desires have cost Jesus! Behold by what exquisite sufferings Jesus has expiated your ambitious designs, your vanity,

and your pride, and at how dear a rate he has purchased for you the graces of humility, patience
and contempt of the world! The barbarous soldiers, eager to inflict all possible torture upon our
patient Saviour, violently press down the crown
upon His brow, by repeated blows, so that the
sharp thorns wound and pierce the most delicate
parts of that adorable Head. My soul, contemplate
this King of Sorrows, and behold the streams of
blood flowing from every part of His wounded
Head, disfiguring and discoloring His amiable
countenance. Oh, how much blood has thy salvation cost Jesus! Compassionate thy suffering
Redeemer, and recognize the fruit of thy hateful
sins in those thorns, those wounds, and those
streams of blood. Each time that thou hast deliberately entertained evil thoughts, so often hast
thou crowned the sacred Head of Jesus with
sharp thorns. Is it possible that thou canst ever
more indulge in vain, blasphemous, and impure
thoughts, or in desires of earthly grandeur, after
reflecting upon Jesus crowned with thorns?

2. The disgraceful character of this torture.

The enemies of Jesus Christ seem to take peculiar satisfaction in making Him a mock King, in
ridiculing His sufferings, and in subjecting Him
to every species of degradation and insult. They
furiously tear off His garments, and clothe Him in
a ragged purple mantle. This outrage is a source
of exquisite suffering to Jesus, for the tearing off
His garments re-opens all the wounds which have

been so lately inflicted by His flagellation, so that fresh blood flows from the lacerated limbs. Oh, how much have the pleasures of our sinful flesh, the delicacy of our bodies, the luxury and vanity of our clothing, cost our sweet Jesus!

They place in His hand a reed as a scepter, to constitute Him a mock King, a King of a theater! Jesus refuses it not, but receives and holds it in His hand, rejoicing by so great a dishonor to merit for you graces of strength and perseverance in virtue, and to purchase for you a heavenly kingdom. In this state Jesus appears to the insolent soldiery a proper subject for mockery, and they proceed to ridicule Him in a manner worthy of their cruelty. They all march before Him, saluting Him in the most derisive terms King of the Jews. They deride Him as a wretched imposter, adding shameful insults and reproaches to the most humiliating expressions of scorn and ridicule; they spit in His face, give him blows, and, taking the reed out of His hand, strike the crown of thorns with it so violently as to enlarge every wound, and cause Him the most exquisite pain. They vie with each other in deriding and insulting Him, and in rendering His sufferings yet more cruel and ignominious. Oh, how ingenious is human cruelty in torturing Jesus! But, in the meantime, His most holy Soul, though overwhelmed with the weight of so much ignominy and suffering, rejoices in offering to His Eternal Father the sacrifice of humiliations so profound, in reparation of the outrages offered to His

Majesty by our sins. Bow down in adoration before this Divine King, return Him thanks for His infinite charity, and promise that you will love Him alone for the remainder of your life.

3. The patience of Jesus.

Amid His bitterest sufferings and most excessive humiliations, Jesus never once opens His mouth to complain. A frightful crown of thorns pierces His head on every side, and causes Him the acutest pain, yet he makes not the slightest complaint of the cruelty of His enemies. What do you say to this example of divine and superhuman patience, O you who are ever seeking after worldly pleasures and sensual gratifications, and who cannot endure even the slight thorn of some small inconvenience or trifling pain? You ought indeed to feel ashamed of living in luxury, when you behold your King, your Creator, and your God crowned with sorrow and ignominy. Do you calculate upon entering Heaven crowned with the roses of pleasure instead of the thorns of mortification, suffering, and penance? Deceptive hope! Jesus Christ beholds Himself abandoned by all— in the power of His cruel enemies, outraged, defied with spittle, buffeted, and smitten, yet He maintains peace of soul, and calmness of demeanor, and makes not the slightest gesture of anger or impatience. And you, wretched worm of the earth, unworthy sinner—you have not yet learned to submit in peace and silence to an insult, injury, or wrong done you by your neighbors! Is it possible that the sight of a God thus loaded with ignominy and suffering, and yet so patient and so humble, should not be sufficient to teach you patience and humility? If you do not imitate the example of Jesus Christ, you will not partake of His glory.

The Fruit

On all those occasions when it is your lot to suffer some inconvenience, annoyance, or illness, or any mortification of your senses and inclinations, imagine that Jesus offers you one of His thorns, and willingly accept and submit to it for love of Him. In time of temptation, and when assailed by evil thoughts, remember Jesus crowned with thorns, cast your eyes mentally upon His pierced head, and resolve that you will never renew His sufferings.

Example

A soul that loves Christ Crucified is ingenious in discovering ways of suffering in imitation of Him. When Saint Paul of the Cross was walking without shoes or stockings through wild and stony paths, sharp thorns would often enter his feet, and he would allow them to run in deeply, being well satisfied to suffer acute pain for the love of his Crucified Lord. Sometimes one of his companions would perceive what had happened, and, being anxious to relieve his pain, would express sorrow for it, and offer to extract the thorn. But then the servant of God would answer that what he suffered was nothing, since Jesus his Redeemer had permitted so many sharp thorns to transfix His most sacred Head. (See his *Life*).

∽ DAY 18 ∽

Jesus Christ Shown by
Pilate to the People

Meditation

PILATE, on beholding the Redeemer of the
world in the lamentable condition to which
His executioners have reduced Him, imagines
that His appearance alone must move the people
to compassion, and therefore takes Him to the
balcony in front of his palace, from whence He
may be seen by the assembled multitude, saying
"Ecce Homo."—"Behold the Man!" Consider:

1. The state in which Jesus is shown to the
people.

He is so deformed and disfigured as scarcely to
preserve the semblance of a man. His face is pale
and bruised with the blows He has received, and
defiled with the spittle—His adorable head is
bending beneath the painful weight of the sharp
thorns, which pierce His brow and form a crown
of sorrow and ignominy—His torn, mangled, and
bleeding frame is clothed with a garment of scorn
and derision. He suffers in every part of His

sacred Body, and His position is one of the deepest degradation. In this state of indescribable shame and confusion, the adorable Son of God is presented by Pilate to the people with these few words: *"Behold the Man!"* As though he had said: "Behold to what a condition the Man whom you accuse of aspiring to royalty is reduced! See whether He is not rather worthy of tears and compassion than of hatred!" And thou, my soul, attentively contemplate this Man-God, the King of Glory, overwhelmed with ignominy, in the presence of so great a multitude, His adorable Body streaming with blood and loaded with shame. He who was the most beautiful of the sons of men, is now the abomination of His people. He has assumed so painful and humiliating an appearance to induce His Father to take pity upon us, and deliver us from the eternal punishments which we have deserved. Love for our souls, and desire for their salvation, have reduced Him to so pitiable a condition. But, on your part, what efforts do you make for the salvation of your soul which has been purchased by Jesus at so dear a rate? Are you anxious to guard its purity and save it from eternal misery? Or are you, on the contrary, willing for a mere trifle to sacrifice your right to that Paradise which Jesus has purchased for you at the price of so many humiliations and sufferings?

2. The feelings aroused in the hearts of the people by the appearance of Jesus.

The sight of the lamentable condition to which the most innocent Redeemer of the world is reduced, would have touched hearts of stone, and ought to inspire the Jews with feelings of compassion and mercy toward our suffering Jesus. But no sooner do they behold Him than they seem to lose every feeling of humanity, and, with the fury of wild beasts, clamorously demand His death, and seek with unexampled fury to deprive Him of that life which is all but extinct in His martyred Body. The diabolical hatred and implacable rage animating them against our blessed Lord urge them on to demand with loud cries *that He should be crucified!* Behold the consequences of allowing a passion once to take possession of the heart! There is no excess into which a man blinded by any one passion may not fall. All passions delight but ruin the soul, and must therefore be combated with untiring energy. Pilate is well aware of the innocence of Jesus, and is by no means willing to yield to the iniquitous wishes of the Jews, but they fiercely and clamorously reply that *according to their law* He ought to die, because He has made Himself the Son of God. The laws of the world condemn Jesus to die. All worldlings who seek solely to gratify their passions exclaim by the voice of the Jews that Jesus must be put to death, that Jesus must be crucified! And do you regulate your conduct by such laws as these? Do you follow the maxims of worldlings? If such is the case, you will very speedily desert Jesus, and seek to crucify Him anew. Jesus beholds the rage of His enemies, He hears their furious outcries, and bitterly deplores their insensibility to His sufferings, but rejoices at the prospect of that Cross on which He is to die for love of me, while I tremble at the very name of crosses and sufferings. Why are my sentiments so contrary to those of Jesus?

3. The feelings which the sight of Jesus Christ should awaken in our hearts.

While the people display no compassion whatever on beholding Jesus, let us imagine that the Eternal Father shows Him to us to excite at least in our hearts feelings of love, veneration, and of desire to imitate Him. Let us imagine that we hear the Eternal Father addressing us in the words of Pilate to the Jews, *"Ecce Homo"*— *"Behold the Man!"* He is your King, the King of wisdom, of love, and of holiness, but also the King of sorrow and ignominy. He has acquired possession of His kingdom by humiliation and suffering; He has purchased it for you at the price of His Blood and of His Wounds: for your sake He has sacrificed His dignity, and permitted Himself to be thus outraged and tormented. Adore this King, be subject to Him, and if you wish to enter His blessed Kingdom, follow Him in the way of the Cross and of suffering. He is desirous of reigning in your hearts, and He has purchased possession of them at the price of a most painful death. Consecrate then to Him all your thoughts and all your affections. *Behold the Man!* He is your

Father; the most sweet, tender and loving of fathers—a Father who, for the love of His children, and in order to restore them to the life of grace which they had lost by sin, has sacrificed His own most precious life on the Cross, and is yet the most despised and abhorred of fathers. Love so good a Father, obey His commands, and never grieve His tender Heart. *Behold the Man!* He is your Master and your Model. Observe the virtues which He practices on this occasion. Extreme mildness amid so many provocations, perfect silence under so many outrages, great humility amid so many insults, and wonderful patience under so many sufferings. Contemplate, and endeavor to imitate Him. Never will you resemble Him in the honors of Paradise, never will you be His companions in glory, if you resemble Him not in His virtues. Resolve to do so by the help of His grace.

The Fruit

Remain for some time with your eyes fixed on a Crucifix, and say to yourself, "Behold the condition to which a God has been reduced for love of me, and to satisfy for my sins." Offer Him all the powers of your soul, and all the senses of your body, in testimony of your love, and determine to use them solely for His glory. Ask Him, through the merits of His humiliations, to bestow upon you the spirit of humility and penance.

Example

The venerable servant of God, Ursula Benincasa, took such great delight in having constantly before her eyes a picture representing Jesus crowned with thorns, and in the state in which He was shown by Pilate to the people, that she had it fastened on her working frame. When working she would frequently breathe forth fervent sighs of love to her suffering Lord, and beseech Him to allow her to partake in His sorrows, and to share His crown of thorns. She caused Crucifixes to be placed in every part of her house, and kept many in her room, so that, whichever way she turned, she might always behold her suffering Redeemer. Having become a Religious, and Superior of a Convent, she ordered each of her nuns to keep in her cell an image of Christ Crucified, and to say at least thirty-three times every day, *"My Crucified Jesus! I repent of all my sins. Have mercy on me, and help me at the hour of my death."* (See her *Life*).

∞ DAY 19 ∞

Jesus Condemned to the Death of the Cross

Meditation

PILATE, seeing that he gains nothing by all his attempts to liberate Jesus, but that, on the contrary, the people are being excited by the high priests to demand that He should be crucified, at last makes up his mind to pronounce sentence, and condemn Our Saviour to the death of the Cross. Consider:

1. The people desire the death of Jesus.

The Jews are not satisfied with the scourging of Jesus, nor yet with His crowning with thorns, nor with His having been overwhelmed with disgrace and ignominy; they require nothing less than his death, and urge Pilate to have Him crucified. You also have desired His death as often as you have sinned, and the voice of your perfidious, malicious will has uttered the cry, *Crucifige,* against your tender Father, Saviour and God, as loudly as ever the Jews did! Oh, what ingratitude and cruelty!

The Jews had sought for Jesus to make Him

king; they had experienced the effects of His benef-
icence; they had received the most signal favors
from His hand, both for soul and body; and now
with unexampled ingratitude they demand that
He should be put to death on the Cross like a malefactor, and cannot even endure the sight of His
adorable Person. Hence they desire Pilate to *take
Him away;* as though they had said, "We cannot
longer endure to behold Him, so hateful and disagreeable is His presence to us!" This is always the
aim of the wicked. They have no wish to know God,
or to contemplate His infinite perfections, and they
will not reflect upon His benefits, goodness and
love for us. If they once did so, they would have no
difficulty in abstaining from sin. The sight of Jesus
reminded the Jews of His miracles and benefi-
cence, and was a reproach to them for their atrocious injustice and fearful ingratitude in desiring
His death. On this account they would not look at
Him whose appearance aroused remorse in their
hearts. You commit sin, offend God, and persecute
Jesus even unto death, because you never will
pause and consider how much Jesus has loved you,
nor how much He has suffered for your sake. You
live in forgetfulness of God, with scarcely any
knowledge of Him, immersed in vanity and idle
curiosity, and absolutely unmindful of your loving
Benefactor and Sovereign Good; hence it follows
that you feel no horror of crying out, by your hateful sins, that He must be crucified, that He must
die. And what has Jesus done to deserve such
treatment at your hands?

2. Pilate condemns Jesus.

Pilate would willingly liberate Jesus, but his courage fails him. He fears to condemn Him because the thought of His evident innocence causes him to tremble. And yet when he hears the people threaten him with the anger of Caesar, Pilate betrays his conscience, and condemns the Just Man, the Holy of Holies, to death, delivering Him up into the hands of His most furious enemies! O accursed human respect! How many times have you, O Christian, put the Son of God to death in your heart by committing sin through human respect? Not to displease a friend, not to lose the favor of a person who is agreeable to you, not to be deprived of some vain transitory honor, not to lose some wretched pleasure, you have committed the monstrous evil of offending God! And yet you knew that He was your Lord, that He had a right to be obeyed and preferred by you to all things else. You knew that He commanded you to sacrifice friends and inclinations alike to His Will and law. How is it possible that you have made more account of a creature than of God, and that, through human respect and fear of men, you have renounced the friendship of God your Father? How is it possible that you can have been more afraid of displeasing men than of outraging the infinite Majesty of God by sin? Bewail your error, and hold human respect in detestation. Pilate trembles and is filled with horror when pronouncing sentence of death against the God of life; yet all his knowledge, remorse of conscience, and the evident proofs he has of the innocence of Jesus, are not sufficient to restrain him from committing so awful a crime, and he consents to the deicide. Indulge in no feelings of anger against Pilate, but rather turn them against yourself, who, in despite of the light of faith, the assistance of grace, and remorse of conscience, have sentenced Jesus Christ to death each time that you have committed mortal sin. And ought not the mere remembrance of this to cause you to die of grief?

3. Jesus Christ accepts death.

Jesus is standing in the position of a criminal before the tribunal of Pilate, while His sentence of death is pronounced. He hears the iniquitous decree by which He is condemned to die as a malefactor upon a Cross, and, reverently bowing down His Divine head, He submissively accepts it, without making the slightest opposition. He complains not of the wrong done Him; He appeals not to the judge who is abandoning Him to the rage of His most cruel enemies; He murmurs not at the injustice of the sentence, and He utters not one word in His own defense, but willingly and joyfully accepts death, for the glory of His Father and for love of us. Do you manifest equal obedience and submission to the orders of Providence, and to the designs of God in your regard? The sacrifices the Almighty requires of you will never be so arduous as to equal the bitterness and ignominy of the sentence of death pronounced against Jesus, and submitted to by Him for love of you, and to save you from eternal death. And cannot you for the love of Jesus accept that trial, or that humiliation, which is death to your self-love and pride? Oh, how great is your ingratitude toward One who has so much loved you! Jesus hears His enemies triumphing and rejoicing at His condemnation to death, and deeply as His most holy Heart grieves over their perfidious malice, yet equally, nay, even far more, does He rejoice at beholding at hand the long sighed-for moment in which He is to sacrifice His life for our salvation. O how deeply are we indebted to our dear Redeemer! How much ought we to love Him who for love of us willingly consents to die upon a Cross! O my sweet Jesus, now at least may I begin in very truth to love Thee!

The Fruit

Human respect, and your own passions, have caused you to become so often, like the Jews, a rebel to your God. Resolve, then, to be vigilant in mortifying your passions, and in despising all human respect, when the good pleasure of God is in question. Never forget your God, the benefits you have received from His hand, His love and His sufferings. Pious thoughts such as these will prevent you from committing sin. Pay great attention to Divine inspirations, and to remorse of conscience, for they are graces by which God proposes either to save you from consenting to sin, or to raise you up if you have fallen.

Example

Tears shed over the Passion of Our Lord are very pleasing to Him. Blessed Johanna of the Cross, who was filled with devotion to the sufferings of Jesus, even from her mother's womb (as was evident from the fact that, while yet a babe, she refused the breast on Fridays), was one day contemplating in spirit the streams of Blood which flowed down the sacred Body of her Crucified Redeemer, and lamenting that it was not granted to her to shed at least a portion of her blood for love of Him who, for her sake, had shed every drop of His, when an Angel appeared, and bade her be comforted, for that Our Lord regarded all the tears shed over His Passion in the light of so many drops of blood. (See her *Life*).

∽ DAY 20 ∽

Jesus Carries His Cross to Mount Calvary

Meditation

N O sooner is Jesus Christ condemned to death, than He is delivered up to the Jews to be crucified. A Cross is hastily prepared, and placed on the shoulders of our Blessed Lord, who issues forth from Jerusalem, bearing that heavy burden, on the road to Calvary. Consider:

1. The manner in which Jesus accepts His Cross. The soldiers, before placing the Cross upon the shoulders of Jesus, tear off the ragged purple mantle which He has worn until then, and *put on Him His own clothes again,* that He may be more easily recognized by all beholders. Thus are the wounds of Jesus re-opened, and the suffering and agony He endures are great in proportion to the length of time during which the mantle has adhered to His open wounds. Can we meditate upon this point of the Passion without pitying our most afflicted Redeemer, who suffers with such admirable patience and humility? For His greater torment, the crown of thorns is left upon His head, and oh, what a continual source of suffering is this crown to Him! The pressure of the Cross against His sacred Head, every movement He makes, and every step He takes, inflict the most acute torture upon Him. And yet Jesus utters not one word of complaint, but wears this painful crown even to His last breath. Be ashamed of your delicacy and unwillingness to endure the slightest trial. All things being thus arranged, and Jesus clothed in His seamless garment, the long and heavy Cross, upon which He is to be nailed, is presented to Him. Jesus lifts His eyes, and beholds it, and as it has ever been the object of His most loving desires, He embraces and tenderly presses it to His bosom; then, exhausted as He is, suffering, weak from loss of blood, and in a condition more nearly resembling death than life, places it upon His trembling, bleeding shoulders. Learn, O my soul, in what manner thou shouldst accept whatever God sends thee. It may be a heavy Cross that He sends thee, but remember that it is imposed upon thee by God Himself. Thou wilt never be called upon to suffer as much as Jesus, and unless thou bearest thy Cross after Him, thou wilt never partake of His glory.

2. The ignominious manner in which Jesus comes forth from the Praetorium.

The Jews hasten to conduct Jesus to death, and in order to satisfy their hatred against the innocent Saviour of the world, they determine that He shall die in the company of malefactors, and thus be supposed to be equal to them in guilt. They therefore immediately bring forward two condemned robbers, and having placed Jesus between them, set forward in procession towards Mount Calvary. The people, hearing the cries of joy and loud acclamations of the soldiers hasten from all sides to behold the mournful spectacle.

Jesus comes forth from the Praetorium, between the two thieves who are His companions in punishment, bound with cords, His sacred Face defiled with blood and spittle, His Head crowned with thorns, and His adorable form bending beneath the heavy weight of the Cross which He is bearing with difficulty upon His shoulders. With what confusion must Jesus have been overwhelmed at being seen by everyone in so disgraceful a position! How indescribably painful for Him, to whom sin is infinitely odious, to be exhibited to all Jerusalem in the character of a criminal about to suffer the penalty of his crimes! And yet He carries His Cross, and submits to the disgrace with so much patience and humility, with such meekness and mildness, that any hearts but those of the hardened Jews would have been touched with compassion.

Jesus, in taking up His Cross, has at the same time taken upon Himself all our sins; and it is to make satisfaction for them that He now willingly embraces this humiliation, and joyfully bears the heavy weight of the wood on which He is to sacrifice His life. Is it not just that you, who are guilty of so many faults by which you have immeasurably increased the weight of the Cross of Christ, and inflicted so much suffering upon Him, should now humbly and submissively bear the Cross of penance and of obedience to the Divine commands? All the streets of the city through which Jesus passes are crowded with people. Everyone watches, and takes pleasure in deriding and insulting Him in His sufferings. All blaspheme Him in the most derisive and disgraceful terms, and there is none to console, comfort, or assist Him. Approach, my soul, approach thy afflicted Redeemer, and by the light of faith recognize in that Man who is thus become the scorn of the people, thy Saviour, thy Father, and thy God, bearing in His own Person the penalty due to thy crimes; shed tears of contrition at His feet, and beware of increasing the weight of His Cross, and inflicting new sorrow upon His tender Heart by committing sin afresh.

3. The unspeakable agony He suffers during this His last journey.

Jesus being much weakened by all the Blood He has shed, is forced to exert the whole of His remaining strength to support the weight of the Cross, and every step He takes adds to His sufferings. He thus ascends the mount, sinking with fatigue, exhausted, and covered with wounds, but no one expresses any compassion for Him. He advances with the utmost difficulty, bearing on His weak and wounded shoulders that heavy

Cross, which overpowers Him by its weight, and re-opens all His wounds, to that the traces of His passage are marked in Blood. Oh, what exquisite torture does our sweet Jesus now endure! Your unworthy pleasures, and the steps you have taken in the paths of iniquity, are the causes of all His sufferings. The executioners strike, and force Him onward with cruel blows; the strength of Jesus fails at length entirely, and, overpowered by excessive suffering and fatigue. He sinks beneath the heavy weight of the Cross. My soul, attentively contemplate thy Saviour falling beneath His Cross, and acknowledge the enormity of thy sins. None but a Man-God could bear their weight, and even He is overwhelmed with the horror and deformity of so hateful a burden. If thou hadst not sinned, the weight borne by Jesus would have been less overpowering. The weight of our sins inflicts more suffering upon Him than His heavy Cross. Compassionate thy Lord thus oppressed with sorrow on account of thy sins.

Jesus having risen from the ground, feels His strength completely failing, and that He can do no more. And yet, He must proceed onward to Mount Calvary! His love for us, and desire to die for our salvation, infuse vigor into that Body now nearly drained of the last drop of Blood. He is sighing for that moment in which He is to offer Himself as a sacrifice to the honor of His Father, and for the redemption of His brethren. O most sweet Jesus! such then is Thy love for me, and shall I still remain insensible and ungrateful to Thee?

The Fruit

There are crosses to be found everywhere, even upon the throne. Seek not to remove or avoid them, and bear them not unwillingly, but, on the contrary, endeavor to render them meritorious. The Cross alone conducts to Heaven, and there is no saint who has not loved it. Therefore, when an affliction or trial befall you, never fail to return God thanks, and let it be your study then to practice the virtues of humility, patience, and resignation, in imitation of Jesus bearing His Cross. Are you desirous of carrying your cross with ease? Carry it in the company of Jesus Christ.

Example

There is no devotion dearer to the lovers of Jesus suffering than that commonly called the *Via Crucis,* the *Way of the Cross.* The servant of God, Sister Mary Minima, of Jesus of Nazareth, used to make the Way of the Cross, if possible, every day, shedding floods of tears, and deeply bewailing the sufferings of her Lord, whom she accompanied in spirit through the whole of His painful journey to Mount Calvary. One day, as she was performing this devotion, and meditating upon Jesus bearing His Cross, she heard Him say to her, *"Look upon Me; assist Me: love Me."* From which circumstance her heart became inflamed with the most eager desire to relieve Jesus in His excessive sufferings. Do you also perform this devotion in a spirit of loving compassion for your suffering Lord. (See her *Life*).

∽ DAY 21 ∾

The Meeting between Jesus and His Blessed Mother

Meditation

OUR blessed Redeemer, on His way to Calvary, has an interview with His most holy Mother, who is following Him, together with the other holy women. Consider:

1. The anguish of heart experienced by Jesus at the sight of Mary.

He beholds her sorrowing, weeping, overwhelmed with the bitterest grief, and when the eyes of the Mother and of the Son meet, how deep a wound is inflicted on the tender Heart of Jesus! Jesus loves Mary as His Mother. Jesus, the most loving of Sons, entertains the most indescribable feelings of affection for Mary, the most amiable of mothers. How great, then, and how bitter must be His grief at beholding this beloved Mother so deeply afflicted and anguish-stricken on His account? Oh, hard indeed must that heart be which does not compassionate Jesus in this new suffering! The Cross of Jesus is heavy, the thorns pierce His sacred Head, His adorable Body is one single wound, but His Heart is transfixed with a sword of still deeper and more painful sorrow, from beholding the interior of the heart of Mary, in which love and compassion imprint, as in a clear mirror all His wounds, His thorns, His Cross, and His sufferings, and thus inflict the keenest anguish. What mind can conceive the indescribable sorrow experienced by the Heart of Jesus at this mournful spectacle! He would willingly bestow upon His Mother a last token of affection, speak one word of comfort to her sorrowing heart, and bid her a last farewell, but the fury of the Jews does not permit Him to linger one moment by her side. But if these two most holy personages speak not with their lips, their eyes and hearts certainly are not silent, but communicate to one another their mutual sorrows. Beseech Jesus to give you a share in His sufferings, and to touch your heart, that so it may be filled with compassion for them, and with contrition for your sins.

2. The grief of Mary on beholding Jesus.

Mary is anxious to bestow upon her adorable Son proofs of the most faithful love, which never forsakes the beloved object even amid the severest trials. She therefore leaves Jerusalem, and follows her dear Son to Mount Calvary, to be present at His most painful sacrifice of Himself. If you really love Jesus, you should follow Him to Mount Calvary, willingly bearing the Cross of your trials for His sake. Mary also bears her heavy Cross, for she bears in her heart an immense weight of sorrow and suffering, which renders her the most afflicted of mothers. Great, nay, incomprehensible, is her love for Jesus, her Son and her God, and therefore proportionably great and incomprehensible is the grief of her soul on beholding His sufferings. Jesus sympathizes in the anguish of Mary, and Mary partakes of all the sufferings of her beloved Son Jesus, which, as so many sharp swords, rend and transfix her virginal heart. But the most acute pain endured by this afflicted Mother, is caused by the appearance of Jesus when He turns to address the holy woman. How is it, O Mary, that thou dost not die of grief and horror? How is it that thy heart does not break with sorrow? She beholds her dear Son sinking with exhaustion, His Body covered with wounds, and streaming with Blood, His head crowned with thorns, His face defiled with spittle, His whole adorable Person trembling, powerless and suffering; His neck encircled with a cord, and His shoulders burdened with the heavy and all but insupportable weight of the Cross. She beholds Him overwhelmed with insults by the people, dragged onward by the soldiers, and His sacred Heart bleeding with agony at the sight of her, His sorrowing Mother. "My Son!" would Mary have said, "My beloved Son!" but her excessive sorrow deprives her of the power of utterance. She would willingly draw nigh to Jesus, relieve His sufferings, and enfold Him in a last embrace, but any such comfort is denied her, and she is permitted to give expression to her feelings by tears alone. My soul, contemplate this most afflicted mother, and understand that her sufferings are occasioned by the cruelty with which thou hast maltreated Jesus in committing sin. Art thou desirous of diminishing her woes, and of alleviating her bitter sufferings? Bewail thy sins, and never more inflict such torments upon her beloved Son. Compassionate her in her sufferings, and love her as thy Mother.

3. The sorrows of Jesus and Mary at the sight of the sins of men.

Jesus suffers, and Mary suffers, but oh, how far more do they suffer from the sins of men than from all the present and future torments of the Passion! In the insensibility and hardheartedness of those crowds of people who line the road to Calvary, and who behold the sufferings of the Son, and the agony of the Mother, without a feeling of compassion for either, they see an image of the ingratitude of so many Christians, perhaps even of yourself, who never bestow even a single thought or feeling of affection upon Jesus Crucified, and upon Mary the Queen of Dolors. In the insults, outrages, and derisive words heaped upon Jesus in His sufferings by His enemies, they see an image of all those sins by which men will, with equal treachery and barbarity, renew His torments. Oh, what words can describe the sufferings of these two most sacred Hearts! The furious rage with which the Jews are hurrying Jesus to be crucified brings before them in strong colors the mortal sins by which multitudes of souls will, to the end of time, crucify Jesus anew. Alas, that Jesus should have beheld me also on that mountain crucifying Him by my sins! Alas, that Mary also should have seen me; for oh, what a source of sorrow was I to her tender heart! Never more, my soul, never more must thy sins renew the bitter anguish then endured by the adorable Hearts of Jesus and Mary.

The Fruit

If you love Mary, never be unmindful of her dolors. If you are desirous of consoling her, save some soul from sin at least by your prayers, and be most careful never to offend her Divine Son. If you wish to please her, imitate her following Jesus in the way of the Cross, by your patience under affliction, and by your pious remembrance of all He suffered for your sake in His painful journey to Calvary.

Example

St. Pellegrino Laziosi [St. Peregrine], of the Order of the Servites of Mary, was distinguished by his devotion to Jesus' suffering, and by his tender love and compassion for the Queen of Dolors. Having retired into a cave near Siena, he for a long time passed whole days and nights in the contemplation of these two great objects of his love.

For the space of thirty years he never sat down, having imposed so severe a penance upon himself in honor of the sufferings of Jesus, and of the sorrows of Mary. Our blessed Lord was so well pleased with this devotion of His faithful servant, that He vouchsafed to manifest by a miracle how acceptable it was to Him. The Saint being under the necessity of having one of his legs cut off by the surgeon on account of a gangrened wound in it, the figure of our Crucified Redeemer unfastened itself from the Cross, and, touching the affected part, instantly healed it. (*Bollandists,* May 1).

∽ DAY 22 ∽

The Pious Women
Lament over Jesus

Meditation

OUR Redeemer is followed by a vast multitude of people, and by some women who weep with compassion over His sufferings. Our blessed Lord, turning to them, addresses them in words full of instruction and tender love. Consider:

1. The pious affection displayed by these women. Crowds of people accompany Jesus, some to insult Him in His sufferings, and some to feast their eyes upon the spectacle of His Crucifixion. Among so many enemies of our Saviour, there are yet a few faithful and compassionate souls who follow Him, and by their tears and sighs give public testimony of the respectful love they bear their suffering Lord. Undaunted by the universal hatred displayed against Jesus by the Jews, undismayed by the rage and malice with which all maltreat the innocent Saviour of the world, they fearlessly stand forward in His favor, and publicly lament over the Just Man, as over a truly worthy object of compassion. Are you one of the few men of faith and piety not afraid of appearing Christians, even where the law of God is disobeyed and trampled under foot? Or do you, on the contrary, yield to cowardly fears, and join the enemies of your Saviour in deriding piety, persecuting innocence and outraging God? On the day of judgment Christ will not acknowledge you if you are now ashamed to acknowledge Him.

The pious women, triumphing over human respect, and overcoming every difficulty, hasten along the road of Calvary to follow Jesus, and render Him the last offices of love and friendship. On seeing Him the victim of such barbarous usage, and covered with wounds and blood, they weep with compassion, and rejoice to offer Jesus the tribute of their tears in return for the Blood which He is shedding so prodigally for the salvation of their souls. Unite in spirit with these pious women, and let your heart be touched at the sight of Jesus covered with wounds, led like a criminal to punishment, and about to sacrifice His life on the Cross. Oh, how sweet and consoling it is to weep over the sufferings of our dear Saviour. Taste, and you will see.

2. The favor with which Jesus accepts the tribute of their tears.

Jesus seeing the compassion felt for Him by these women, and the tears shed by them over His sufferings, is pleased to accept and reward the expression of their love. Learn, hence, how acceptable is the offering of our compassion and affection to our suffering Lord, and how sensibly His Divine Heart is grieved by the ingratitude and hardheartedness of those who shed not a single tear over His Crucifixion and Death.

Jesus, although overwhelmed, soul and body, with the most excruciating sufferings, although fainting and sinking with exhaustion, is yet insensible to His own agony, forgetful of Himself, and occupied solely with the consolation and instruction of the daughters of Jerusalem. He beholds their tears, and though He sees that they spring from in imperfect faith, yet He is pleased with their humble sorrow, and vouchsafes to reward them by exciting feelings of love and compunction in their hearts. He turns to them in the most benign manner, addresses them in sweet and persuasive accents, and while instructing them in the means of rendering their tears profitable, infuses into their souls particular graces and secret inspirations. Thus is Jesus ever good and beneficent in our regard, and ever occupied with our interests. Oh, how many graces would He bestow upon you, if you were but to meditate devoutly upon His Passion! Many tears have you frequently shed over a slight annoyance or illness, or for the death of a friend; but have you ever shed any over the sufferings which Jesus endured for your sake? Perhaps you have never paid Him the tribute of one single sigh. Bewail your thoughtlessness and want of love, and henceforward gratify the Heart of Jesus, to whom tears of compassion for His sufferings are so very acceptable.

3. The words addressed by Jesus to the women.

It is the Will of Jesus Christ that we should compassionate Him in His sufferings, but it is also His Will that our motives in compassionating Him should be similar to His own in dying for us. He suffers on account of our sins, and He desires that our compassion for Him should also have reference to them. Therefore it is that, turning to the holy women, He says, "*Weep not for me,* as though I were going to die for myself, but weep for the cause of my Passion and death, which is sin. *Weep for yourselves and for your children,* for whom I am going to die, that by my death I may make satisfaction for their sins and for yours." As though He had said, "I praise the love you have for me, I accept the offering of your tears, but unless you make reparation for your sins by tears of true repentance, my Passion and death will be of no avail to you." "Look at me," says Jesus to you also, O Christians, "and reflect upon yourselves, since if I endure such bitter torments for sins not my own, what eternal punishments must not be looked for from Divine Justice by those who neglect to cancel their offenses by tears of true repentance?" Shed tears of compunction over your sins which have transformed the Son of God into a Man of sorrows; your tears will then be of real service to you, and your compassion for Jesus in His sufferings will be of lasting benefit to your soul. They will be blessed tears indeed, if you mingle them with the Blood of Jesus, and cleanse your soul from all its defilements.

The Fruit

Examine this day which is your most habitual failing, and determine seriously to correct it. Make frequent acts of contrition for your sins, and offer in satisfaction for them the blood shed by Jesus on His way to Calvary. Receive all the trials and tribulations of life as a penance for your sins. You may thus easily pay the debts you owe Divine Justice.

Example

Blessed Clare of Monte Falco was filled from her childhood with such tender devotion and ardent love for Jesus Crucified, and so eager a desire of suffering, that when only six years of age she would macerate her innocent body by the most excessive mortifications. Her bed was always the bare ground or a hard board. The floor and walls of her room were stained with blood, and bore testimony to the innocent cruelty with which she frequently took the discipline in memory of the sufferings of Jesus. The Passion was the ordinary subject of her meditations, for she would say, "Can anyone who has once beheld Jesus on the Cross ever think of any other object?" Her ardent desire of suffering for the love of Jesus

Crucified induced her to implore Him most fervently to give her some share in the pains and torments of His Passion. Our blessed Redeemer appeared to her one day, and told her that her devotion to His sufferings was most pleasing to Him, and that all the instruments of His Passion should be imprinted on her heart; which in effect took place miraculously, so that after her death the wonderful marks were distinctly visible. (See her *Life*).

∾ DAY 23 ∾

Jesus Is Assisted by Simon of Cyrene to Bear the Cross

Meditation

THE high priests, fearing lest Jesus should expire from fatigue and suffering in ascending the mountain, take the Cross from His shoulders, and force one Simon of Cyrene, who is by chance passing that way, to carry it for Him. Consider:

1. Wherefore Jesus consents to be assisted in carrying the Cross.

Our Redeemer might, by a miracle, infuse strength into His frame sufficient to enable Him to carry His welcome, long-desired Cross, even to the summit of Mount Calvary. He has already worked other miracles to support sinking nature, and to prevent Himself from expiring at the time of the scourging and during His agony and bloody sweat. He might add this one more to the number. But such is not His Will. It is His Will to have companions to bear the Cross with Him. It is His Will that others should feel the weight of His

Cross, and this is why He sinks down and requires assistance, and not because He is weary of bearing His Cross, or that He finds its weight insupportable. His consent that another should relieve Him of His Cross arises from no desire of unburdening His sacred shoulders, but is a mystery intended to teach us that He is pleased to share His sufferings with all His elect. On the other hand, Jesus is, at the same time, ready to bear His Cross so long as to fall several times beneath its weight, and even finally to expire upon it. And with what degree of constancy do you bear your Cross. Do you persevere in virtue? Are you firm and constant in your resolution to follow Jesus Christ, and to suffer with Him and for Him? Remember that whoever does not take up his Cross and follow Jesus, is not worthy of Him. Whoever has not partaken of His sufferings will not partake of His glory. Jesus desires to associate us with Himself in His eternal happiness, and for that reason it is His Will that we, in the person of Simon of Cyrene, should assist Him to carry His Cross. Therefore, if it is cruelty on the part of the Jews to relieve Jesus of His burden, only because they desire to see Him die the death of the Cross, on His part it is love for you, zeal for your salvation, and a burning desire to make you partake of those sufferings by which He is meriting eternal glory.

2. The happiness of the Cyrenian in being chosen to assist Jesus in bearing His Cross.

Among all the multitude of people following Jesus Christ to Mount Calvary, not one man offers to assist Him in bearing His Cross. All look upon it with horror as a public mark of infamy. Not one of the many disciples and friends of our blessed Redeemer will risk his reputation so far, or has courage sufficient to relieve our suffering Jesus of the heavy burden beneath which He is sinking. Oh, how many there are in the world who call themselves followers of Christ, but, the moment an opportunity offers of suffering anything for His sake, take to flight, make excuses, and declare themselves, by their actions, the enemies of the Cross of Christ! Are you one of these? Remember that to bear the Cross with Christ is not a counsel only, but an obligation for all who wish to save their souls. While the Jews are seeking for someone to carry the Cross of Jesus, they fall in with a stranger from the city of Cyrene, who is passing that way, and him they force to take up the Cross. Thus is this man singled out by Providence to be honored with bearing the Cross of Jesus. How fortunate is he in being able to relieve our dear Redeemer of His burden! What a happiness to have to ascend Mount Calvary in His company—to partake of His sufferings, His ignominy, and His fatigues! What an honor to bear this Cross, which has been already so tenderly embraced by Jesus, and sprinkled with His Divine Blood! My soul, if thou hadst been in the place of Simon of Cyrene, and hadst known who and what Jesus was, as thou knowest now, wouldst thou not most willingly have assisted Him to carry His Cross? Wouldst thou not have considered it a happiness to bear that heavy Cross upon thy own shoulders, to relieve the agonizing Son of God? Most certainly thou wouldst. Well, if thou bearest thy trials patiently, if thou dost struggle generously against thy temptations, thou wilt enjoy an honor similar to that of the Cyrenean. All our sufferings are portions of the Cross of Jesus. They have all in the first instance afflicted His blessed Soul and Body. He has experienced all the sufferings which you now endure. He has borne the sorrows which afflict you. You will diminish the burden laid on Jesus, you will relieve His sufferings, if you bear your Cross willingly and joyfully for love of Him. Promise our sweet Jesus that you will do so from this moment.

3. In what manner a Christian should bear the Cross.

The Gospel does not say that Simon of Cyrene refused to take up the Cross he was required to bear, or that he murmured or lamented over his fate. Behold the example which you should follow. The crosses of our own choice are good, but those sent us by Providence are better, from whatever source they may proceed. To accept them in silence, receive them without complaint, and bear them with patience, will render them meritorious, and make us true followers of Jesus Christ. Simon of Cyrene bears the Cross after Jesus, keeping Him always before his eyes.

Oh, how joyfully should we suffer did we always keep Jesus Crucified before our eyes! When we contemplate Our Saviour covered with blood and wounds, expiating our sins in His own Person, at the price of so much suffering, how willingly do we bear our cross, overcome our depraved appetites, resist our evil inclinations and avoid sin! Every Cross seems light, all sufferings easy, when we bear them in union with Jesus. Endeavor then always to remain united to Jesus in your sufferings.

Finally, Simon of Cyrene bears the Cross of Jesus to assist and relieve Him, and bears it even to the summit of Mount Calvary. How many persons bear the Cross, feel all its weight, and faint from fatigue, but derive no advantage from it to their souls, because it is not the Cross of Jesus that they are bearing. They suffer, but for the world; they suffer, but to content their own whims; they make the most painful sacrifices, but for anything rather than the love of Jesus. No merit will you ever have in your sufferings unless you suffer for the sake of Jesus. Neither will your sufferings ever be rewarded if you persevere not to the end in suffering for Jesus. You must follow Jesus even to the summit of Mount Calvary, that is to say, with fidelity even unto death.

The Fruit

The crosses imposed upon men by the world are not found heavy, because men love the world.

Love Jesus Christ, and you will patiently bear the crosses He sends you. Everything that is painful to the flesh, disagreeable to the senses, or displeasing to self-love, is a Cross. Embrace all these little opportunities of suffering, and you will be bearing the Cross of Christ. Refuse not to relieve the poor and afflicted for the love of Jesus, and He will accept as given to Himself whatever consolation or assistance you charitably bestow upon your suffering neighbor.

Example

Blessed Veronica Giuliani, who from her earliest childhood was most devout to the Passion of Jesus Christ, and who, when in her novitiate among the Capuchinesses, was filled with a very eager desire of suffering for His sake, was one day ordered by her mistress to carry water to the infirmary. Now there were two flights of very steep stairs to be ascended from the place where the water was drawn, to the infirmary, and the servant of God, whose fervor knew no bounds, carried up more than thirty pitchers full, so that her feet were dreadfully galled, from the number of times she had to ascend and descend the stairs, and she was completely exhausted and ready to faint. While she was in this state our Divine Redeemer appeared to her, bearing His Cross, and said, in touching accents, "Look at the Cross which I am bearing; observe how heavy it is." At this sight the soul of the blessed novice leaped for joy, so that she felt her strength restored, and her heart burning with eagerness to suffer yet more for the love of Jesus. Imagine that Jesus addresses the like words to you when oppressed with weariness, and you will experience their virtue. (See *Life*).

∽ **DAY 24** ∽

Jesus Nailed to the Cross

Meditation

JESUS having reached the top of Mount Calvary, the Jews will not allow a moment's delay, but most barbarously and cruelly fasten Him with nails to the Cross. Consider:

1. The sufferings of Jesus before His Crucifixion.

Jesus has arrived at the end of His journeys on reaching the summit of Calvary, but He has not attained the termination of His sufferings, which henceforward become truly unmeasured. His enemies throng around, while each and all freely insult and curse Him as a malefactor, who now at last is to suffer the penalty of His crimes. The Divine and patient Victim remains perfectly silent, and fixing His eyes and thoughts upon the Cross, contemplates the scaffold upon which He is soon to yield up His last breath, and joyfully offers up His life as a sacrifice for the salvation of mankind. Jesus suffers in every part of His agonizing frame, save in His tongue, but He permits not this member to continue longer without its

share of torment. It is the custom to give all condemned criminals about to be executed some
refreshing and comforting beverage. But even
this last office of humanity and compassion is not
fulfilled towards Jesus Christ in His state of utter
exhaustion and suffering, and the soldiers barbarously offer Him wine mingled with bitter gall,
to torture His palate and stomach. Such is the
beverage which you have presented to Jesus by
your evil habits, censorious and pretended piety,
sensual pleasures, and innumerable sins. They
are the bitter gall which you have offered to your
Lord, even when He was quenching your thirst
with the sweet waters of His love and goodness.
Now, at least, offer your suffering Redeemer the
refreshment of your tears—tears of sincere sorrow and tender compassion. No sooner has Jesus
tasted the bitter and disgusting liquid than the
executioners strip off His garment with cruel violence. My soul, look on thy Saviour, and compassionate Him in these new sufferings. Owing to the
quantity of blood and the countless wounds which
cover His sacred Body, the garments had again
adhered to His lacerated flesh, so that on their
being torn off, all His wounds are re-opened, and
His sufferings become quite indescribable, while
the Blood flows to the ground in streams. Oh, see
how Jesus sheds every drop of His Blood for your
salvation! And thou, my soul thou for whom thy
Saviour sheds such torrents of blood, thou for
whom this Man of Sorrows endures so much, wilt
thou not shed one tear, nor breathe one sigh for

all His sufferings? Wilt thou be hardhearted
toward thy Crucified Jesus alone?

2. The obedience of Jesus in placing Himself
upon the Cross.

The Cross is already lying on the ground, the
altar is prepared on which the adorable Victim is
to ascend to be sacrificed. The executioners command Jesus to lie down upon the Cross, and the
instant He receives the order, in deference to His
Divine Father, He bends His knees, reverently
bows down His Head, and wishing to be obedient
even to the most ignominious of deaths, lies down
on that hard bed of suffering and infamy. By this
great act of obedience does Jesus make satisfaction for the disobedience with which we have so
often violated the commands of God. See, my soul,
see how Jesus manifests no repugnance to obey
the cruel order. There is no need of employing force
to make Him obey it. He willingly, and of His own
accord, stretches Himself out upon the Cross,
places His lacerated and bleeding Body in the
proper position, presents His hands and His feet
to be nailed, and raising His eyes to Heaven offers
Himself in sacrifice to His Eternal Father for the
salvation of the whole world, and even of my poor
soul, fervently beseeching Him to pardon our sins
through the merits of His obedience. You who are
so willing to obey the commands of the world, of
the flesh, and of your own concupiscence, and on
the other hand so stubborn and rebellious to the
law of God, what can you say on beholding this

most wonderful example of obedience in the Son of the Most High? How many excuses, difficulties, and pretexts do you bring forward by way of exempting yourselves from the observance of the law? You are creatures, why then refuse to subject yourselves to the commands of the Creator? You are servants, why then disobey the ordinances of your celestial Master? To teach you the important virtue of obedience, Jesus has subjected Himself even to the ignominious death of the Cross. Can it cost you as much to obey God as it has cost Jesus to obey His Divine Father for the salvation of your soul?

3. The sufferings of Jesus in His Crucifixion.

Jesus having stretched forth His hands on the Cross, as though to fold all sinners in His embraces, and reconcile them with God, the executioners fasten them to the wood with large nails, by dint of violent and repeated blows of a heavy hammer. These nails pierce entirely through, tearing and crushing flesh, nerves, veins, arteries, and all that make any resistance. Inexpressible are the sufferings of our blessed Jesus, and so great is His agony that He is all but ready to expire from utter exhaustion and intense anguish. In the meantime, the Blood of our sweet Redeemer, that Blood which He is offering to His Eternal Father for me, flows forth in copious streams. Harder than a rock must your heart be, if you are not moved to tears at so mournful a spectacle. Draw nigh to Jesus and reverently ask

Him what are those wounds in His hands and feet, and He will answer that they are the work of your sins and the pledges of His love. He will tell you that, to cancel your sinful deeds, He has allowed His most sacred hands to be pierced through with nails. Read then in these wounds the history of your sinfulness, and detest it, read in them the history of His love, and be grateful for it. The hands of our dying Redeemer being nailed to the Cross, the same torture is inflicted on His feet. By reason of the violence with which the executioners stretch His Body, and the cruel manner in which they strike and hammer the large nail that is to transfix both feet, Jesus endures unspeakable torture, and asks you to afford Him some consolation by shedding at least one tear of compassion, or breathing one sigh of affection, at the sight of His sufferings. Will you refuse that much to Jesus, who asks for it from His Cross? See with what patience, meekness, and silence He endures the most excruciating tortures, without uttering one word of complaint, either of the nails which so painfully tear His flesh, or of the executioners who treat Him as inhumanly as though He were the worst of malefactors. He is your Leader whom you must seek to resemble, if you desire to save your soul. What resemblance do you bear to Jesus, you who lead a delicate, sensual life—you who are passionate and impatient under the slightest suffering? Ah, my sweet Jesus! I adore thy precious wounds, and through their merits do I implore grace to imitate Thee.

The Fruit

Renew this day your determination of obeying God at any cost, and of ever preferring His Divine Will before all else. Whenever you feel any repugnance to obey man for the love of God, remember the obedience with which Jesus Christ submitted to the commands of His executioners themselves. Make it a rule to dwell frequently each day in the wounds of Jesus often paying them homage by acts of adoration and love, and taking refuge within them in all dangers and temptations.

Example

The remembrance of the most painful Crucifixion of Jesus inspires the heart of a Christian with love for God and desire to suffer for His sake. Blessed Christina of Spoleto was one day meditating upon the sufferings of Jesus, and the point she was considering happened to be the dreadful wound made by the nail in the feet of Jesus. "Oh, ungrateful wretch that thou art!" she said to herself, "behold how much Blood He has shed for love of thee; and what has thou done to prove thy love and gratitude for such infinite goodness?" So saying, being filled with holy fervor, she took a large nail from the wall, and pierced her feet entirely through with it, too happy thus to return Jesus blood for blood, and wound for wound. Jesus asks not so much of you, but at least you may inflict some penance for love of Him upon your hands, which have committed so many sins, and upon your feet, which have taken so many steps in the paths of iniquity. (*Bollandists,* 14th Feb.). That you may frequently call to mind the wounds of Jesus Christ, imitate the example of the venerable Father Alphonsus of Orosco, an Augustinian monk, who was accustomed, whenever he heard the clock strike, to remember the blows of the hammer nailing down the feet and hands of Jesus (See his *Life*).

∾ DAY 25 ∾

Jesus Elevated on His Cross
In the Sight of All

Meditation

THE executioners having fastened Jesus with nails to the Cross, raise Him in the air between two thieves in the presence of all the people. Pause awhile, and gaze upon your dying Saviour, with deep compassion and earnest devotion. Consider:

1. His bodily sufferings.

The vibration of the Cross when raised in the air reopens the wounds of that torn and lacerated Body, thus inflicting tortures of the most acute nature upon our blessed Jesus. Raised thus on high, and hanging on three nails, our dear Lord rests solely upon the deep and momentarily increasing wounds of His hands and feet. In this state, the thought alone of which makes us shudder, does Jesus pass the last three hours of His life. Oh, what anguish, what indescribable, incomprehensible sufferings, does Jesus endure in so painful a situation! And ought not this consideration to arouse in you feelings of the deepest love for that goodness and charity which has induced Him to ascend the Cross, and endure such countless sufferings for love of you, to heal your infirmities, and save you from Hell? How hard must your heart be, if you are not touched by such a spectacle! There is not a single portion of the Body of Jesus, from the crown of His head to the sole of His foot, that can be called whole, and that has not its own particular suffering, as He hangs upon the Cross. His head is crowned with thorns, and He has not where to lay it; His adorable face is defiled with spittle, and overspread with the pallid hue of death; His eyes are bloodshot, His flesh lacerated, His bones may be numbered, His hands and feet are pierced with nails, and every part of His Body is torn and streaming with blood. My soul, behold the Blood which, when applied to thee in the Sacraments, has so often cleansed thee from thy sins! Behold the wounds which thy sins have so frequently opened afresh! Behold the condition to which the Son of God, thy Father and Saviour, is reduced for love of thee! Behold what excruciating sufferings He is enduring to make satisfaction for thy sins!

2. The opprobrium with which He is overwhelmed.

The insults and opprobrious words with which Jesus is loaded, equal the excessive sufferings He endures in His Body, and, before His death, He is truly satiated with them. The Jews, having crucified two thieves together with Him, elevate Him on the Cross between them in the sight of all the people, that so He may appear as the worst malefactor of the three. Oh, with what confusion must the Son of God, the Holy of Holies, have been overwhelmed on beholding Himself thus shamefully dishonored before so large a multitude! What deep sorrow must have filled His sacred Heart on seeing His good name and honor thus infamously vilified and degraded! And yet, our suffering Lord submits to everything with the most admirable patience and unexampled meekness. Behold what your pride has cost Jesus, since to cure it in you, and make satisfaction for it, He has endured such terrible infamy.

His enemies, not yet satisfied, and being devoid of every feeling of humanity, insult Him in His sufferings, mock Him, and load Him with curses and blasphemies, deriding His patience, and defying Him in insulting language, *to come down from the Cross!* All mock and reproach Him, and vie with one another, by the most insulting gestures and language, in making Jesus truly the outcast of the people, and satiating Him with outrages. What pain must such disgraceful insults have occasioned the Heart of our innocent Lord! He sees His enemies all rejoicing and triumphing at His sufferings. He might in one instant have struck them dead, and thus have proved Himself to be the Almighty God, suffering and dying only because such is His Will. And yet our most meek Lord, with unshaken fortitude, submits to be thus dishonored, without expressing the slightest emotion or anger, and without answering a single word. He beholds His honor attacked in its most tender point, and He well knows the evil intentions with which the Jews are insulting and deriding Him, yet He shows no resentment, but suffers in humility and silence. Learn from such an heroic example not to resent the evil that is done you, not to indulge in anger, nor to revenge the injuries you receive from others. How can you call yourself a Christian, if you do not imitate the example left you by Jesus Christ on the Cross?

3. The acute interior anguish of the Soul of Jesus. The exterior sufferings of our Blessed Redeemer are occasioned by the hatred of His enemies, but the interior sufferings of His Soul are caused by His love toward you. So excessive are they, that of them alone, out of all His tortures, does our Saviour mildly complain to His Heavenly Father. Jesus might sweeten His sufferings, as He has since sweetened those of His martyrs; but it is His Will to drink the bitter chalice of His Passion without any alleviation or comfort; it is His Will to die plunged in an abyss of mortal anguish, weariness, sadness, and affliction, and with His holy Soul overwhelmed with sorrow. And if He receives any consolation from the Divinity to support Him through His Passion, it is only that He may suffer the more. Understand now at least what mortal sin is, since, in order to make satisfaction for it, a God-man dies thus immersed in a sea of sorrow. The circumstance of His most blessed Body being exposed naked before the eyes of all, is a source of great confusion to Him. Deeply also is His Soul afflicted at beholding Himself placed between two thieves, and at hearing the disgraceful epithets and derisive words showered upon Him. The hatred, ingratitude, and hardheartedness of His beloved people grieve His merciful heart. Your want of love, your forgetfulness of His sufferings, your ingratitude for all His charity, the manner in which you have abused and trampled His Blood underfoot, overwhelm His sacred Soul with bitter sorrow. His blessed Soul is soon to be separated from His Body by the most infamous and ignominious of deaths, and His infinitely precious life is about to be sacrificed like that of a malefactor upon a disgraceful Cross. Oh, deep and inexpressible, indeed, is the interior anguish of Jesus! And yet He accepts all, willingly suffers the whole bitterness of His most dolorous Passion, and offers it up on the altar of the Cross to His Eternal Father for the salvation of mankind. And will you not joyfully sacrifice such or such a passion, or burst of anger, or guilty friendship, for the sake of your soul and out of gratitude to Jesus? For the love of Him who for your sake submitted to the painful separation of soul and body, will you not fly forever from such or such an occasion of sin, or such and such objects of your attachment, which absorb affections due solely to your most loving Lord? Ah, yes, otherwise too great would be your ingratitude toward Him who has suffered so much for you!

The Fruit

Whenever you meditate, or look upon the Crucifix, say to yourself, *"Behold the condition to which my sins have reduced the Son of God!"* and make acts of repentance and confidence in His mercy. When tempted to commit any sin, direct your thoughts to Jesus hanging on the Cross, and say, *"Jesus Crucified! and I about to commit sin? Can this be? Never! never!"* There can be no remedy more efficacious against temptations of the flesh than the remembrance of the humiliations and sufferings endured by Jesus on the Cross. Let such be your habitual thoughts, that you may avail yourself of them to some purpose when you stand in need.

Example

Our Divine Saviour appeared once to St. Bridget in the state in which He was when nailed to the Cross, all covered with the Blood that was streaming from His wounds. The Saint being overwhelmed with sorrow at such a sight, exclaimed in a transport of love, "Ah, Lord! Who has reduced Thee to so mournful a condition?" "Those," replied the Saviour of the world, "who despise My law, and, unmoved by all I have suffered for them, repay My love only by ingratitude." So deep an impression did this vision make upon the heart of the Saint, that she could never think of the Passion without shedding floods of tears. The bleeding form of her Saviour was ever present to her mind; wherever she was it was always before her eyes, and when at work the abundance of her tears frequently forced her to pause. She was most ingenious in finding out methods of afflicting and macerating her flesh in memory of the sufferings of her Redeemer. She had a wound in her body, which she reopened every Friday, dropping burning wax upon it, thereby to nourish in her heart a lively remembrance of the sufferings of Jesus. Learn from this Saint frequently to remember the Passion of your Saviour, and to practice some mortification for His love. (See her *Life*).

Jesus Crucified
Prays for His Enemies

Meditation

OUR Divine Lord, hanging on the Cross in the sight of the assembled multitudes, insulted, scorned, and blasphemed by His enemies, turns to His Eternal Father, and beseeches Him to *forgive them, for they know not what they do.* Consider:

1. The charity with which Jesus prays.

After a prolonged period of silence, our dying Saviour at length opens His lips, to teach us the most sublime lesson of love from the pulpit of the Cross. It is the first time that Jesus has spoken from His Cross, and the first words He utters are to implore pardon for His enemies, while they are in the very act of most barbarously depriving Him of life. He forgets all His own sufferings in His solicitude to apply a remedy to the spiritual wounds of his executioners. Not all the bitter torments He is enduring cause Him such exquisite pain as the thought of their damnation. He remembers not by whose hands His sufferings are

179

inflicted; He remembers only for whom He is dying, and He procures the eternal salvation of His very crucifiers! Sin is hateful to Jesus; He is dying to destroy it; but the sinner is most dear to Him; He is dying for his salvation, and in death is only desirous of affording proofs to His persecutors of the inscrutable depths of His love for them. Then, turning to His Divine Father, "Most beloved Father," He exclaims with His dying accents, "to Thee I offer this Blood, these Wounds, this Cross, to move Thee to pardon My enemies, who have inflicted upon Me so cruel a death." Oh, surprising charity! The thought of the eternal perdition of the souls of His crucifiers is a greater source of suffering to Jesus than His own most bitter Passion! He is expiring in the most excruciating torments, and in death implores grace and pardon for His murderers! Can we conceive more burning love than this, which is neither extinguished nor damped by even the overflowing waters of boundless sorrow? Truly this is a sublime lesson of what your conduct toward those who injure or offend you should be. How can you have the heart to desire to revenge yourselves upon your enemies, when Jesus, with such tender charity, is solely occupied with obtaining the pardon of those who have crucified Him? Very possibly your enemy may not deserve that you should pardon him, but the Blood and Wounds of Jesus Crucified have merited that you should grant that pardon for His sake. The slightest feeling of hatred entertained against your neighbor wounds the loving Heart of

Jesus, and is an obstacle to the remission of your own sins.

2. For whom Jesus prays.

Not only does Jesus pray for those who are crucifying and blaspheming Him, but He likewise prays for all sinners, for all who have contributed to His sufferings and death. May not the most wretched sinners take courage at the thought of this prayer of Jesus? For in it He includes not merely His executioners, accusers, and judges; that is to say, not only the Jews who so clamorously demanded His death, but all sinners without exception, since all who have committed sin have thereby been the cause of His death. Yes, my soul, every time that thou hast sinned thou hast renewed the cause of the death of the Son of God, thou hast crucified Him anew; and by every fresh sin thou committest thou renderest thyself guilty of His death. And shall not sin, which has crucified Jesus, be henceforth most hateful to me? But oh, how sweet and how deserving of love must be my Divine Jesus, who prays for me, even while I am desiring His death! Ah, sweet Jesus! In the very height of Thy suffering, in Thy mortal agony, Thou art mindful of sinners, Thou art mindful of me! Are not even my innumerable sins and base ingratitude sufficient to banish me from Thy loving Heart? Are not all my sins present to Thy mind, being as they are the very cause of Thy death? And still Thou dost implore Thy Eternal Father to forgive me! But through the blessed effects of that prayer, Thy death, which is caused by my sins, has become my hope and my salvation. Art thou a sinner? What canst thou fear, when Jesus Christ Himself is the Great Advocate who prays for thee, and from His Cross beseeches His Father to pardon thee? Come, come, O sinner, cast thyself with entire confidence at the feet of Jesus, bathe them with thy tears, and then, if sincerely penitent, thou wilt be secure of forgiveness and Heaven. But if thou persistest in sin, His Blood will be thy condemnation.

3. The excuse alleged by Jesus in His prayer for His enemies.

Jesus might have taken awful vengeance upon His enemies from the Cross, and exterminated them in one moment from the face of the earth; but He prefers exhibiting Himself in the character of a God of peace and mercy, and giving proof of the most tender solicitous charity. To move His Father to have compassion on those who are insulting and deriding Him by the most impious expressions of scorn, He seeks to excuse and palliate their guilt by saying that *they know not what they do.* They have given free vent to their hatred of His sacred Person by the most atrocious calumnies; they have consummated the most fearful injustice by crucifying Him; they are even now seeking to load Him with contumely by their insulting gestures and derisive words; and yet Jesus in His infinite charity pities and excuses their sin, and fulfills the loving office of an Advocate by having recourse to Divine clemency in their behalf. He hides their wickedness beneath the torrents of His own Blood, and implores His Father to accept the excuse of their ignorance, willful though it is, in attenuation of their guilt and malice. Oh, how great is the clemency and goodness of God our Redeemer! Such, my soul, is the lesson taught thee by the example of thy dying Saviour. Not only shouldst thou forgive thy enemy, or whoever has done thee an injury, but thou shouldst also do him all the good in thy power, pity and excuse him, and desire that he may one day attain the possession of eternal happiness. Ah, what would become of me, had Jesus treated me as I treat my neighbor, when, for a slight injury or affront, I resolve to be avenged, and indulge in thoughts of hatred and anger? My most sweet Jesus, I beseech Thee to enkindle in my heart the flames of a charity like unto Thine, which may teach me how to love and pity everyone who does me an injury. I love my neighbor for Thy sake. I forgive all who may have offended me from the bottom of my heart; and I beseech Thee, O Father of mercies, to cancel their debts, and shower forth Thy graces upon them.

The Fruit

Imitate Jesus praying from His Cross for His enemies, if you wish to have any part in the pardon He then sought to obtain for you. Be reconciled with your brother, if you wish to make your peace with God. Delay not, for if you are obstinate in sin, you will die impenitent. Excuse those who persecute you; suffer in silence; forget and forgive. Hate sin, but not the sinner, because for him did Christ die, and for him did He sacrifice His life.

Example

A glance at the Crucifix is a powerful incentive to the pardon of injuries. St. Philip Neri, finding the most tender and urgent solicitations of no avail in persuading a certain young man to pardon an injury which had been done him, took a Crucifix, and said with great earnestness, "Look upon this image, and remember how our Divine Lord shed the last drop of His Blood for love of thee, and how on His Cross He prayed to His Eternal Father for the very men who had crucified Him!" The young man was struck by these words, and far more by the sight of Jesus on the Cross. He trembled all over, and answered with many tears, "Behold, Father, I am now most willing to pardon every injury, and to make all the reparation that lies in my power." If you feel any difficulty in pardoning an injury, imagine that Jesus implores you from His Cross to forgive it for love of Him. (See *Life of St. P. Neri*).

∽ DAY 27 ∽

Jesus from His Cross Bestows Mary upon Us as Our Mother

Meditation

1. THE hour of the death of Jesus is fast approaching, and He beholds from His Cross His most dear and loving Mother, who is standing at its foot, assisting at His last sufferings in deep but silent agony, and He would address her for the last time. Bending down His sacred Head, turning his dying eyes toward her, and indicating by a glance His beloved disciple, John, His pallid lips breathe forth the words, *"Woman, behold thy son";* by which He bestows all the faithful in the person of John upon her as her children. Such loving solicitude evinced for her by Jesus at this last awful hour is some consolation to Mary, but oh, what new anguish fills her heart on hearing that we poor sinners are given her in the place of Jesus the Man-God, and that she is to receive us as children in His stead! Her most amiable, beloved, and holy Son Jesus is taken from her, and ungrateful, wicked men, His crucifiers, given her in exchange! Oh, how deep is the anguish of her immaculate heart! She is desirous of replying to the words of her Divine Son, or of addressing John, but at that very moment she feels her maternal heart overflowing with new love, and with the deepest emotions of charity she accepts as her children the faithful of all ages in the person of the beloved disciple John; "for these, O woman," whispers a secret voice, "these shall be thy children." She beholds them at this time deformed with sin, the enemies of God, and objects of His wrath, nevertheless she accepts them! Oh, great indeed is the goodness of Mary, who, with tender and compassionate love, then receives her new children, and embraces them with all the loving solicitude of a Mother. Then, O Mary, even so ungrateful a sinner as myself has been given to thee as a child, and received by thee as such! How can my heart ever testify sufficient gratitude to thee, or be filled with love and veneration commensurate with thy charity! O happy sinners, remember what a Mother you have, remember whose children you are! Your Mother is Mary, the Mother of God; a Mother full of grace, a Mother the mirror of purity and holiness. It is not fitting that so holy a Mother should have sinful children. Are you desirous of being her true children? Fulfill the obligations of children in her regard, and never grieve her maternal heart by your hateful sins.

2. Jesus, then addressing John, and indicating Mary by a glance, says, in loving accents, *"Behold thy Mother."* As though He had said, "By My death thou dost lose thy Father, but behold I leave thee My Mother in My place; I bestow her upon thee and upon all the faithful in thy person, that you may all regard her as your Mother." Jesus is not satisfied with saying to Mary, *"Behold thy son"* in the person of His beloved disciple, John; but He also addresses these words to John: *"Behold thy Mother,"* that the gift being reciprocal, the sentiments of love and confidence may be reciprocal too. Oh, how great is the gift bestowed upon us by Jesus in this His last will and testament! Our dear Saviour has nothing else on earth to leave us but His own most holy Mother. His Body He has delivered up to the fury of His enemies, His Blood He has shed for the redemption of the world, His garments the soldiers have divided among themselves; nothing therefore remains for Him to bequeath, save His most blessed Mother, and her He leaves to John and to all Christians in his person. He bequeaths this tender Mother to us at the very moment when her soul is pierced by a double-edged sword of grief, and her heart distracted between anguish for the death of her Son, and desire for the salvation of men. O most amiable Redeemer, how precious is the legacy which Thou leavest us in the last hours of Thy life! While Thou art expiring, overwhelmed with ignominy and suffering, Thou dost bestow upon us the happiness of having Thee for our Elder Brother, and Mary for our Mother. I humbly beseech Thee, since Mary is my Mother, to give me grace to regard her as such, and to serve and love her with all the tenderness of a true son.

Take courage, devout soul, lift up thine eyes to our Crucified Jesus, listen to His voice, and hear how lovingly He says to thee, "Son *behold thy Mother.*" Look at this Mother with the tenderest feelings of affection, and know that Jesus has placed in her hands all the blessings His mercy is willing to bestow upon us. No one is saved but through Mary, no one receives any blessing but by the hands of Mary, no one obtains pardon but through the intercession of Mary. Gratefully acknowledge the goodness of Jesus, have recourse with confidence to Mary, and let thy conduct be that of a son in her regard.

3. Thus enriched by the possession of so great a treasure, John, having in the name of all the faithful accepted Mary as a Mother, takes her to his own home after the death and burial of Jesus, bestows upon her all the anxious care due to a parent, and respects, honors, and serves her with the most filial devotion.

Similar are the duties which you must also fulfill as a child of Mary. You must entertain for her sentiments of profound respect, tender love and filial confidence, and your desires and inclinations must ever be conformable to hers. She is the Mother of Purity and Queen of Virgins, and it is by purity of heart and morals that you will please her. Her whole life never displayed anything but holiness, innocence, and purity; and she will ever bestow upon you her most loving protection and particular patronage, she will ever be to you the tenderest of Mothers, if, in imitation of her, you lead a pure, holy, and innocent life. You will experience the effects of her maternal love if you are in all things a docile and devoted child. Listen how she says to you from the foot of the Cross, where she is sorrowfully attending the last agonies of her dying Son, "Behold, I am your Mother." Look at her suffering on account of those sins which have crucified Jesus, and weep at the sight of the bitter anguish with which they have filled her heart. Promise never more to commit those sins which crucify her Son anew, and cause her to be the most afflicted of Mothers. Sweet Mother! Through that inexpressible sorrow which thou didst suffer at the foot of the Cross on account of my sins, obtain for me grace to be henceforward a dutiful child to thee, and never more by my sins to become guilty of the death of thy most amiable Son Jesus; obtain for me grace to love thee constantly, to serve thee with the utmost fidelity, and to honor thee with heartfelt devotion, so that through the merits of the death of Jesus, and thy own deep sorrow, I may one day attain the happiness of praising and blessing my God and thee eternally in Heaven.

The Fruit

Next to Jesus, let your whole confidence be given to Mary, and suffer not one single hour of the day to pass without having recourse to her. But your devotion to Mary must mainly consist in delighting her pure heart by your love of modesty, purity and humility; virtues so inexpressibly dear to her. You will never be really devout to her, unless you try to please her; and an impure, contaminated, proud heart never can be pleasing in the eyes of the Mother of Purity. In your endeavors to acquire the virtues of humility and modesty, let it be your intention to imitate the most blessed Virgin, and you will be fulfilling the duties of a son in her regard.

Example

St. John Nepomucene was the child of prayer, for it was through the intercession of the Blessed Virgin, to whom his parents had had recourse, that a son was granted to their fervent and earnest prayers. The name of John was bestowed upon him in honor of that disciple to whom Mary was given as a Mother by Jesus. And truly did Mary show herself a Mother to him, for she obtained his recovery from a dangerous illness in his childhood. As John grew older, he faithfully fulfilled every duty of a true child of Mary, for he tenderly and fervently loved, honored, and served her, and in every necessity she was his sweetest refuge. Being repeatedly tempted by King Wenceslaus to break the sacred seal of Confession, and threatened with death on account of his persevering refusal to accede to so impious a request, he undertook a pilgrimage to a venerated shrine of his dear Mother, there to implore her assistance in the assaults to which he was exposed. Mary did not fail to assist her faithful servant, and obtained for him such signal graces that, when his constancy was again put to the proof, he triumphed over every temptation, and, in consequence, was put to death; thus terminating a life which had been wholly employed in the love and service of Mary, by a glorious martyrdom. (See his *Life*). Accustom yourself in all temptations to have recourse to Mary, and you will experience the effects of her intercession.

∽ **DAY 28** ∽

Jesus Crucified Complains
Of Being Forsaken by
His Eternal Father

Meditation

TOWARDS the ninth hour, that is to say, after having been three hours upon the Cross, our dying Jesus cries out with a loud voice, *"My God, My God, why hast Thou forsaken Me?"* Consider:

1. What does Jesus intend to teach us by this mournful cry of complaint?

In all the bitter torments of His Passion, Jesus has never uttered a single word of complaint, but in the last moments of His life He cries out with a loud and mournful voice, that we may understand that His exterior and interior sufferings have now reached their utmost height. What man is there so hardhearted as not to compassionate our dying, suffering Redeemer? Not one complaint has He uttered in the midst of all His torments, but now, when about to die, He reverently complains to His Divine Father, *"Why hast Thou forsaken Me?"* to make known to us the excess of anguish which He is enduring at being thus forsaken, and that all mankind may be fully aware of the inexpressible sufferings which the salvation of our souls has cost Him. Oh, how much are we indebted to the tender love He bears us! Jesus complains, not that He is forsaken by the Divinity, nor that the Eternal Father is divided from His most beloved Son; but as man, that His suffering humanity feels as though destitute of help or consolation, and, as it were, plunged into a sea of inexpressible sorrow, that to all it may be made known that, God though He is, His sufferings are not thereby alleviated or diminished in the slightest degree, but rather increased and rendered more acute; also, that we may understand how terrible must be the rigor of Divine justice, which requires that He should be abandoned to all the fury of His enemies, to endure every imaginable torment, and finally, to undergo the most ignominious and cruel death of the Cross. This inexpressibly painful feeling of dereliction, which thus elicits a complaint even from the Son of God, is the shadow of the sufferings experienced by the damned in Hell, when in the midst of their torments they are, moreover, conscious that they are hated by God, who was once their Father, but is henceforward their most implacable enemy. This last thought fills up the measure of their eternal fury, anguish, and despair. Implore your sweet Jesus never to deprive you of His grace in this world, that so you may not incur the dreadful misfortune of being eternally forsaken by Him.

2. The painful effects of this dereliction.

Almighty God usually bestows upon martyrs delightful alleviations of their sufferings, by infusing into their souls sweet interior consolations, so that they rejoice in torments, and go to meet the most cruel deaths exultingly. But Jesus, amid all His sufferings, is deprived of any consolations to temper the bitterness of His anguish. His soul is steeped in all the bitterness that has been or ever will be experienced by the martyrs, and yet is left without the slightest consolation. Jesus, while enduring this dereliction, has to taste the whole bitterness of the chalice of His Passion without one drop of refreshing sweetness. To the exterior sufferings which he endures in His whole Person, in His body, head, hands, and feet, are added the interior torments of mental agony, sorrow, fear, sadness, and most terrible desolation of spirit. All these sufferings, which have been most acute during the whole course of His Passion, reach their extreme height on Mount Calvary. Thus does Jesus become in very truth the Man of Sorrows, the King of Martyrs, and the Most Afflicted of Men. My soul, canst thou meditate upon the excessive sufferings endured by the most holy Soul of thy dying Redeemer, and not be enamored with His unbounded love in thus submitting to them for thy sake? Art thou not moved even to tears of compassion when thou rememberest the part thy sins also have had in inflicting the pangs of martyrdom upon His most loving Heart? Knowest thou of what Jesus complains most bitterly on the Cross? To see that His Blood, His Passion and Death will be of avail but to few! He laments and grieves at the sight of the small number of those who will profit by the Blood which He sheds so lavishly for all. This is the source of the deep sorrow which oppresses and overwhelms the Heart of Jesus. O my dear Redeemer, permit not that I should ever be one of that numerous host of reprobates, who, by their own fault, render Thy Passion and Death of no avail! Grant, sweet Jesus, that I may never be separated from Thee by accursed sin, and that I may one day come to enjoy in Heaven the blessed effects of Thy Death which has merited it for me.

3. The sentiments of Jesus in His dereliction.

Jesus Christ, although abandoned by His Father to the mercy of His most furious enemies, to the whole bitterness of His torments, and to the most ignominious death, nevertheless casts Himself entirely, and without reserve, into the arms of this same beloved Father. He had taught us how to live; on the Cross He teaches us how to die. His whole Soul had always been absorbed in God; He had ever been entirely resigned to the Divine Will, and had reposed with the most perfect trust in the arms of His Father. At the moment of death, He yields up His spirit to God its Creator, and commends it to the all-merciful Providence of His beloved Father. Imitate Jesus in life and in death. Live so as to be able to say with perfect confidence at the hour of death, *"Into Thy hands, O Lord, I commend my spirit."* In the meantime, accustom yourself often to yield up to God your body, your soul, and all you possess. He is our Father, and the very best of Fathers: He cannot forsake us. Our names are inscribed on His loving Heart, and He never can forget us. His hands have formed these bodies of ours, and from Him have we received our souls, which He created to His own image. There is nothing that can be denied us by a God who has given us His own beloved Son, and delivered Him up to death for our sakes. Often remind Jesus of all that your soul has cost Him, and beseech Him to save it; recommend it to His Heart transfixed with a spear, implore Him to watch over it, never to abandon it, and, above all, to preserve it from sin, and bestow upon it the gift of His love.

The Fruit

When you are deprived of all consolation or comfort in misfortune or suffering, reflect that Jesus is bestowing upon you some small portion of that anguish which He endured in His dereliction, thus to render you more like unto Himself. Be not discouraged, faint not, if you experience no sensible pleasure, but rather a feeling of repugnance, in the service of God. Look at Jesus suffering on the Cross, and let this sight be your sweetest encouragement and best incentive to perseverance in those works of piety which you have undertaken for the love of God.

Example

Devotion to the most sacred Passion of Jesus is a mark of predestination. Blessed James of Bevagna, a Dominican friar, was most devout from his earliest childhood to Jesus Crucified, and being one day disturbed by an importunate feeling of fear concerning his eternal salvation, threw himself in a suppliant posture at the feet of his suffering Lord, to pray for grace and consolation. Jesus lovingly spoke to him from the Crucifix, saying, "This Blood, O my son, shall be to thee a mark of predestination;" and at the same moment so copious a stream of Blood flowed from the Crucifix as to bathe the whole face and dress of the blessed man. So great a favor filled his heart with a sweet feeling of confidence that he should be saved, and with an earnest desire of loving his Crucified Lord more and more, and of being forever united to Him in Heaven, a happiness to which he afterwards in fact, attained. (See his *Life*).

∽ DAY 29 ∽

Thirst of Jesus on the Cross

Meditation

1. THE last moments of our dying Redeemer are at hand. His throat being parched, and His whole Body consumed with inward fever owing to the immense quantity of blood He has lost, and the innumerable tortures and sufferings He has endured, He exclaims in a mournful voice, *"I thirst!"*

Long has He suffered this thirst, and patiently has he forborne to utter a word of complaint but yet, when now at length He reveals it, even in the tone of a suppliant imploring relief, there is not found one man who will give Him a drop of water to refresh His burning lips! The God who created the rivers, and supplied the sea with fountains of water; the God who miraculously assuaged the thirst of a million of Jews in the desert—that God is without even a drop of water to moisten His parched lips! Thus does our Divine Saviour expiate in His own Person our gluttony and excessive delicacy! Thus does He endure the penalty of the sins we commit by our intemperance in eating and drinking. A soldier now raised to the mouth of Our Lord a sponge soaked in vinegar. Can you point out any culprit treated with such refinement of cruelty as this exercised upon the innocent Son of God in the midst of His most excruciating sufferings? My soul, compassionate thy sweet Jesus. He says, *"I thirst,"* and yet they do not even give Him a drop of water to moisten his lips! But little does God require of you to satisfy His Divine Heart, and yet you refuse Him even that little! At what time does Jesus say, *"I thirst"?* When about to die, when plunged in an abyss of suffering, when about to consummate His great sacrifice for our redemption! At what time do you refuse God the little He asks of you? At the very moment when He is most liberally loading you with benefits of every description! Oh, how great is your ingratitude. From whence does Jesus say, *"I thirst?"* From the Cross, on which He has been languishing for three long hours. The very place from which He speaks ought to be sufficient to move you to compassion. At the sight of a God hanging for your sake upon a Cross, and imploring you to correct some fault, break off some improper friendship, or fly from some occasion of sin, can you turn away, can you refuse Him that consolation? Ah, reflect at least before uttering a refusal which will be a source of so much suffering to Him!

2. Besides this corporal thirst, Jesus suffers from another spiritual species of thirst, which cannot be so easily assuaged.

Jesus thirsts for our eternal salvation. He thirsts for souls. This is the thirst of which he complains, and which is consuming His very life's Blood. Jesus most passionately desires that the Blood He has shed should benefit mankind by saving them from Hell; and yet He foreknows that there will be many eternally lost, notwithstanding all his love and all His sufferings. Oh, truly does this thirst consume the loving Heart of Jesus, and its sacred heat slowly but surely deprives Him of life.

My soul, reflect now what things thy desires tend to, and what thou dost thirst after. No doubt thou thirstest after worldly goods, after honors, pleasures, comforts, and amusements, but thou thirstest not after thy salvation; thou art not desirous of gaining Heaven, of entering into the possession of that eternal, undying bliss which Jesus has purchased for thee at so dear a rate. Jesus Crucified thirsts in an especial manner after thy salvation and progress in Divine love. If thou hadst been present on Mount Calvary, and hadst heard our Redeemer saying, *"I thirst,"* wouldst thou not have relieved His sufferings by giving Him a little water? Know that even at the present moment it is in thy power to relieve His burning thirst. He says to thee from the Cross, "My son, *I thirst* for thy soul." Art thou desirous of affording thy Redeemer some solace in His sufferings from thirst? Offer Him thy thoughts by frequent consideration on His goodness and sufferings. Give Him thy heart with all its affections by constant protestations that thou lovest Him above all things, and will ever love Him in preference to all created objects. Give Him thy soul with all its powers, and often renew thy resolution to work out thy eternal salvation, however much it may cost thee, and hope that thy efforts may be crowned with success, through the merits of His Passion. Thus mayest thou relieve Jesus in His thirst.

3. Consider a third species of thirst endured by Jesus.

The thirst to suffer yet more for the glory of His beloved Father, and the salvation of souls. Jesus has drunk the bitter chalice of His Passion, even to the dregs, and yet He thirsts to suffer even more for love of us. Be filled with admiration at the ardent charity of Jesus, which causes His sacred Heart to be consumed by such a thirst of love, and thank Him for His great goodness in suffering so much for your sake, and desiring to suffer yet more. There can be no doubt that Jesus would have prolonged His bitter sufferings, had not the Will of His Father disposed otherwise, so great was the love He bore your souls. Are you filled with a thirst of labor and suffering for the love of Jesus? Do you thirst with a desire to struggle and fight manfully to save your soul? Perhaps your thirst is the thirst of the world, the flesh and earthly goods, a thirst which overwhelms the Heart of Jesus with bitterness. Jesus loves His Eternal Father with an infinite love, and rejoices that, for His greater glory, His body is slowly consumed with suffering, and that His spirit continues to drink the bitter chalice of fresh afflictions. He rejoices that His sacrifice is prolonged through every species of ignominy, in order to honor His Father, and that His life is slowly departing amidst agony and suffering, that so His obedience to the Divine Will may be yet further exercised, and His beloved Father more and more glorified. Now cast a glance upon yourself. Do you joyfully endure the sufferings with which life is strewn? Do you love God in the midst of your trials? Do you kiss the hand which chastises you? Do you desire to glorify God by the sacrifice of your patience? Do you thirst for God to be honored by yourself and all others? Do you thirst after the performance of good and virtuous actions, which alone can give satisfaction and joy to the Heart of Jesus? Examine yourself, and resolve to amend.

The Fruit

The remembrance of the thirst of Jesus on the Cross, and of the gall and vinegar given Him to drink, should serve you as an incentive to mortification of the palate, and as a lesson in sobriety and temperance. Dwell in thought upon your past life, and bitterly deplore that you have so often given Jesus gall and vinegar to drink, by your sinful deeds. Entertain a most earnest and persevering desire to save your soul, and thirst eagerly after that eternal Fountain of life which is prepared for you in Heaven.

Example

The faithful followers of Jesus Crucified willingly deprived themselves, for His love, of even the most innocent gratifications that creatures can afford them. One day in the height of summer Saint Paul of the Cross was returning with a fellow-religious from a mission which he had been giving, and, owing to the extreme heat of the weather, he was suffering greatly from thirst, when suddenly they came to a clear fountain of water, which seemed to invite them to drink. The servant of God turned to his companion, and said to him, smiling, "Shall we now perform an act of mortification by abstaining from this water? For the love of Jesus enduring such burning thirst on the Cross, let us make a sacrifice of this gratification of our palate." His fervent companion immediately assented to the proposal, which was forthwith acted upon. This act of mortification was so pleasing in the sight of our Divine Lord, that He speedily rewarded His servant by abundant spiritual favors. (See his *Life*).

∾ DAY 30 ∾

Jesus Dies on the Cross

Meditation

JESUS after having commended His Spirit to His Father, after being three hours on the Cross in agony of body and desolation of mind, at length bows His head and dies. Consider:

1. Who is it that dies?

He is the Son of God, the only begotten of the most High, who is immense and infinite in all His adorable perfections. He is the God of Glory; God most loving, most holy. The ocean of all good dies for thee, a creature most vile, most wicked, a sink of every vice, a sea of miseries, a monster of ingratitude. So it is: the Creator dies for the creature; the Lord for the servant; God for man. And art thou not struck with wonder at seeing a God dying for thee, solely on account of the love He bears thee! Where is thy emotion, where is thy astonishment, at the sight of such a death, such condescension! *A God has died for man.* This thought was the sweetest, this reflection was the most endearing to the Saints. This was the powerful motive to the love of God. *A God has died for man.* This is suggestive of the confusion and despair of the damned in Hell. "A God has died for me," will the damned soul exclaim, "and yet I burn, I despair in those flames. I cannot doubt of His love, if He has died upon the Cross to save me. Therefore, if I am damned, it is all through my own malice." Ah, deservedly does that soul burn eternally who has been ungrateful and frowardly heedless of a God Crucified and dying for man! My soul, wouldst thou rather burn forever in the unquenchable fire, than burn now with the love of that God who has died for thee on the Cross? And is it possible that, after having beheld God dying for thy love, thou wilt not cease to offend Him, to maltreat Him, to despise His tender charity? Draw near, my soul, to the foot of the Cross, where cold and bloodless hangs the Body of thy dead Jesus; repent of thy past ingratitude; thank Him for having died for thee, and freed thee from eternal pains; put thy trust in His Blood, and in His sacred Wounds, and promise Him never more to draw thyself away from His love.

2. How does He die?

He dies, after having poured forth in cruel anguish all the sacred Blood in His veins. He dies, satiated with insults, with reproaches and ignominies. He dies, plunged in an ocean of inexplicable pains and torments. He dies consumed, not so much by the raging fire of His sufferings, as by the living furnace of His charity. Which of us can wish to live except in order to love our Jesus? Which of us would like to suffer except in order to give Him pleasure? Who will dare to make Him die over again by accursed sin? Jesus dies, bowing His head in sign of obedience and submission to His Eternal Father. He could have prolonged His life, and even abolished death altogether, but He was pleased to die, and allow the force and atrocity of His pains to slay Him, in order that His obedience might reach to death itself. By His obedience he repairs the damages caused by the first fatal disobedience; He restores to the Divine Majesty the honor that had been robbed, and puts man again in possession of Paradise. God does not require of you an obedience that will cost you your life; yet how remiss are you in obeying? It may be, indeed, that the observance of some precept will cost you something? But will you not obey God, your Lord, your Sovereign Lord? Will not you, a vile creature, do this, seeing Jesus has obeyed even unto death? Jesus bows His head towards us, to express the lovingness of the invitation He gives us to approach Him. But, ah! who accepts so sweet, so loving an invitation? How long is it since Jesus invited you to penance? How often has He entreated you to come and ask pardon? And do you defer coming to One who is so anxious to receive you! Shall you, to satisfy a wrong desire, delay to approach Jesus calling you from the Cross? Resolve this moment to amend.

3. Where does He die?

He dies on the Cross, suspended by three nails, between two thieves, covered with wounds, in the presence of an immense multitude. Behold the excess of a God loving. One sigh, one tear of His, would have been sufficient to redeem the world. That would not satisfy the love of Jesus. He wished for death—the death of the Cross. Fix thy gaze, my soul, upon the adorable lifeless Body of thy Jesus, which still hangs from the Cross. See this beautiful countenance, pale, livid, defiled with blood and spittle; this head pierced with thorns; those hands and feet perforated with big nails; those members rent and torn until the bones may be numbered. At the sight, the sky is covered with heavy darkness, the earth is shook, all creation emits a voice of sorrow and mourning. How is thy heart moved towards its good God, its dear Father, its loving Brother, just expired for your sake? The number of wounds opened in His sacred Body are so many mouths which speak and preach of love. Canst thou doubt of being loved by Jesus? Canst thou live without making a return? My soul, thy value is the life of a God. Thou owest thy life to the Son of God, who gave His for thee on the Cross. What enormous injustice would it be if thou gavest thy love to the world, to the flesh, to the devils, thy cruel enemies, and deniest it to Jesus? O my Jesus! I am no longer mine, nor do I wish to be another's, but only Thine, who hast died for me, and Thine I wish to be for eternity. My soul has cost Thee much. Grant that I may know its value, that I may esteem it, and no longer give it away to sin and the devil. Grant that I may spend the remainder of my life in serving Thee and loving Thee with all my heart.

The Fruit

Look often at your Crucifix, and say with affectionate devotion, *"A God died on the Cross for me."* Kiss often His sacred feet, bathing them with tears of true contrition. The Crucifix will be the only object of comfort and consolation that can be presented to Thee at the hour of death. Try now so to act that the love and the Wounds of Jesus serve not to reproach thee at that terrible moment.

Example

Devotion to the sufferings of Jesus procures us a holy death. The blessed Joachim Piccolomini, of the order of Servites, having had during life a tender devotion, and kept up a loving remembrance of the Passion of our Lord, and not having had the opportunity of shedding his blood for Him by martyrdom, begged earnestly of the Blessed Virgin to procure for him the privilege of dying on Good Friday, in order that he might thus have, at least, the happiness of giving up his life on the same day on which Jesus laid down His upon the Cross. The loving Mother was pleased at the petition. On the very day he prayed for, while assisting at the function, and the Passion was being sung, he was buried in the thought of the pains and sufferings of Jesus Crucified, and just as the words, "He gave up the ghost," were pronounced, he sweetly rendered his soul up to his Maker, by a death which excited the wonder and holy envy of all present. (*Annal. de Serv. Mariæ*).

∽ DAY 31 ∽

The Side of Jesus
Wounded by a Spear

Meditation

OUR blessed Saviour having expired, a soldier, more cruel and impious than the rest, imagining that He may yet be alive, wounds Him in the side with a lance. Consider:

1. The cruelty displayed towards Jesus on this occasion.

The barbarity of the enemies of Jesus is not satiated by all the inhuman tortures inflicted upon His living Body, but, more cruel than death itself, they turn their rage against the sacred Body of their dead Redeemer. A man, however wicked he may have been, is an object of compassion when once he has given his life in expiation of his crimes. The outrages offered to Jesus alone are endless, the insults heaped upon His sacred Person alone are unlimited. Jesus is already dead, why then open His side with a lance? Why is not the hatred borne Him by the Jews at last extinguished? Why is their cruelty not yet satiated by all the sufferings which have been inflicted upon their innocent Saviour? Behold how that sharp lance, directed by eager hands, inflicts a deep wound upon the breast of Jesus, and pierces through and through His adorable Heart. Oh, cruel spear! But oh, far more cruel hands that direct it! How frequently have you, O Sinner, not merely crucified Jesus anew by sin, but persisted in wounding and lacerating His most holy Heart over and over again by your continual offenses! Repeatedly have you thus cruelly and impiously outraged your loving Redeemer. How many times have you re-opened that wound? Detest your malice, bewail your ingratitude, and cleanse all the stains wherewith your soul is defiled, in that Blood and water which issues from the side of your Redeemer.

Jesus feels no pain from the wound at the moment of its infliction, but He suffered it by anticipation, and by the knowledge He had of the atrocious cruelty of the man who would inflict it; still He willingly accepted this indignity and submitted to so barbarous an outrage. Jesus spares not Himself in any way where the salvation of your soul is concerned, whereas, oh, how ungenerous and niggardly are you in His regard! Ah, such is not the manner in which you should correspond with the infinite love of Jesus, who has deigned to suffer for your sake with so much generosity!

2. The love displayed by Jesus for us.

The Son of God was not satisfied with giving us proofs of His love during life, but it was His Will to give us additional proofs of it even after death. It was His Will thereby to show us that His love was not quenched by death. Therefore He permitted that His sacred side should be opened with a spear after His death, so that we might behold His divine Heart pierced for love of us. Thus was a door opened for us, through which we might enter, and behold the ever living, ever burning love of the Heart of Jesus, even after death. His sufferings might deprive Him of life, but not of love, which, like a mighty fire, burned more brightly and clearly still, when fed with the fuel of sufferings. Do I desire to increase in love for Jesus, I need but fix my eyes upon Him as He hangs dead on the Cross for love of me, and behold how His sacred Body has been lacerated and immolated for my sake. Those wounds which bleed no longer because every vein is emptied of the last drop of its blood, tell us loudly how great, how excessive, is the love of God for us, since it has reduced Him to such a condition for our sake. But why add a fresh wound to the lacerated Body, from which the soul is already separated? Oh, truly precious wound, inflicted by reason of the excessive charity of a God, whose desire it is to make known to us how great, even after death, is His love for man! His Heart is a furnace of love, which not all the waters of the sea can ever extinguish. Oh, is there any one to be found, who can contemplate that open side, that tender, wounded, loving Heart, without feeling himself obliged to return love for love? Enter, my soul, enter into the burning furnace of the tender Heart of Jesus, enter it frequently in spirit, and there thy incredible hardness of heart will be softened, and thy icy coldness warmed; thou wilt be inflamed with holy love for thy God. Behold the last drop of warm blood issuing from that sacred Heart, and bathing the soldier who has inflicted the wound! The scourges had not drawn that last drop, neither had the thorns, or the nails, but now, at last, the spear opens it a passage, and it flows forth! O surprising and excessive charity of Jesus! Who gives even the last drop of His Heart's blood, and gives it for the good of those who inflict the wound upon Him! And are you so fearful of bestowing too much upon Jesus, if you bestow all your love upon Him, that you are obliged to share it with a thousand vain objects? Permit me, O my Jesus, to kiss Thy wounded side, and to enter into Thy Divine Heart, where thou mayest destroy my malice in the flames of its charity, transform me totally into Thyself, and fill my soul with Thy Divine love.

3. The mystery therein represented.

From the side of Adam asleep, the Almighty took a rib, of which He formed Eve, the mother of all the living, thereby representing in figure what would be accomplished in the death of Jesus. The death of our Redeemer is but the sleep of the Second Adam, the Repairer of the evils brought upon the world by the first. Therefore, while He is sleeping the sleep of love upon the Cross, His side is pierced by the lance, in order that the Church,

His beloved Spouse, the Mother of all the faithful, may come forth from His side, that is to say, from His adorable Heart. Behold of how great a Mother your faith makes you the happy son! She derives her existence from the most pure Heart of a Man-God. Must not your origin be Divine also, since you are the son of such a Mother? What therefore can be more suitable, since you derive your existence from the most loving Heart of Jesus, than that you should return whence you came forth, and should be unable to find true rest or happiness, save in the Heart of your Lord? From that wounded Heart has likewise flowed the water which sanctified you in Baptism, and which has so often cleansed you from your sins in Confession. Comprehend, if possible, the price, the value, the dignity, and merit of holy Baptism, and the excellence of the august title of a Christian, which it bestows upon you. Through it you are born again to a new life of grace, you are put in possession of the precious inheritance of the sons of God, you acquire a right to the eternal inheritance of Heaven, you become one of the people of God, the brother of Jesus Christ, his co-heir, and a member of His mystical Body, the Church. So numerous, therefore, are the favors, so noble the prerogatives, which you derive from the wounded side of Jesus! What gratitude do you feel toward your Divine Redeemer for blessings so great and innumerable? Have you ever even thought of them with the slightest emotions of gratitude? How often have you thanked your Lord for His infinite goodness and mercy? Strange as it may seem, it yet is a fact, that Christians live and die without having perhaps once returned God thanks for so extraordinary a favor as that of being children of the true Church of Jesus Christ, or having even considered the grace of being Christians as any extraordinary favor! Value so great a happiness as it deserves, and be grateful for it to Jesus, through whose wounded Heart it has been bestowed upon you.

The Fruit

Consecrate yourself this day to the love of the sacred Heart of Jesus—the center of all hearts. In all your trials and temptations, take refuge in the side of your Redeemer, endeavoring to make most fervent and lively acts of love for His adorable Heart. Return God thanks every morning and evening, for the singular favor He has bestowed upon you in making you a Christian, and a member of His Church. Glory in being, in appearing, and in professing yourself a Christian on every occasion. Do not disgrace the august and venerable character bestowed upon you in Baptism, by committing sin, or by leading a life unworthy of a Christian.

Example

Blessed Francis Lippi, a Carmelite friar, was most devout to the Passion of Jesus Christ, and accustomed to spend several hours each day in meditating upon it, with many tears. It happened one day, that being engaged in this pious exercise, and considering how excessive were the sufferings of his Jesus on the Cross, and how great was the cruelty of those who pierced His side with a spear after death, he wished that his eyes might be changed into two fountains of tears, that so he might weep unrestrainedly over the sufferings and outrages endured by his loving Redeemer; when, behold, there appeared unto him Jesus nailed to the Cross, covered with blood, and His side pierced with a spear! The following words were then addressed to him in a voice faint with exhaustion: *"Behold, O Francis, how much I have suffered for the love of man, and what an ungrateful return he yet makes Me for all My sufferings."* The vision then disappeared. At this mournful spectacle the blessed man wept bitterly over the sufferings of his sweet Jesus, and, taking an iron chain, scourged his body severely, until he had made his blood flow in streams for the love of Him who for his sake had shed even the last drop of His own, and he meanwhile, exclaimed in sorrowful accents, "It is I, O Lord, it is I who am the cause of Thy sufferings; it is I who am the cause of Thy bitter Passion!" (See his *Life*). Repeat these or similar words whenever you look at the Crucifix.

EXERCISES OF
DEVOTION

EXERCISES OF
DEVOTION

✑ EXERCISE 1 ✑

Incentives to Devotion toward The Five Adorable Wounds of Our Saviour Jesus Christ

1. *The Wounds of Jesus Christ bear eternal testimony to His infinite love for us, and are fountains of Charity, according to the expression of St. Bernard.* And, in fact, what stronger proofs could we have of the infinite love of Jesus than those five Wounds, which He permitted to be made in His hands, feet, and side, that in them, as in so many written words, we might read the immensity of His love? One single drop of His most precious Blood would have been sufficient, and a thousand times more than sufficient, for our Redemption, but not for His love. It was His Will that His Blood should flow from five copious fountains, that so He might shed every drop of it for our salvation. Yet more; no sooner had our loving Redeemer breathed His last, than, in order to make us understand that His love was stronger than death, He permitted His side to be opened with a spear, and His sacred Heart pierced with a deep wound, that so He might bestow upon us the

219

few remaining drops of Blood which the scourges and nails had failed to draw forth from His veins. "It was not so much the lance," says St. Cyprian, "which inflicted the Wound upon the side of Jesus, as His love for us." The lance was but the instrument of His love, which was desirous of thus bestowing His Heart upon us. Oh, how loudly do these Wounds proclaim to us that great, or rather, infinite, has been the love of Jesus for us! How strongly do they remind us of all He has suffered for our salvation! It has been the will of Jesus to preserve in His glorified Body the marks of His Wounds as a perpetual remembrance of the great love He has borne us, and of all He has done for our sakes, and as incentives to urge Him to do yet more, and preserve and increase in us the gifts of His grace. Now, how is it possible that with so many incentives to love, our hearts should still remain cold, and unwilling even sometimes to remember, reflect upon, venerate, honor, and love the adorable Wounds of so loving a Redeemer? Jesus has purchased our hearts and affections at the exorbitant price of His Wounds and Blood, and shall we refuse to give them to Him, shall we refuse to employ our hearts in loving Him, and our affections in honoring and venerating His most holy Wounds? Such fearful ingratitude on the part of a Christian would indeed be most painful to the sweet and adorable Heart of Jesus! And, in fact, the most acute and bitter anguish endured by that sacred Heart, was, says St. Bernard, caused by the thought of the ingratitude of man, who would so seldom call to mind His Wounds and His Passion. Dedicate your heart, then, with the tenderest feelings of devotion, to the Wounds of your Redeemer, which are the everlasting pledges of His love for you. Imitate the example of St. Augustine, who used to beseech Jesus Crucified to inscribe His sacred Wounds in his heart with one of His blood-stained nails, that he might thus have these marks of the love of his God continually present to his mind.

2. *The Wounds of Jesus are fountains of Grace, Mercy, and Salvation.* From them did the price of our Redemption flow, to satisfy Divine Justice for our sins. From them flowed forth the plenitude of the Divine benedictions and mercies, by which our souls were to be enriched, and their salvation rendered an infinitely less arduous task. From them did the Sacraments derive their thrice-blessed origin—the Sacraments which cleanse, purify, and sanctify us, and the celestial waters of which irrigate our hearts with their precious streams, and impart fecundity to the vineyard of Holy Church. These Wounds constitute an asylum, in which we may take refuge, lest we perish with the reprobate, and lose our souls. They are the dearest, and at the same time the most secure pledges of our eternal salvation, which Jesus has bestowed upon us. Whoever desires to know how great was, and is, the anxiety of Jesus for our salvation, need but look at His most sacred Wounds. What deep emotions of gratitude ought not such reflections to awaken in the hearts of all Christians? What affection, what tender devotion, ought they not to feel towards these most holy Wounds? How earnestly should they strive to love and adore them with the utmost reverence, and thus give expression to their unbounded gratitude. Blessed James of Bevagna, being disturbed by fears concerning his salvation, implored Jesus to bestow upon him a pledge of Heaven, the sole object of his desires. His loving Lord, to console him, gave him a paper signed with the Blood that flowed from His Wounds, saying, "Let this Blood be to thee a pledge of thy salvation."

3. *The Wounds of Jesus furnish us with powerful motives for hope.* Our divine Redeemer has been pleased to retain the marks of His Wounds in His glorified Body, in order to inspire sinners with confidence. His office in Heaven, says St. Paul, is to make continual intercession for us to His Eternal Father. His Wounds are so many tongues ever speaking in our favor. He offers them to His Father, imploring His clemency in our behalf, with powerful efficacy. If our sins demand vengeance, the Wounds of Jesus cry out still more loudly for pity and mercy, and the voice of His Wounds drowns the voice of our sins. They make reparation for those offenses which would otherwise call down the just anger of God upon sinners. They fulfill the merciful office of perpetual advocates and intercessors in our behalf, and implore grace and mercy for us. Let us, then, unite our supplications to their powerful voices, and when we pray and ask favors through the merits of these Wounds, we may be sure of obtaining all that we ask. Let us, then, unite ourselves closely to the most holy Wounds of our Saviour; let us have recourse to them with lively hope and entire confidence, and doubt not that our prayers will be heard. For us have these Wounds been made, and for our sakes has Jesus retained them as marks of glory, to make known to us that our names being thus inscribed in characters of blood, He will never forget us. "No," says St. Augustine, "our Lord willeth not the eternal loss of those souls which He has purchased at so dear a rate." "Jesus," adds St. Bernard, "was pleased to ascend into Heaven with His arms and hands extended, that all might see His sacred Wounds, and seeing, might adore them, and adoring, might place all their hopes in them."

4. *Through the Wounds of Jesus Christ we have been reconciled to God, our sins have been pardoned, and we have been released from those bonds which detained our souls in a state of servitude to the Devil.* By the Blood that flowed from these adorable Wounds were our sins remitted, our souls purified from their stains, and the life of grace bestowed on penitent sinners. Through these precious Wounds the decree of our condemnation has been cancelled, and the merciful sentence of our pardon and absolution written in its stead.

However great may be our debts, we may find in the Wounds of our Crucified Jesus wherewith to pay to the full all that may be owing by sinful men to Divine justice. The sacred bank is open, the ransom-money ready, and whoever refuses to profit by it must be resolved to die in his sins. Does your conscience reproach you with the enormity of your sins, and the slightness of the penance you have done for them? Take courage, fear not, hasten to the Wounds of Jesus, and there you will find wherewith to make atonement. Draw nigh to those Wounds with faith and love, bury your sins in them with feelings of heartfelt contrition, wash yourself in the Divine Blood flowing from them, and you will be cleansed from all your stains. But whoever, on the other hand, is obstinate in sin, or refuses to have recourse to the Wounds of his Redeemer, will close to himself those fountains of pardon and reconciliation, and be lost for all eternity. At the hour of death, he will hear these severe words of reproof from the lips of his wounded Lord: "These Wounds were the work of thy hands—for thy sake were they made—and yet thou wouldst not even so much as look at them, much less approach, and hide thyself within them." And what could we, wretched creatures, answer at that awful moment? Let us then at once provide against so fearful a misfortune, and devote all the love and affection of our hearts to the most holy Wounds of Jesus Christ.

5. *The Wounds of Jesus invite us to repentance,*

inspire us with horror for sin, and produce in us a change of life. Even the hard-hearted crucifiers of Jesus, on beholding Him dead and covered with wounds, were touched at the sight, repented, and shed tears of compunction. And is there a man to be found, who, on contemplating the Wounds of his Crucified Lord, recognizing in them the work of his hands, the effect of his malice, and the malignity of his sins, which, like cruel executioners, inflicted such Wounds—is there a man, I say, who will not be moved to repentance? Can any one behold the excruciating torments endured by his mangled Lord, see such copious streams of Blood flowing from His lacerated limbs and pierced Heart, and not bitterly bewail his sins with tears of sorrow? Can anyone have the heart to renew by sin those Wounds which Jesus was pleased to receive in His blessed Body, on account of sin? Are you really anxious to amend? Do you sincerely desire to bewail your ill-spent life? Never allow a day to pass without a few moments' contemplation of the Wounds of your Redeemer, and you will there behold how great an evil sin is, which inflicted on your soul wounds that could not be healed but with the salutary balm distilled from the Wounds of the Son of God. These Wounds will also show you how great is the hatred God bears to sin, since He visited it with such severity upon the humanity of His only begotten Son. How would it be possible for any Christian, who often contemplates Jesus fastened with nails to the Cross, and pierced with the lance, to take plea-

sure in those sins which inflicted such Wounds
upon the Son of God? Could such a man commit
sin, and not rather be filled with the deepest
abhorrence for it? But we must contemplate Him
attentively, and for a due space of time, not hurriedly and with a mere passing glance, as was
done on Mount Calvary by the Pharisees, who yet
remained as hardened and obstinate as ever.
Earthly goods allure, our passions seduce us, and
sin tyrannizes over us, only because we do not fix
the eyes of our mind upon the Wounds of our Crucified Jesus. Penance alarms us, and we regard it
almost with horror, solely because we do not consider how much suffering, and how many wounds
were inflicted upon Jesus for sins not His own.
Frequently read the enormity of your sins in the
Wounds of your Crucified Lord, and you will
detest and do penance for them.

6. *The Wounds of Jesus make known the infinite
value of Heaven, which they have opened to us.
Heaven is the price of the Wounds and Blood of the
Son of God.* Jesus Christ did not think the sovereign beatitude and glory of Heaven too dearly purchased at the price of unspeakable tortures, and
by suffering His sacred flesh to be mangled by
nails, thorns, and scourges. Great indeed must be
the value of that which cost the Son of God so
dear! And yet we esteem it so little, as to be even
ready to renounce our claim to it, as, in fact, so
many of us do, for the sake of some wretched pleasure or despicable interest! Ye blind and deluded

children of men, contemplate the Wounds of your Crucified God, and see in what manner the gates of the kingdom of glory have been opened to you! See what it has cost Him to place you in possession of it, and understand, if possible, how infinite a benefit was bestowed upon you by the Son of God when He purchased for you Heaven, which you had lost by sin! St. Bernard, being greatly disturbed at the hour of death by a strong temptation to fear that he never should obtain Heaven, put the tempter to flight with these words: "It is true that what I have done to gain Heaven is nothing; it is also true that I am undeserving of it; but I hope to obtain it because the Blood and Wounds of my Redeemer have purchased it for me." Enter in spirit into these sacred Wounds, and you will comprehend the value and sublimity of that eternal felicity which they have acquired for you, and you will learn to detach your heart from the earth and from creatures, so as to place all your affections and desires upon Heaven. Be filled with gratitude for those adorable Wounds, which have purchased such a treasure for you, and frequently adore, bless, and venerate them with the liveliest feelings of gratitude. Often gratefully address Jesus Crucified in these words of St. Augustine: *"O Jesus! Thy Wounds are my merits;"* or in those of St. Jerome: *"The Blood which flows from Thy Wounds, O Lord, is to me the key of Heaven."*

7. *The Wounds of Jesus Christ have delivered us from the slavery of the devil and of Hell.* If you had been delivered from slavery among the Turks, what love would have inflamed your heart for the merciful benefactor who had saved you! Now, Jesus Christ has freed you by His Wounds and death from the slavery of a far more cruel and terrible tyrant—the devil. He has saved you from the dreadful torments of Hell; what gratitude should you not then feel for so loving a Saviour? With what emotions of love and devotion should you not contemplate His most holy Wounds, which have broken asunder your chains, and extinguished the flames of Hell, to which you were condemned, by the Blood flowing from them? Cast your eyes upon Hell, and then upon these most sacred Wounds—upon Hell, to see what you had deserved; upon the Wounds of Jesus, to thank Him who has saved you from it, and to behold in what manner He has saved you. Your creation cost God nothing, but your redemption cost Him Wounds, Blood, Life itself. And can you remain indifferent to so much goodness? Will you not frequently kiss those adorable Wounds with the liveliest sentiments of affection? Will you not return earnest thanks for your liberation from eternal damnation? But the greatest proof of gratitude that you can offer these Wounds—the highest gratification you can give your wounded Redeemer, is to endeavor to avoid sin, which subjects you anew to the slavery of the devil, and imperils your eternal salvation; to direct all your efforts and to seek by every means in your power to save your soul, in order to go to Heaven, where you may forever bless those Wounds of love, and enjoy the happiness of which they are the price, in the society of the holy Angels and Saints. Daily adore the Wounds of your Redeemer, and protest before each of them that you are determined, at whatever cost, to save your soul. And if the devil brings to your mind the sins of your past life, and Hell claims you for its own because you once merited a place in its dark dungeons, look at the Wounds of your Crucified Lord, and listen to their voice, encouraging you not to fear, because the Blood which flowed from them has power to quench the flames enkindled by your sins.

8. *The Wounds of Jesus Christ impart to us strength whereby to combat our enemies.* Our life on earth is a continual warfare. We have to fight against the devils who, by their deceits, evil suggestions and temptations, lay snares for us on every side, and violently assault and attack us in order to make us fall into sin, and thence headlong into Hell. The Wounds of Jesus are prefigured, according to the Fathers, by those five small stones which the shepherd David selected to vanquish and kill the giant Goliath. In like manner, when you are armed with, and shielded by these five Wounds, you will be enabled to triumph over all the efforts of Hell. If you take shelter within these Wounds, as within so many strong fortresses, the spirit of evil will have no power over you. The world with its flatteries, vanities, terrors and menaces, makes war upon us without ceasing, spreads dangers in our path, lays a thousand snares to rob us of our innocence, and presents us at every turn with occasions of sin and incentives to allure us to our fall. Who will be saved where it is so easy to be lost? He only who takes refuge in the Wounds of Jesus. *"Here do I live secure,"* says St. Bernard, *"here have I nought to fear. In this harbor of refuge do I find salvation."* The other enemy of our soul is the flesh, a domestic, yet bitter enemy; disguised, but the more powerful on that account, which by allurements and deceptive flatteries seeks to poison our hearts and ruin our souls for eternity. Oh, what havoc does not this enemy make among Christians! How many poor souls are lost for ever through the hateful vice of impurity! Is it your desire to be liberated from the venomous fangs of this monster? Are you anxious to extinguish the flames of impurity lighted up by the flesh, and to excite in your souls the love of holy chastity? Be devout to the Wounds of your Crucified Lord. It is all but impossible that any man who, in time of temptation to sins of the flesh, thinks of the Wounds of his Redeemer, should have the heart to consent to that very sin for which Jesus made satisfaction by so many sufferings and Wounds in His immaculate flesh. Be devout to the Wounds of Jesus, and choose them for your dwelling-place by day and by night. Have recourse to them with confidence in time of temptation and you will infallibly come off victorious. If Christians were to profess a more tender devotion to the holy

Wounds of their Crucified Lord, they would be stronger against the enemies of their salvation, and would not fall so miserably into the unhappy abyss of sin. All the Saints have experienced the powerful efficacy of this devotion in enabling a soul to overcome temptations. You also will surely experience the same if from this day you consecrate yourself to it.

9. *The Wounds of Jesus are burning furnaces of Charity, which inflame all hearts with the holy love of God, and are the remedy for all our spiritual infirmities.* Flames of love issue from these Wounds, consuming all the Saints of Heaven in the burning fire of charity. These blessed furnaces enkindle in the Saints on earth ardent fires of love, ravishing their hearts. How can it be otherwise than that the wounded Heart of Jesus, all on fire as it is with charity, should communicate its blessed heat to whoever approaches it? On one occasion, St. Catherine of Genoa beheld in a vision the Heart of Jesus, with so many flames issuing from it, through the Wound in the side, that she fainted away from the excessive warmth and unbearable heat of this blessed fire. And if such is the effect produced by the mere contemplation of these blessed Wounds, which all breathe forth flames of love, what would it be if we entered into them, and dwelt there? "Certainly," says St. Laurence Justinian, "if your heart were harder than adamant, the sacred fire which burns in these Wounds would soften it, and enkindle flames of love within you." Jesus invites you to enter into His holy Wounds; draw nigh to them, then, with the liveliest feelings of devotion, unite your heart to them, and you will experience what heavenly sweetness, what delicious consolations, they will infuse into your soul. Then all the joys of earth will become insipid; the love of God alone will give pleasure and happiness, and suffering for Jesus will be sweet and delightful. St. Mary Magdalen of Pazzi once beheld the Blessed Virgin holding in her hand a vase, which she was filling with a precious liquid from the side of Jesus, and this liquid was the love of God. Do you thirst after these Heavenly waters? Approach the wounded side of Jesus, entertain a lively devotion toward the Wounds of your Redeemer, often enter into them by devout meditation, and you will find there wherewith to cure all your spiritual maladies, however dangerous and deep-rooted they may be. "No!" exclaims St. Bernard, "there is no medicine more efficacious for healing the wounds of the soul than devotion to, and meditation upon, the Wounds of our Crucified God." He who attentively thinks of the Wounds of Jesus Christ, and meditates upon all the sufferings endured by Jesus in these Wounds, will place a guard over his eyes, bridle his tongue, mortifying his taste, bring his body under subjection, repress his passions, and refuse to gratify the vain desires of his heart. Here may we find a remedy for all bad habits and evil inclinations. "Give but one glance at your Crucified God, look at His Wounds," says St.

Augustine, "if you are desirous of being made whole of those spiritual maladies which sin has brought upon your soul." You are sick in body, in soul, in your powers, and in your senses. Jesus and His most holy Wounds are the medicine by which you may be restored to health. From these blessed Wounds is distilled that precious balsam which heals all spiritual infirmities. By them is the soul comforted and strengthened to perform acts of virtue, to suffer willingly, and to endure death itself, for the love of her Lord. From them did the holy martyrs obtain courage and strength to suffer all their torments with undaunted constancy. From them did the holy penitents learn how to endure their life-long austerities. Become acquainted, then, by your own happy experience, with all the advantages of this devotion; enter into the Wounds of Jesus Christ; be most devout to them, and in them you will find a hidden treasure; in them all your desires will be fully satiated, and you will no longer set any value upon aught the world can afford you.

10. *In the last place, the Wounds of Jesus procure us a holy death, open to us the gates of Heaven, and introduce us into a state of everlasting glory and happiness.* Our death is the great affair which we have on hand, and on which depends a happy or a miserable eternity. The whole time of our existence here below is given us by God to prepare for a holy death; and what better disposition can we have to ensure our dying happily than that of having always professed a constant and tender devotion to the holy Wounds of Jesus Christ? A holy life is the best preparation and most secure means for obtaining the happiness of dying the death of the saints. Now, devotion to the Wounds of Jesus Christ causes us to lead a holy life, because these most sacred Wounds enkindle the love of God in our souls, infuse into us a penitential spirit, restrain us from sin, fill us with hope, stimulate us to virtue, render us strong against our enemies, and impart all possible good to the soul. Therefore, through this devotion, that is to say, through the Wounds of our Crucified Lord, which we have loved, venerated, and adored in life, we shall surely obtain a holy death. For this reason is it that the Wounds of our Redeemer are styled by St. Bonaventure, *The gates of Heaven,* because it is through them that the devout soul passes into eternal glory. St. Edmund, when about to die, asked for a Crucifix, and kissed its Wounds, saying, "Behold the wood on which I hope to reach the port of eternal salvation"; and very shortly after he went to receive the reward of his hope, and of the devotion which he had always felt towards those most holy Wounds. A like happy fate may be hoped for by all who are truly devout to the Wounds of their Crucified Lord. Oh, what consolation will be theirs at the hour of death, when the blessed Crucifix is presented to them! Oh, what confidence of salvation will be awakened in their hearts on beholding those Wounds into which they have so often entered in spirit during life, and which have ever been the dearest objects of their affections and of their devotion. The sight of the Crucifix will sweeten the sorrows of death, give us strength to bear all its accompanying sufferings, and mitigate the horrors of our last agony. The most holy Wounds of Jesus will strengthen, console, and comfort the soul in its last tremendous journey, and will introduce it into the joys of Heaven. Happy the soul which, by means of such slight homage offered to the Wounds of Jesus—by means of a little devotion and affection bestowed upon the Wounds of so loving a Redeemer—thus enters into possession of eternal, infinite, everlasting happiness! If you desire so enviable a fate, consecrate yourself from this day to devotion to the Wounds of Jesus Crucified; let it be your chosen devotion, and let not a day pass without offering your sincerest homage to these adorable Wounds, dedicated yourself to their love and veneration, and renewing your determination to persevere therein to the end of your life. In them you find a rule whereby you may regulate your whole life, and the means of sanctifying your every action. Listen to the words of Jesus Himself. St. Mechtildis, being one day engaged in the contemplation of the Wounds of her Redeemer, was filled with a most earnest desire to know what she could do in their honor that would give the greatest satisfaction to the Heart of Jesus. Our blessed Lord spoke to her, and gave her the following useful lesson: "In return for the Wounds of My feet,

thou must offer Me all thy affections and desires;
for the Wounds of My hands, thou must offer Me
thy works; for the Wounds of My side, thou must
offer Me perfect conformity of thy will with Mine."
Can any Christian who lives in this manner, lead
any other than the life of a saint? Can he die any
other than the death of the saints? Put this lesson
of Our Lord into practice, while you are reciting
the Rosary of the Five most holy Wounds of Jesus
our Redeemer.

⌘ EXERCISE 2 ⌘

A Short Account of the Rosary of the Five Wounds of Jesus Christ

BLESSED Angela of Foligno being one day engaged in fervent prayer, and earnestly beseeching her Lord to make known to her what she could do that would be eminently acceptable to Him, Jesus Christ appeared to her, and informed her that nothing could be more acceptable in His sight than the devout contemplation of His sacred Wounds. (See her *Life*). Let then these adorable Wounds be the objects of your devout contemplation, the subjects of your thoughts, and the daily matter of your meditations. And in order that your method of adoring, venerating, and meditating upon these blessed Wounds may be at once easy and clearly defined, I here propose that you should make use of the short and pious devotion commonly called *The Rosary of the Five Wounds*. Among all the pious practices which have arisen in the Church for the purpose of adoring and venerating the Wounds of Jesus, we may say that the Rosary of the Five

Wounds, if recited in dispositions comformable to
the spirit of its institution, is a devotion the most
pleasing to Jesus, the most advantageous to the
faithful, and authorized in the most especial manner by the Popes, who have attached many indulgences to its recital. Hence it is that persons
remarkable for their learning and piety have ever
been most zealous for the promotion of this devotion, by making known its importance, showing
its utility, and perpetuating its practice.

It was instituted at Rome, according to Bartoli,
at the beginning of the seventeenth century, and
was diffused and propagated in many countries
by the Fathers of the Society of Jesus, at the
earnest request of Father Vincent Caraffa, the
seventh General of the same Society, with great
benefit to souls, and a great increase of glory to
the Wounds of Our Saviour. Several Popes sanc-
tioned it, and enriched it with many privileges
and special favors. This Rosary consisted then, as
now, of five stations, at each of which were recited
five *Paters* [*Our Fathers*] in honor of the five
Wounds of Our Saviour, and one *Ave* [*Hail Mary*]
in honor of the Dolors of Mary. In order to facilitate so useful a practice, and make it general
among the faithful, Father Paul Aloysius of the
Blessed Virgin, the sixth General of the Passionists, a zealous apostolic missionary, perceiving
that many of the less fervent among Christians
were deterred from making use of it by its great
length, requested Pope Leo XII to decree that it
should for the future consist of only twenty-five

Glorias [*Glory be to the Father . . .*] (five being recited at each station), together with one *Ave* in honor of the Dolors of the Blessed Virgin Mary, to which the Venerable Supreme Pontiff graciously consented, confirming at the same time all the indulgences which had been previously granted by Pius VII, of holy memory, to the Rosary when it consisted of twenty-five *Paters*, by the decree published December 20, 1823.

There is scarcely a town in Italy where this devotion is not practiced by the faithful, mainly through the efforts of the Passionist Fathers, who always promoted, and still continue to promote it, to the utmost of their power, according to the spirit of their Institute. In many parts of France also this short but devout practice in honor of the Wounds of Jesus has become a common devotion; and the fact that many zealous priests of that kingdom have faculties for blessing the Rosary, facilitates its spread.*

So easy and advantageous a method of honoring the holy Wounds of Jesus being within your reach, your want of devotion would indeed be most inexcusable if you neglected to make use of it, and daily to offer so slight a tribute of veneration and adoration to these same most precious

---

*Since the Passionist Fathers have come into the United Kingdom this devotion has become very common among the faithful [1927]. It is to be hoped that it will become still more widely spread now that it is one of the duties of the members of the Confraternity of the Most Holy Cross and Passion, lately established in all the churches of the Passionists.

Wounds. Adopt, therefore, this devout practice, and while repeating the Rosary, bestow five loving glances upon the adorable Wounds of your Redeemer, reflect on the sufferings endured by Him in His pierced hands and feet, and thank Him for all the love He has borne you.

A Method of Devoutly Reciting the Rosary of the Five Wounds of Jesus

Begin by humbly reciting the usual prayer, "Incline unto my aid, O God," etc.,* on your knees before a Crucifix, to beg Our Lord to assist you. Then, if agreeable and convenient, say the following:

Prayer before a Crucifix

O EVER good and sweetest Jesus, behold I here fall down upon my knees before Thee, and with all the powers of my soul do beg and beseech Thee to inspire my heart with lively feelings of faith, hope and charity, with a true repentance for my sins, with a will resolved to amend, and with a heart full of affection and sorrow, while I consider within myself, and contemplate in mind, Thy five most precious Wounds; fixing my eyes upon those words long since uttered by the lips of the prophet David, *They have pierced my hands and feet; they have numbered all my bones.* Amen.

---

*See p. 358. —*Publisher,* 2002.

Note that whoever, after having confessed and communicated, shall repeat the above prayer to Our Crucified Lord before a Crucifix, praying at the same time for the necessities of the Church, etc., may gain a Plenary Indulgence, applicable to the souls in Purgatory. By grant of Clement VIII, Benedict XIV, and finally, of Pius VII, in 1807.*

In the first station, you must meditate upon the sufferings endured by Jesus from the Wound of His Left Foot, and implore the remission of your sins.

In the second station, meditate upon the sufferings of Jesus from the Wound of His Right Foot, and ask for the graces of final perseverance and of a holy death.

In the third station, meditate upon the sufferings of Jesus from the Wound of His Left Hand, and beseech Him to save you from Hell.

In the fourth station, meditate upon the sufferings of Jesus from the Wound in His Right Hand,

---

*These grants of indulgences, as well as those on the following pages (at least the partial indulgences specifying durations of time), would seem to have been abolished by the Apostolic Constitution of Pope Paul VI, "The Doctrine of Indulgences," January 1, 1967, as given in the *Enchiridion of Indulgences* (1968)—although the Passionist Order *may* have obtained the privilege of retaining the plenary indulgences specified here. The *Enchiridion* specifies the indulgences for the Prayer before a Crucifix as follows:

A *plenary indulgence* is granted on each Friday of Lent and Passiontide to the faithful who after Communion piously recite the above prayer before an image of Christ crucified; on other days of the year the indulgence is *partial*. (No. 22). —Publisher, 2002.

and ask Him to bestow upon you the joys of Heaven.

In the fifth and last station, you must, while contemplating the most sacred Wound in His Side, meditate upon the immense love borne by the blessed Heart of Jesus, and ask for grace to love God.

At each station recite five *Glorias*, in memory and honor of the five most holy Wounds of your Redeemer, and one *Ave* in honor of the sorrowing heart of the Blessed Virgin.

Blessed Hermann, a Dominican friar, was accustomed to address five *Our Fathers* to the Wounds of Jesus; and then five *Hail Marys* to the Blessed Virgin, that she might in his name salute the Wounds of her Divine Son in the same manner as she adored them on the Cross and adores them in their glorified state in Heaven. He thus supplied for all deficiencies in the reverence and honor he paid to the adorable Wounds of his Redeemer. When, therefore, you render homage to the Wounds of Christ by saying the Rosary here described, beseech Mary to render it in your name, and then you may feel sure that Jesus will be well pleased with the homage offered to Him. You may have this intention, as well as that of honoring the sorrows of the Blessed Virgin, in reciting the *Hail Mary* attached to each station of the Rosary. If you are desirous of moving the Divine Mercy to grant you, through the Wounds of your Redeemer, the five important favors you ask, you must endeavor to recite this Rosary with the utmost fervor, and in a true spirit of devotion and recollection. Heavenly favors will be bestowed upon you in proportion to your dispositions in these respects. Such, in fact, was the signification of a vision with which St. Frances of Rome was once favored. She beheld Heaven, and in the center of it Our Lord, whose five Wounds were radiant with light. This light was shed forth upon all men, in mysterious diversity to each. For some received light from one Wound only, others from the rays of two, others from three, others, again, from four, and a very few from all five; because few there are who venerate these holy Wounds with all the dispositions required. (See her *Life*). Let me exhort you to be of the number of these few.

Indulgences granted by the Sovereign Pontiffs* Leo XII and Pius IX to those who recite the Beads of the Sacred Wounds of Our Lord Jesus Christ

1. An Indulgence of one year, which may be gained once a day.

2. A Plenary Indulgence for those who recite ten times in the month. This Indulgence may be gained by approaching the Sacraments, and praying according to the intention of his Holiness the Pope on the following days: One of the Fridays of the month of March, whichever may be chosen; on the Feasts of the Nativity, Circumcision and Epiphany, the most Holy Name of Jesus, the Resurrection and Ascension of Our Lord, Corpus

---

*See footnote on p. 241. —*Publisher,* 2002.

Christi, the Transfiguration, the Feasts of the Finding and Exaltation of the Holy Cross, or any day within their octaves.

Whoever shall recite it from Passion Sunday to Holy Saturday inclusively may gain a Plenary Indulgence on the day in which they fulfill their Easter duty; on the other days, viz., from Passion Sunday to Holy Saturday inclusively, they will gain for the recital each day an indulgence of seven years and as many quarantines [periods of 40 days]. All these indulgences may be applied to the souls in Purgatory.*

*N. B.—In order to gain the above indulgences, the chaplet or beads must be blessed by the General of the Congregation of the Passionists, or by some other priest authorized by him, as all the priests of the Congregation of the Passion are.**

Acts of Adoration Addressed to Each of the Five Most Holy Wounds of Jesus Crucified, and which May Be Made Use of in the Rosary

1. I humbly adore Thee, O most holy Wound of the Left Foot of my Lord, and implore Thee, my Crucified Jesus, through the pain Thou didst endure in it, and through the Blood which Thou didst shed from it, to grant me the remission of my most grievous offenses, and preserve me from ever again committing them, giving me strength

---

*See footnote on p. 241. —*Publisher,* 2002.

to resist every temptation, even unto death. And I beseech thee, most Blessed Virgin, through the anguish which thy soul endured on account of this Wound, to intercede for me, that my prayer may be heard.

2. I most humbly adore Thee, O holy Wound of the Right Foot of my Redeemer, and I beseech Thee, my Crucified Jesus, to grant me the precious gift of perseverance in Thy grace to the last moment of my life, and that of a holy death. And thou, O Mary, my sweet Mother, who didst suffer in thy soul what thy beloved Son endured in His Body, be my Advocate, and obtain this great favor for me.

3. I humbly adore Thee, O most sacred Wound of the Left Hand of my Saviour, and with a heart filled with tender gratitude for the sufferings Thou didst endure, I beseech Thee, my Crucified Jesus, to deliver me in Thy mercy from the eternal punishment of Hell. And thou, most sorrowful Virgin, who didst endure overwhelming anguish with so great constancy at the foot of the Cross, vouchsafe to ask of thy Son for me the grace not to be condemned to the abode of everlasting torments.

4. I most humbly adore Thee, O Blessed Wound of the Right Hand of my Lord, and with my whole heart do beg of Thee my Crucified Jesus, by the Blood Thou didst shed from it, to grant that on the great day of General Judgment I may find myself in the number of the elect, on Thy right hand, and hear myself summoned by Thy own sweet invitation, to enter into the joys of Heaven. And thou, O Mary, my loving Mother, never cease assisting me by thy powerful intercession, that so I may be made worthy to come and behold thee in Heaven, and in union with thee to praise and bless my God continually.

5. I adore Thee with my whole soul, most sweet Wound of the sacred Side of my Redeemer, and I beseech Thee, my Crucified Jesus, through its merits, and those of all the Blood shed by it, that Thou wouldst enkindle in my heart the most ardent love for Thy infinite goodness. And thou, O Immaculate Virgin, Mother of fair love, and Advocate of sinners, through that anguish which thou didst endure when the Side of thy beloved Son was wounded, obtain for me the gift of that love, and imprint in my soul the memory of His Wounds, and of thy bitter anguish.

A Prayer which St. Francis Xavier Was Accustomed to Recite

MY LORD Jesus Christ, through those most holy Wounds which Thou didst endure on the Cross for love of us, I beseech Thee succor Thy servants whom Thou hast redeemed with Thy Precious Blood.

A Short Prayer to Mary
The Queen of Sorrows

MOST afflicted Mother of grace and mercy, by that great love which induced thee to assist with unshaken firmness at the foot of the Cross, at the last agony of thy beloved Son, and by all the sufferings there endured by thy virginal heart, I beseech thee to assist me with thy especial patronage at the hour of my death, that so, through thy assistance, I may die the death of the just, and come happily to enjoy in Heaven the fruit of the Wounds of Jesus my Redeemer.

Here say seven *Hail Marys* in memory of the Seven Dolors of the Blessed Virgin, adding after each *Hail Mary* the little verse:

> *Sancta Mater istud agas,*
> *Crucifixi fige plagas*
> *Cordi meo valide.*
>
> Holy Mother, pierce me through;
> In my heart each wound renew,
> Of my Saviour crucified.

*Pius VII, by his Brief of December 1, 1816, has granted to all the faithful who, with a contrite heart, recite the seven Hail Marys with the verse above named, three hundred days' Indulgence, to be gained once a day, and to all who shall recite them daily for a month, a Plenary Indulgence.**

---

*See footnote on p. 241. —*Publisher,* 2002.

∾ EXERCISE 3 ∾

A Devout Practical Method of Visiting the Holy Crucifix

For the Morning

ALL pious persons who really love Jesus, their Crucified Spouse, keep a Crucifix in some quiet and suitable part of the house, and cannot, as it were, exist without frequently visiting, contemplating, and revering the blessed image of that true Lover, who solely for their sakes allowed Himself to be put to death on so painful and disgraceful a gibbet; and from this spectacle they derive not only most sweet and copious fruits of spiritual consolations, and grace to amend their own faults, but it is also most likely that they obtain many graces for those whom they recommend at such times to the Divine Majesty. Whoever, therefore, is anxious to perform this devotion in such a manner as to derive solid benefit from it should:

1. Set apart some convenient hour of the morning, and without ever changing it, except in cases of absolute necessity, go regularly, with the greatest devotion and recollection, to present himself before the image of Jesus Crucified, and after having kissed it with the utmost love and tenderness, let him:

2. Fix his eyes upon those streams of Blood shed by his loving Redeemer on the Cross, offer Him his soul, defiled as it is with innumerable stains of sin, beseeching Him to deign to wash and cleanse it from the filth of sin, and make it everlastingly pure and holy in His sight.

3. Let him offer and present, in remembrance of the Head of Our Lord crowned with thorns, the Pope, all the prelates of Holy Church, and all Christian princes, fervently imploring Him, through the excessive sufferings caused by the thorns, to bestow upon them grace to set before their subjects good and edifying example, and willingly to bear all the trials and difficulties pertaining to the care of others, in order that all may unite in the service and praise of His Divine Majesty in this world, and finally come to the eternal possession of Him in the next.

4. Contemplating the Wound of the Right Hand, let him make an offering of all his relations, benefactors and friends, beseeching Our Lord to bestow upon them His holy benediction, and to grant them continual peace and prosperity.

5. Let him present to the Left Hand all those

who wish him evil, or have any aversion to him, beseeching Our Lord in His mercy to pardon them, and give him grace ever to render them good for evil.

6. As an offering to the Right Foot, he should present to Our Lord all good and virtuous persons who are walking in the path that leads to Heaven, beseeching Him to bestow upon them perseverance in their good works, that so, at the Day of Judgment, they may deserve to be placed at His right hand, in the company of His elect.

7. Let him salute the Left Foot, by representing to Our Lord all those who are in mortal sin, and are traveling along the crooked paths which lead to destruction, that He may bestow upon them grace to change their lives, and return to the straight road of salvation.

8. When venerating the sacred Wound of the Side, let him recommend to Our Lord the Holy Church His beloved Spouse, who owes her origin to His pierced Side, and beseech Him to increase the flow of His Divine Spirit, and defend and protect her from the treachery of heretics and other wicked and perfidious enemies.

9. When reflecting upon the burning thirst endured by Jesus on the Cross, he should pray for those persons in particular who desire or stand in need of his prayers, that they may be consoled, and their requests granted by His Divine Majesty.

10. Looking upon the Cross, he should pray to Our Lord for all religious, that they may have grace easily and joyfully to follow Christ Crucified, bearing the Cross of entire self-mortification.

11. When meditating upon the scourging at the pillar, and the insults and blows endured by Jesus, he should pray to God for the conversion of Jews, Gentiles, heretics, and all sinners, that they may never more persecute Christ, nor insult and deride Him by their perverse opinions, heresies, infidelity and hardness of heart.

12. When contemplating the sorrow and agony of spirit suffered by Jesus Christ, he should recommend to Our Lord all persons in trouble, temptation, or suffering, that He may bestow upon them the gift of perfect patience; he should also pray for souls in their agony, that they may happily pass from time to eternity.

For the Evening

Imagine, in the first place, that your Angel guardian is calling and inviting you to visit your Divine Spouse, who is bleeding and dying for your sake on Mount Calvary, and who is desirous of speaking to your heart by showing Himself to you.

1. When you behold Jesus nailed to the hard wood

of the Cross, kneel down, and devoutly fixing your eyes upon Him, tenderly kiss the Wounds of His sacred Feet; then, thanking Him for all the steps He has taken for love of you, beg Him to give you grace to follow Him, in suffering whatever trials may befall you, for His sake, and ever to walk in the straight way of His commandments.

2. Kiss the Wound of His side, and while returning Him thanks for having permitted it to be made, for the sake of showing you His Heart transfixed with love, beseech Him to give you grace to correspond with His love by loving and serving Him with your whole heart.

3. Kiss His blessed Hands which performed so many wonders, return Him your most grateful thanks for the innumerable benefits bestowed on you during the whole course of your life, and beseech Him to give you grace always to persevere in good works, and in things worthy of eternal life.

4. Venerate and kiss His adorable Head crowned with sharp thorns, and beg pardon for the innumerable thoughts of vanity, anger, sloth, and love of worldly vanities, in which you have indulged during your past life, and beg Him to give you grace to have ever in your heart holy thoughts, affections, and earnest desires for salvation.

5. Kiss that Mouth which tasted the bitter gall,

and from which words of eternal life ever flowed; thank Him for the sacred lessons which the Divine Majesty of God has been pleased to leave you in the holy Gospel, and for those which have been taught you by His servants, and beseech Him to give you grace to have them constantly present to your mind, so as to profit by them, and that you may for the future restrain your tongue from speaking evil, and employ it in hourly praising, blessing, and adoring His infinite goodness.

Conclude this devotion with these words which Saint Francis Xavier, holding a Crucifix in his hand, pronounced at the moment of death: *"Jesu Filii Dei, miserere nobis"*—"Jesus, Son of God, have mercy on us."

∽ EXERCISE 4 ∽

Three Devout Meditations Intended to Awaken Feelings Of Compassion in the Heart of a Christian for Mary, The Queen of Dolors

DAY 1

Mary on Mount Calvary Before the Death of Her Son

Meditation

1. *Her sufferings in the Crucifixion of her Son.*

Never has any mother or pure creature suffered a more painful martyrdom than that endured by Mary in beholding her most beloved Son barbarously crucified under her very eyes. Full of faith, and overflowing with generous love for Jesus, she had hastened to Calvary, in order to be at once a witness, companion, and partaker of His painful and ignominious Passion; and now, when she beholds Him in the hands of His merciless executioners, who are violently tearing off

His clothes, and thus reopening all His wounds—now, when she beholds Him, His sacred Body lacerated and bleeding, lie down upon the hard bed of the Cross, what must be the anguish of her tender and loving heart? What a sword of grief must have pierced her most holy soul, on beholding her Son in a state so worthy of compassion, yet receiving nought but insults, outrages, and cruelty, and become an object of horror and malediction to the people who surround Him! Mother of sorrows! I compassionate thy most afflicted heart, and beg of thee to allow me to share its anguish.

The sufferings of Mary exceed all measure, when Jesus being stretched upon the Cross, His barbarous executioners proceed to pierce His hands and feet with large nails, and then to raise Him on high in the sight of all, suspended on that tree of suffering. What a sight for a Mother—and for the Mother of such a Son! How great and how deep must have been her interior anguish! If we, who have not the faith, the love, nor the heart of Mary, yet feel overcome with sorrow and compassion, when we only reflect upon the Crucifixion of Jesus, what must have been the feelings of Mary, who saw it all with her own eyes—of Mary, whose faith and love for Jesus were so strong and burning? And yet, her noble heart remains unmoved, calm, and resigned to the Divine Will, even amidst these excessive trials. Learn from Mary to bear with resignation the sufferings of this life. An extraordinary grace comforts and supports her, lest she should expire beneath the weight of so much affliction. Compassionate this most sorrowful Mother, to whose sufferings you have greatly contributed by so frequently crucifying her innocent Son Jesus by your sins.

2. *Her grief at the sufferings of her Son.*

Mary, being permitted to do so, draws nigh to the Cross on which her beloved Son is hanging in agony, that she may assist at the last moments of His life. She stands beneath the Cross, deeply immersed in the consideration of the Wounds and sufferings of her Divine Son. Her eyes are fixed upon Him, and each time she looks upon His dying countenance, upon His suffering face, upon His agonizing body, the sword of grief anew wounds, pierces, and rends her heart; yet she sheds not a tear. She listens to the last words of Jesus, she sees Him painfully breathe forth His last sighs, her eyes meet His last loving glances; and who shall say what feelings overwhelm the heart of this afflicted Mother, during the last agony of her beloved Son! She would fain afford some relief to her dying Jesus, wipe His Divine face, support His tortured head, or alleviate His sufferings in some degree; but nothing of the kind is allowed her; she is only permitted to taste of the whole bitterness of His chalice, and by her sufferings to augment those of her Son. O what heroic fortitude does not Mary display amidst so much agony! But, oh, what a martyrdom does not her maternal heart endure during those hours of anguish, when, standing at the foot of the Cross, she gathers up in it the last drops of precious Blood shed by her expiring Jesus!

O true martyr—or, rather, more than martyr! O Queen of Dolors, if we would understand in any degree how much thou didst suffer in the agonies of Jesus, or fathom the depth of that sea of sorrow which overwhelmed thee, it would be necessary for us to have a heart as loving, as deeply enamored of Jesus, as thine! Give it unto me, O sweet Mother, and engrave on it the Wounds of Jesus Crucified, and thy bitter sufferings, that so, both the one and the other may ever be the dearest objects of my love and compassion.

3. *Her sufferings on account of the thirst of her Son on the Cross.*

Beneath the altar of the Cross, on which, through His exceeding great charity, Jesus is offering the painful sacrifice of His life, Mary stands offering also the dolorous sacrifice of her anguish-stricken heart. Numerous as the Wounds inflicted by the nails which pierce the hands and feet of Jesus, and by the thorns which encircle His head, and all the wounds which cover His whole body, so numerous are those formed in the virginal heart of Mary, which participates, in a manner peculiar to itself, in all the sufferings of her Son; with Him is wounded, lacerated, and tortured, and with Him agonizes and languishes for three entire hours on the Cross. In the height of her desolation, she hears our dying Redeemer raise His voice, and exclaim, *"Sitio!"*—I thirst!

What tongue can express the thousand conflicting emotions which fill the bleeding heart of Mary at this moment? Love, compassion, tenderness, amazement, desire of administering this last comfort to her dying, Crucified Son, agitate her heart, so as to increase her anguish. "Ah, my Son!" exclaims Mary, "could I but quench Thy thirst with my tears! But even this comfort is denied me. Will the poor alleviation of a drop of water be refused to a God-man, dying amid such unspeakable sufferings, and must I, His sorrowing Mother, be forced to witness all His agony, and the barbarity of His enemies?" Distracted with thoughts such as these, the heart of the afflicted Mother is overwhelmed with the waves of a sea of sorrow. Hard indeed must that heart be which is not touched and moved to tears of compassion at the thought of the martyrdom which Mary endures, and the agonies of which are immeasurably increased, when she beholds the perfidious Jews put the finishing stroke to their inhumanity and cruelty by offering our Redeemer in His thirst the refreshment of vinegar. It would be necessary for us to know all the tenderness, perfection, and burning love of the heart of such a Mother to understand the anguish she endures on beholding her dear Son deprived in His dying hour of even the wretched refreshment of a drop of water to relieve His thirst. Are you desirous of consoling Mary? Weep with tears of sincere repentance over your sins, which deluged the loving Heart of Jesus with an ocean of bitterness. Have a tender and compassionate remembrance of the sufferings of this most afflicted Mother, and never more renew them by those sins with which you have so often wounded her maternal heart.

The Fruit

Be not satisfied with a mere sterile and unfruitful compassion for Mary, the Queen of Dolors, but seek to participate in her sufferings by loving and imitating her. The Blessed Virgin endured a long and cruel martyrdom in her heart for our sakes, and for love of us. Frequently, and with feelings of tender love, contemplate her standing at the foot of the Cross, and join her in bewailing and weeping over sin, which, by causing the death of Jesus, rent in twain the heart of Mary. Pledge your heart to this Mother of sorrows, by some habitual act of devotion and mortification, in remembrance and in honor of her bitter sufferings. Also, endure something for love of her, imitating her patience, resignation, and silence.

Example

Saint Camillus de Lellis, who had the greatest devotion during life to the Passion of Jesus and the sorrows of Mary, was desirous that in his last agony these two great objects of his devotion should be constantly before his eyes. He caused to be painted a beautiful picture representing Christ Crucified shedding Blood from His five Wounds, the Blessed Virgin standing at the foot of the Cross praying for himself, and by her whole countenance and demeanor expressing the excess of her interior anguish, and himself kneeling on the ground pronouncing these words: *"Parce famulo tuo quem pretioso sanguine redemisti"*—"Spare Thy servant whom Thou hast redeemed by Thy precious Blood." With his eyes, and still more with his heart, fixed on the contemplation of Jesus dying upon a Cross, and of Mary suffering at its foot, he sweetly breathed forth his soul into the hands of his Redeemer. Every Christian ought to form in his own heart a similar devout image, in order always to have a lively remembrance of the Passion of his Lord, and of the sorrows of Mary his dear Mother, if he is desirous of dying with so sweet a security of eternal happiness. (See *Life of Saint Camillus*).

DAY 2

Mary on Mount Calvary at the Time Of the Death of Jesus

Meditation

1. *Her grief at beholding her Son dying on the Cross.*

It was always considered the very height of barbarity, and the severest of punishments, for children to be obliged to be spectators of the sufferings and death of their parents. Understand, then, if it be possible, what excessive suffering, what mortal anguish, must have been endured by the most holy Virgin, who was the tenderest of Mothers, and the most ardent lover of Jesus, on beholding with her own eyes her beloved Lord, her God and her all, covered with wounds, satiated with tortures, and yielding up His blessed Soul upon an infamous gibbet after three hours' painful agony! Was ever martyrdom so cruel as that endured by Mary for love of us? But was there ever ingratitude, hardness of heart, and want of love to be compared to yours in regard of this most afflicted Mother, whose sufferings you contemplate without the slightest emotion of tenderness or compassion? Such was the price at which Mary purchased the title of our Mother, and at which she acquired a right to the name of Queen of Martyrs, the price of the most bitter anguish. Others have been martyrs because they have died for Christ; Mary has been more, by dying with Christ, without, however, ceasing to live. In other martyrs the great love they had for God tempered the pain of their torments; in Mary, the great love she bore to Jesus increased the pangs of her martyrdom. The sword of grief which pierced her heart during the time of the Passion and death of her Son, without giving her the consolation of dying, served her as the most dreadful martyrdom. O heart of Mary, transformed into a sea of bitterness, an abyss of suffering, I compassionate and love thee!

When Jesus expires, Mary, with the utmost

generosity of heart, makes a full and entire sacrifice of her dear Son to God. She offers this adorable Victim to the justice of the Eternal Father in satisfaction for our sins, and for the salvation of each individual, and to this offering she unites that of her own unspeakable sorrow. Thus does Mary merit the title of Co-operatrix in our redemption. Behold how much your sins and your salvation have cost Mary; understand what obligations you are under to this most afflicted Mother, and never be wanting in love, gratitude, and compassion for her.

2. *Her sufferings on account of the Wound given to her Son with the spear.*

Jesus having expired, a cruel soldier opens His side with a spear, and pierces His Heart. This is the last Wound received by our Redeemer, and which, as it were, puts the seal to His dolorous Passion. It manifests the cruelty of the Jews, the tender charity of Our Lord, and the deep anguish of Mary, in a clearer light. Jesus feels not the wound inflicted by the lance because He is dead, but when the lance passes through His sacred side, it cruelly wounds the heart of Mary, whose whole soul is thereby rent with anguish.

A long and painful martyrdom has Mary endured in the Crucifixion and death of her beloved Son, since she was closely united to Him by love, and through love and compassion feels all His sufferings in her heart. But now, when she beholds human cruelty becoming more and more heartless, and unsatiated yet with the innocent Blood of her Crucified Jesus, her anguish reaches its height. Now is fulfilled that prophecy which announced that the heart of Mary should be pierced with a sword of grief, and the cruel spear in lacerating the side, and transfixing the Heart of Jesus, at the same time rends and pierces the heart of the most sorrowful of Mothers, and inflicts a wound deep enough to have caused her death from sorrow alone. Compassionate this Queen of Martyrs, and reflect that, each time you have sinned, you have inflicted anew these two deep wounds upon the Hearts of Jesus and Mary. Deep was the affliction of Mary at seeing with her own eyes the cruel spear-thrust aimed at her Crucified Jesus, but equally deep was it when she beheld with the eyes of her soul how frequently you would by sin reopen the wound of that side to which you owe your existence, and wound that Heart which has so loved you. This was the sword that transfixed and inflicted the sharpest pain upon her tender heart. Bewail your cruelty, and detest sin, for which Jesus suffered and Mary wept so much. As a means of showing you the enormity of sin, the sight of Mary at the foot of the Cross is second to nothing but that of Jesus Crucified. Often cast the eyes of tender, loving compassion upon this most afflicted Mother, and such a spectacle will soften the hardness of your heart, and draw copious streams of tears from your eyes.

3. *Her grief on receiving in her arms the dead Body of her Son.*

It did not suffice for the accomplishment of the designs of the Eternal Father upon Mary that she should consent to the painful sacrifice of her Son, or that she should be a spectator at the foot of the Cross of the agony and death of the world's Redeemer; but in order that she might be the most sorrowful of Mothers, and the Queen of Martyrs, she was to reach the height of suffering, and endure the most bitter of all desolations. After she had seen her beloved Son suffer the most cruel tortures, and expire by an ignominious death, His mangled Body was taken down and placed in her arms, as she sat at the foot of the ignominious tree. Oh, that we could obtain an insight but for a moment into the heart of this Mother, and thus acquire some idea of the excess of her anguish at the moment of receiving that lifeless Body within her arms! But it is incomprehensible, and, in point of fact, we never could come to a due appreciation of it. Then it was that, as she gazed upon those sacred limbs become one single wound, that head pierced with so many thorns, that pale bleeding face, that open side, her grief no longer knew any bounds, and, as a torrent, overwhelmed her suffering soul. Then it was that to the bitterness of her anguish was added the sorrow of not being able to die of grief, and being thus deprived of the sole consolation of sacrificing her life together with Jesus. We may compassionate the sufferings of Mary, but never describe them.

Pause for a moment, and with heart and mind contemplate that most afflicted Mother, with the dead Body of her Son in her arms, impressing a thousand kisses on His precious wounds, to satisfy her love and overwhelming grief. Behold how she presses Him to her heart. "O my beloved Son," she exclaims, "with what indescribable barbarity have men treated Thee! To what a deplorable condition have the sins of the world reduced Thee! What a Mother of Sorrows have sinners made me." Contemplate this Saviour of mankind lying dead in her arms, and say, if you can, that you are not the author of His death! Is there a wound in that sacred Body which is not the work of your hands and the effect of your malice? Then it is you who have pierced the heart of Mary with a sword of grief, it is you who have overwhelmed her soul with anguish and bitterness. What an ungrateful, cruel son have you been to so loving a Mother! Now at least bewail your perfidy, and resolve, from this day forward, entirely to renounce sin, and to consecrate yourself anew to the love and compassion of Jesus Crucified, and of Mary the Queen of Sorrows.

The Fruit

Hard-hearted, or intolerably ungrateful, must that Christian be who either never reflects upon, or is never touched by all that the most holy Virgin has suffered for our sakes. How many die without having even thought of it! Repair such irreligious forgetfulness by a determination to devote a few minutes daily to the remembrance of the dolors of Mary. Never omit your practices of piety in honor of this Mother of Sorrows. The best of these, and the one most pleasing to Mary, is that of loving her adorable Son, frequently meditating on His Passion, and avoiding sin, which cost Jesus and Mary so dear. Make it a rule constantly thus to gratify her heart, and ask of Our Lord grace for this purpose through the bitter sufferings of Mary.

Example

Mary rewards those who are devout to her sorrows with singular favors. Blessed Antonio Patrizi of Siena, of the Order of the Servants of Mary, was accustomed to recite, every day until his death, five hundred *Hail Marys*, in order thus as he said, to soothe with the angelical salutation his dear Mother's sorrows, to which he was most especially devout. He frequently meditated upon her sorrows with tears of devotion, and was accustomed to say that all our prayers ought to be accompanied by some few tears of compassion for the most holy Virgin Queen of Dolors. The sole occupation of his life was to promote devotion to the Queen of Martyrs by preaching and example, and she, on her part, repaid the tender love of this her devoted servant by innumerable favors. He being on one occasion suddenly seized with a fainting-fit, Mary appeared and refreshed him with a nosegay of beautiful roses. She herself informed him of his approaching passage to eternity a few days before his death, and comforted and consoled him with her special assistance at the moment of his departure hence. Finally, his good Mother, to reward him for the many *Hail Marys* with which he had honored her sorrows, caused a beautiful lily, in the leaves of which were written in golden characters the words, *Ave Maria*, to issue from the mouth of his uncorrupted body forty years after his death. (See *Bollandists,* May 13th).

DAY 3

Desolation of Mary After the Death of Jesus

Meditation

1. *Her grief at the burial of her Crucified Son.*

It still remained to the disconsolate Mother to drink the last drop of that chalice of sorrow from which indescribable bitterness had so long been poured forth into her virginal heart. And this last drop consisted in being deprived of the consolation of any longer beholding the sacred remains of her beloved Son, by their being enclosed in the holy sepulcher. Joseph and Nicodemus, being desirous of rendering this office to the sacred Body of their Crucified Redeemer, reverently take It from the arms of Mary, and, after having embalmed It with precious ointments, enclose It in a new sepulcher, thus hiding It in some sort from the view of the desolate Mother. Now, indeed, most truly can we say that there is no sorrow like unto the sorrow of Mary, and that her desolation is as great as the sea. In her other afflictions, indescribably bitter as they were to her most holy heart, the visible presence of her beloved Son, and the fact of being able to gaze at Him, was, if not an alleviation to her anguish, at least a source of great consolation, giving her strength to be His companion in suffering. But now the adorable Body of her Jesus is removed from her sight, and she can no longer behold Him. Oh, what words can tell the deep affliction, the bitter anguish her soul suffers! Oh, if you could see into her afflicted heart, and behold the fearful agony it endures at this separation from the dead Body of her Jesus, when placed in the sepulcher, how many tears of love and compassion would you not shed over the most sorrowful of Mothers! See now how, the sepulcher being closed up, Mary buries all her affections, all her thoughts, and her heart also, together with the Body of her Crucified Son. See how, unable to tear herself from that loved tomb, which contains her only Treasure, she kisses it a thousand times, and would willingly die there, so as not to be separated from the Dear Object of her love; and there, in fact, she would have died of pure sorrow, had not God by a real miracle preserved her life. Is it possible that the sight of such excessive sufferings, and so painful a martyrdom of your loving Mother, should yet find you insensible? Are you aware who it is that has occasioned so much suffering to Mary, who it is that has deprived her of her only Son? Yourself; by your sins. What cause have you then for tears, and for fulfilling the pious office of consoling the afflicted Mother in her desolation for the loss of her Divine Son!

2. *Her grief from the remembrance of the Passion of her Son.*

The world's Redeemer being buried, Mary departed from the sepulcher in body, but there left her heart, the dolorous Passion and cruel death of her innocent Son being deeply engraved in her soul. As she passed along those streets still marked with His precious Blood, as she met the ungrateful people who were the authors of this impious Deicide, not one, but a thousand swords transfixed anew the heart of the desolate Mother. Mournfully, sorrowfully, she enters her humble dwelling, and there, as she beholds no more the beloved Object of all her affections, and is no more blessed with the sweet visible presence of her dear Son, can words ever describe, or heart understand, what painful feelings are aroused in her mind, or what sighs of anguish break forth from her troubled heart? Her sole occupation, night and day, is to call to mind, over and over again, the long series of sufferings endured by her Son Jesus. The image of that Flower of Nazareth, so cruelly tortured, is ever present to her thoughts, and the weight of her sorrow becomes every instant more oppressive. The blows, the buffets, the insults heaped upon Jesus are vividly impressed on her mind. She beholds the deep wounds inflicted on His most holy Body by the scourges, the thorns, and the nails. She imagines she still hears the last accents of the voice of her dying Son. She reflects upon the hatred, the cruelty, and the ingratitude with which the chosen people have treated their Redeemer and their God, and, at remembrances so painful, excessive indeed must have been the depth of anguish endured by her loving soul, thus encompassed by a sea of bitterness! And what are the sentiments with which you call to mind all that a God has suffered for you? With what feelings do you contemplate a God upon the Cross agonizing and dying for your salvation? Learn from Mary how to meditate upon the sufferings of Jesus; beg her to imprint them upon your heart, and to inspire you with those feelings of love, compassion, and sorrow with which she meditated upon them; and when you meditate upon them, forget not to give a glance at the sorrowful heart of Mary, so as to dedicate your own ever more and more to her love, to the imitation of her virtues, and to compassion for her sufferings.

3. *Her grief on account of the sins and ingratitude of men.*

The sword of grief which inflicted one of the greatest pains upon the virginal heart of Mary, and rendered her martyrdom more bitter, and her desolation more complete after the death and burial of Jesus, was her foresight of the sins of men, and her foreknowledge of their ungrateful forgetfulness of all that had been done for them. Oh, the sight of all those followers of the Crucified God, who would by sin re-open His wounds, renew His sufferings, and display the most unheard-of cruelty against Him, her innocent Son and their loving Father, could not but have been a source of bitter suffering to her heart. Ah, perhaps this Mother of Dolors beheld you among the number, and shed tears of sorrow over the malice with which you have so frequently offended Jesus. When she reflects how many would pervert this Divine Blood, the price of their salvation, to their own damnation; when she beholds how many souls, purchased at the price of the life of a Man-God, would be cast into Hell to burn in unquenchable fire; when she reflects upon the hardness of heart and obstinacy of the Jews, who, in defiance of innumerable prodigies, so many signs of the world's Redeemer, would not be convinced and converted, but would persist in their malice and voluntary blindness, what inexpressible anguish must overwhelm her soul! She beholds in spirit all Christians, who have been given to her as her children in an especial manner by Jesus dying on the Cross; she beholds them ungrateful to His love, forgetful of His goodness, unmindful of the numerous benefits which have been bestowed on them through His Passion, and not even giving one glance of compassion, or one devout thought, upon their suffering Redeemer, but rebelliously refusing Him that heart and that love which He has purchased at the price of so much blood and so many torments. Oh, how so painful a sight transfixes and overwhelms the heart of the Virgin Mother with acute sorrow! How many miracles of goodness and mercy has not Jesus worked in your favor, and have you ever determined to correspond with them, and thus to console the afflicted heart of Mary, your loving Mother, who has brought you forth to a life of grace at the foot of the Cross? Have you ever thought of the debt you have incurred of venerating, respecting, and loving her with all the affection of your heart, and of constantly bearing in mind all she has suffered?

Begin from this day forward, and deliver your Mother from that sword of ingratitude and want of love for her which has so wounded her heart.

The Fruit

Reproach yourself with having been until now so unfeeling and so ungrateful towards the holy Virgin Queen of Dolors, and determine never to let a day pass without offering her the tribute of some devout thought, feeling of affection, or pious practice in her honor. Devotion to the sorrows of Mary was ever the favorite devotion of all the Saints; let it be yours also. Often repeat to yourself, *"Mary has loved me, and has delivered up her Son to death for my sake."* It will not be difficult for this thought to excite in your heart feelings of love and gratitude toward this most afflicted Mother. Unite your trials, sufferings, and crosses to hers, and bear them as she has borne hers, suffering in imitation of her with patience and silence, for love of Jesus.

Example

St. Paul of the Cross, being singularly devout to the Passion of Jesus, was so also to the Dolors of Mary, which he bore, as it were, engraven in his heart; and he would most fervently seek on every occasion to inspire all men with a filial devotion and a tender and loving compassion for the Queen of Martyrs. It was from herself in person that he acquired the wonderful knowledge he possessed of the extent and depth of her sorrows, for she appeared to him one day, her heart transfixed with a sword, and her eyes overflowing with tears, while she made known to him the excess of her sufferings.

One Good Friday, the holy servant of God being urged by his companion to take some slight refreshment, began to weep bitterly exclaiming, "How would you, dear brother, have me eat, when thinking of the sufferings of holy Mary? Oh, what bitter anguish did Mary endure in the loss of her beloved Son! What indescribable sorrow on returning to Bethania, after the burial of her adorable Son!" And here, immersed anew in the contemplation of her sufferings, and bursting forth into tears and sighs, he did most truly find it impossible to taste any food whatsoever. (See his *Life*).

∾ EXERCISE 5 ∾

The Sacrifice of the Mass
And How to Assist at It Well

MASS is an action the most holy and sublime of all the actions of religion: it is most glorious to God and profitable to men. Jesus Christ here renews the great mystery of our Redemption. He becomes our Victim, offering Himself really in this unbloody Sacrifice, through the hands of the Priest; and giving thus to His Father infinite glory, He applies to each of us in particular the merits of the adorable Blood which He has shed for our salvation. The Sacrifice of the Mass is not only the most perfect act of religion, and the greatest wonder of religion itself, but it is, so to speak, a compendium of all religion. The grandest sacrifices of the Old Law were only poor shadows and figures of the majesty, the dignity, and the excellence of the Sacrifice of the New Law. The Mass is, properly, the treasure of the Church, the masterpiece of the wisdom and mercy of God.

The Church can count about twenty million martyrs, who, by shedding their blood for the Faith, have become so many victims immolated to the living God. What an honor would the voluntary sacrifice of all creatures put together give to God! Yet, all these acts of religion, and a hundred others still more perfect, and offered by the noblest of creatures, would not bear a comparison with the excellence of the Sacrifice of Jesus Christ upon our altars. God is more honored by one single Mass than He could be by all the actions of Angels and of men, no matter how fervent, perfect, or heroic they might be. The spotless Victim that is offered in Sacrifice is of merit proportional to the Majesty to whom it is offered. Has God been offended? Do we need new assistance? Do we groan under the tyranny of our passions? Do we languish under oppressive and painful disease? Do we wish to thank God for His benefits? Have we to satisfy His justice? We find abundantly in this Sacrifice wherewith to supply all our necessities, satisfy all our duties, and pay all our debts. The Mass is a universal remedy, the tree of life and immortality. God receives here the homage of the beloved Son in whom He is well pleased. Here is a Victim which disarms Divine wrath. This is a Sacrifice of propitiation which cannot fail of being acceptable. We, by uniting ourselves to Our Lord, who is here in the quality of Mediator between us and His Father, immolate ourselves with Him; and the joining of our prayers with His mediation enhances their value immensely, and their acceptance in the sight of God.

Such truths as these have infused into the faithful a singular devotion, the highest esteem, and a most profound respect for the Sacrifice of the Mass; and they ought also to create in us the desire of assisting at it with sentiments of a solid and sincere piety; yea, with the same dispositions we should have had had we been present at the Sacrifice that was consummated on Calvary. With what faith, with what fervor, with what recollection and compunction, should we not have assisted at the Sacrifice which Jesus Christ then offered in person to His Eternal Father? Well then, in the Mass the same Sacrifice is renewed, though in a different manner. To assist at it, therefore, with want of reverence, with willful distractions, without exterior composure or interior respect, would be to repeat as far as in us lies the insults of Calvary, and to dishonor our faith.

To avoid so great a misfortune, try to be present at Mass with the disposition of a Christian and the spirit of Jesus Christ. Offer it with Him and like Him. Enter the church penetrated with deep respect; preserve in it a recollection that nothing may be able to disturb. Have no other thought, no other inclination, than that of honoring God, and thereby providing for your own eternal interests.

A Devout Method of Hearing Mass

The method of assisting at the holy Sacrifice of the Mass which appears to me the most fitting, and most in conformity with the spirit of the Church, is to unite oneself to the sentiments and intentions of the Priest. He offers this Sacrifice in fulfillment for the four principal duties which we are all obliged to render to God, and which are the four ends for which Jesus Christ Himself offers this Sacrifice by the hands of the Priest.

The *first duty* is to praise and adore the infinite Majesty of God; the *second*, to satisfy His Divine justice for all our sins; the *third*, to thank Him for all the benefits we have received from His liberality; the *fourth*, to expose our wants to Him, as to the Author and Source of all graces. Now here is the method of fulfilling these four great duties. Apply yourself to read and reflect on the four following offerings; endeavor to realize their sense, and to make them with the greatest possible fervor.

In the **beginning of Mass,** when the Priest humbly recites the Confiteor, make a brief examen of conscience, exciting yourself to an act of contrition, and begging of Our Lord pardon for your sins. Implore the assistance of the Holy Ghost, and of our blessed Lady, to hear holy Mass with all the respect and devotion of which you are capable. Then divide the Mass into four parts, in each of which you shall apply yourself to fulfill one of the four above-named duties.

In the **first part,** which includes the beginning of Mass to the end of the Gospel, apply your mind to **adore and praise the infinite Majesty of God**—worthy of honor and of infinite praises; and with feelings of profound humility say:

O MY GOD, I adore Thee and acknowledge Thee as my Lord and Master. I protest that whatever I have, whatever I am, is entirely Thine, and that I have received it from Thee.

But as Thy Sovereign Majesty deserves an honor and requires an infinite homage which I am utterly incapable of rendering, I offer to Thee the humiliations and the homage which Jesus renders Thee on this altar.

I desire, O my God, to do what Jesus Christ does in this adorable Sacrifice; I humble myself, and bow with Him before Thy supreme Majesty. I adore Thee with the same sentiments of humility as my Jesus adores Thee. I embrace with all my heart the submission with which He has infinitely honored Thee for me.

Here shut your book, and continue the same or similar acts of devotion in your mind.

In the **second part** of the Mass, which begins with the end of the Gospel and continues to the Elevation, in order to **make satisfaction for the immense debt of your sins**, say with sentiments of profound humility:

B EHOLD, O God, in me a traitor who has so often been in revolt against Thee. Penetrated with the deepest grief, I detest all my sins, and in satisfaction for them I present to Thee the adorable Victim who is offered upon this altar. I offer Thee all the merits of Jesus Christ, His

Blood and His Passion. And since on this altar He becomes my Mediator and my Advocate, and with the voice of His Precious Blood implores mercy for me, I unite my voice to that of His adorable Blood, and crave pardon for all the enormous sins which I have committed. The Blood of Jesus appeals for Thy mercy, and my heart, penetrated with grief, implores it likewise.

O God of my heart, if my tears do not move Thee to compassion for me, let the sighs of Thy beloved Son move Thee. Yes, my God, I hope that by the virtue of His precious Blood Thou wilt pardon all my iniquities, which I wish to continue to bewail until the hour of my death.

Here give free vent to the feelings of your heart.

In the **third part** of the Mass, from the Elevation to the Communion, considering yourself enriched with so many benefits by the liberality of your God, **offer Him in requital Jesus Christ**, saying with tender feelings:

GOD of my heart! Behold me at Thy feet overwhelmed with the immense weight of the benefits, general and particular, which with such kindness Thou hast bestowed upon me. I confess that in my regard Thy mercies are infinite, but still I am ready to make a full return for them. In gratitude, and in requital for all I owe Thee, I present to Thee by the hands of the Priest this Divine Blood, this Precious Body, this Victim Immaculate. This offering is sufficient to compensate for all the gifts Thou hast bestowed upon me, because Its worth and Its value are infinite.

O all ye Angels and Saints of Paradise, help me to thank my God, and offer to Him, in thanksgiving for all the benefits which He has bestowed, not only this Mass, but all the Masses which are being celebrated this day on earth, so that by their means I may perfectly compensate His lovingkindness for all the graces which He has given me—for those which at every moment He confers, and for those which He will vouchsafe to give me.

Continue in these devout sentiments as long as you can. Invite the whole of Paradise to thank God for you, making your prayer to those Saints to whom you pay the greatest devotion.

In the **fourth part** of the Mass, from the Communion to the end, when you shall have made either your Spiritual or Sacramental Communion, concentrate your faith on the God who is within you, and, with a lively ardor, **ask Him for all the graces of which you have need**, for in this moment Jesus Christ unites Himself to you and prays for you. Dilate, open, unfold, therefore, your heart, and do not limit either your desires or your confidence. Say to Him, with profound humility:

O GOD of my soul, I acknowledge myself unworthy of Thy favors. I confess my unworthiness with all sincerity; considering the multitude and enormity of my sins, I do not deserve to be heard by Thee; but wilt Thou reject the prayer which Thy adorable Son makes to Thee for me on this altar, where He offers His life and His Blood for me? O God of my heart! Accept the prayer of Jesus which He pours forth to Thine adorable Majesty for me, and, for His sake, grant me all those graces which Thou knowest to be necessary for my salvation. And now, more than ever, do I dare to implore of Thee a general forgiveness of all my sins, and the grace of final perseverance. Through the merits of Jesus Christ, I beg of Thee all the virtues necessary for me, and all the efficacious assistance which I need in order to become a Saint and to work out my salvation.

I also ask of Thee the conversion of all infidels and sinners, the liberation of the souls from Purgatory, and the eternal salvation of all the souls redeemed with the Blood of Jesus Christ.

Here continue to ask graces for yourself, for your friends and benefactors, and for all your relations; pray for holy Church, for Christian princes, for the Holy Father; but make your prayers with the certainty that, being united with those of Jesus Christ, they will be heard.

At the **end of Mass, thank God** for the favors He has granted you. Leave the church with the same feeling of **compunction** as if you were coming down from Mount Calvary.

Make from this moment the resolution to use

this easy and simple method of hearing Mass, by which you will perceive, in a short time, that your soul will become enriched with singular graces.

∽ EXERCISE 6 ∽

Practical Instructions for Making a Good Confession

MANY Christians regard Confession in the light of an unimportant act of piety, if not a mere ceremony. They imagine that it is sufficient to strike their breasts, relate their sins to their Confessor, recite with their lips the slight penance enjoined them, and do nothing more. Hence it is that so many go even frequently to Confession, but so few amend, and consequently derive little or no benefit from the Sacrament.

Whoever fails to make a *good* Confession [i.e., makes a bad Confession] after having committed mortal sin, has closed to himself the two gates of Paradise—Innocence and Repentance—and therefore will be lost (unless he repairs the evil done by a second, good Confession).* Be, then, most thoroughly convinced of the immense importance of this Sacrament, and be filled with an earnest desire of approaching it worthily, bestowing the utmost care and attention upon your preparation for this

---

*See footnote on p. 285. —*Publisher*, 2002.

great duty, if you desire to obtain eternal salvation.

Confession is one of the seven Sacraments instituted by Christ; it is called the *Sacrament of Penance,* and by its means alone can he who has committed mortal sin after Baptism hope to save his soul;* therefore it is called by the holy Council of Trent: *the second plank after shipwreck.*

In this Sacrament Jesus Christ has deposited His Precious Blood, that it may be to our souls as a salutary bath wherein they may be cleansed from all the stains of sin, their wounds closed, their maladies cured, their weakness strengthened, and grace unto salvation imparted to them. This Divine Blood is dispensed to us by the priest in the holy absolution, and is abundantly poured forth upon all souls approaching the tribunal of Confession with proper dispositions. Oh, how blessed is our lot in being able at so low a cost to regain Heaven, which we have lost through our own fault! What does it cost you, O Christian, to receive this Sacrament, in which the soul is cleansed from all its stains, even were it defiled by

---

*Note: "A person in mortal sin can regain the state of grace before receiving the Sacrament of Penance by making an act of perfect contrition with the sincere purpose of going to Confession." (*Baltimore Catechism*, Official Revised Edition, no. 403). "Our contrition is perfect when we are sorry for our sins because sin offends God, whom we love above all things for His own sake." (no. 399). "Our contrition is imperfect when we are sorry for our sins because they are hateful in themselves or because we fear God's punishment." (no. 400). "To receive the Sacrament of Penance worthily, imperfect contrition is sufficient." (no. 401). —*Publisher*, 2002.

all the sins that have ever been committed from the creation of the world? Far more did its institution cost Jesus Christ, for it cost Him scourges, thorns, nails, a Cross—in one word, His Passion and Death. But for you to reap the whole fruit of the Passion and Blood of your Redeemer, you need but make one act of true contrition, "shed but one tear" of true repentance, and, in short, make a good Confession. And yet Christians are so negligent and indolent in approaching this Sacrament of reconciliation, pardon, and peace! They prove, indeed, how little they care about their own salvation, or value the most Precious Blood of Jesus, which was shed for their salvation.

Go often to Confession, dear Christian; and if you have incurred the dreadful misfortune of falling into mortal sin, go to Confession without any delay. Do not have the presumption to live one single moment in a state of mortal sin, because death might surprise you in this state, and precipitate you into Hell forever. By means of a good Confession your soul is released from the slavery of the devil; the chains of sin are burst asunder, and your name is effaced from the gloomy records of Hell, where it was written. You are in one instant transferred from the enemy into the child of God, the co-heir of Christ, the heir to Heaven; you become the beloved of blessed Mary, the friend of the Angels, the companion of the Saints. You become once more capable of acquiring merits for life eternal; you regain that grace and those blessings which you had lost by sin, and fresh and ever-increasing strength is imparted to you, to preserve you from falling anew. All Heaven is glorified when the sinner confesses his sins and is converted to God with his whole heart.

Often go to Confession, even when your soul is not burdened with mortal sin, because by good and frequent Confessions the soul is still more strengthened to keep at a distance from sin, is enlightened, filled with ever-increasing graces and the gifts of the Holy Ghost, is in better disposition for receiving the favors of God, acquires new light to discover the temptations of the devil and strength to overcome them; she is cleansed yet more and more from her daily stains, and approaches nearer to the sanctity required of a true Christian. St. Catherine, St. Bridget, St. Charles and St. Ignatius confessed every day; St. Francis Borgia confessed twice a day, once before saying Mass, and once before going to bed.

It would be a very excellent thing for you to make a rule to go to Confession once a week.

On the other hand, whenever you go to Confession, exert the utmost care and diligence that you may well and worthily approach this Sacrament.

To make a **good Confession, five things are required,** viz.: Examination of Conscience; Contrition (sorrow for sin committed); Purpose of Amendment (determination never more to commit sin); Confession (a declaration of your sins to the priest), and willingness to perform the Penance enjoined.

Examination of Conscience

The examination of your conscience should be made with the same degree of care and attention with which you would set about an affair of the greatest importance. In order, therefore, that your efforts may be crowned with success, you must beg Almighty God to bestow upon you light and grace, through the merits of Jesus Christ. In proportion to the length of time which has elapsed since your last Confession, and to the nature of your employments and the duties of your calling, you should devote more or less time to your examination.

Examine, in the first place, what length of time has passed since your last Confession—whether you have performed your Penance, and whether or not you have put in practice the advice given you by your confessor. Then read through, one by one, the Commandments of God and of the Church, to see whether you have transgressed any of them by thought, word, deed, or omission. Examine yourself upon the seven capital sins, and upon the obligations of your position and state of life. To assist your memory, you may likewise call to mind in what places you have been, with whom you have conversed, or upon what business you have been engaged. When you have remembered your sins, bear in mind their number, that you may be able to tell your confessor.*

---

*Note: A good Examination of Conscience is to be found in the book: *Confession: Its Fruitful Practice*, TAN, Rockford, IL, 2000. —*Publisher*, 2002.

Contrition

When you have concluded your examination, you must proceed to excite contrition—the most important part of this Sacrament.

For want of contrition, innumerable Confessions are either sacrilegious or invalid; the penitent so often breaks his promises to God, and falls again so easily into the same faults, and many souls are eternally lost. Contrition is that true and lively sorrow which the soul has for all the sins it has committed, with a firm determination never to commit them any more.

1. It must be *sovereign,* for sin must be more hateful to the soul than any other evil. Therefore, if you wish to make a good Confession, you ought to hate sin above every evil, and be in the disposition to accept any suffering or trial rather than return to your sins and offend God, the Fountain of Justice and all True Good.

2. It must be *universal*—that is to say, you must detest and repent of all the sins you have committed—at least of all that were mortal sins.

3. It must be *supernatural*—that is to say, proceeding from the grace of God, and conceived through a motive revealed by the light of faith, such as having deserved Hell, lost Heaven, etc. If you repent of your sins because by them you have offended God, the Sovereign Good—because you have displeased a God infinitely worthy of being loved—your sorrow will be *perfect contrition*—it will be that of a son who is deeply grieved at having offended his good Father. Happy will you be if your sorrow be of this exalted kind!

Many Christians spend a long time in examining their consciences, and in making long and often unnecessary narrations to the confessor, and then bestow little or no time upon considering the malice of their sins, and upon bewailing and detesting them. Christians such as these, says St. Gregory, act like a wounded man who shows his wounds to the doctor with the utmost anxiety and care, and then will not make use of the remedies prescribed. It is not so much thinking, nor so much speaking of your sins that will procure their pardon, but heartfelt sorrow and detestation of them. And since the most difficult, and, at the same time, most necessary part of Penance is to conceive this true sorrow for sin, I will lay before you, in the following Preparation for Confession, various considerations composed of motives and acts, which you must read slowly and attentively, meditating upon them one by one, so that each may sink deeply into your heart, and thus excite you to repentance.

Purpose of Amendment

Purpose of amendment is a firm and fixed resolution never more to offend God. Many fail in the purpose of amendment, especially habitual and relapsing sinners, and in consequence fall again so speedily into the sins they have confessed, and offend God.

Your purpose of amendment must be:

1. *Firm*—that is to say, you should have an earnest, strong, resolute, lively, and true determination never more to commit sin. Confession does not mean the mere relation of your sins to your confessor, as a narration, but it means an entire change of will, a change of affections, a change of desires, a hatred of the sins that you have hitherto loved—in short, a change of life. And after so many Confessions, have you changed your life?

2. *Universal*—that is to say, you must resolve never again to commit sin.

3. *Efficacious*—that is to say, you must not only resolve that, with God's grace, you will never again commit sin, but you should also consider what would be the proper means of preventing a relapse; you must plan to avoid all voluntary near occasions of sin, and you should endeavor most earnestly to eradicate your evil habits. If you do not resolve in this manner, your purpose of amendment will be in words only.

Confession or Accusation of Sins

Confession or *Accusation of Sins* is the declaration to an authorized confessor of the sins which you have committed. It must be:

1. *Entire.* You must accuse yourself of all the mortal sins which you are certain of having committed—and you should also confess any mortal sins you are doubtful of having committed—exactly as you see them in your conscience to be, and which you have not as yet duly confessed. You must confess your mortal sins with their kind and number, neither more nor less, if you can, or at least as nearly as you can remember. It is good to confess your venial sins also.

2. *Sincere*—That is to say, you must not excuse, disguise, or justify your sins. How many Christians, in the very act by which they think to unburden their conscience, load it still more heavily, because they do not sincerely accuse themselves of their sins, and after Confession are more guilty than before? What does it avail you to deceive the confessor into giving you absolution, by confessing a smaller number of sins, concealing the others through shame, or by not telling them such as they truly are? Acting thus, you only draw down upon yourself the anger of God. For the sake of not saying a few words to your Confessor, who is bound to inviolable secrecy, who is your spiritual Father, who loves your soul, who pities your weakness, who is the minister of Jesus Christ, and who has been by Him entrusted with this office to hear and assist poor sinners, you are willing to go to Hell, and be lost for all eternity. What madness!

The Sacramental Penance

The sacramental penance is a satisfaction imposed by the Confessor, after hearing in Confession the sins of the penitent. In the ancient canons of the Church, very severe penances of years and years were imposed for one single mortal sin. The Church has most wisely moderated such excessive severity, and confessors usually impose very slight penances. Nevertheless, if the fervor of Christians has grown cold, sin has not lost its malice, or grown less reprehensible, neither has Divine justice become less rigorous; therefore, besides accepting and performing the penance enjoined you by your confessor, you should endeavor to add some voluntary ones, to satisfy the justice of God, or you should at least seek to gain some of the indulgences which are so plentiful in the Church. Be not of the number of those who are dissatisfied, and even refuse to accept the penance enjoined by the confessor, from the mere apprehension of its being too severe. Is it much, indeed, after having committed so many sins, and having repeatedly merited the bitter torments of Hell, to have to perform a short penance? If Christians possessed true faith, they not only would never refuse or neglect to perform the penances enjoined them, but would even ask for more. For it must be remembered that the sacramental penance is of far greater value, and releases you from much more temporal punishment, than any that is performed through your own choice, because it derives peculiar value and virtue from the Sacrament, and from the merits of Jesus Christ. Humbly accept then the penance imposed upon you, and perform it as soon as possible in a spirit of devotion and sincere contrition.

PREPARATION FOR CONFESSION

On the day when you are to go to Confession, hasten, if possible, to the church before entering upon any other business, and there retire on one side to the foot of some Crucifix, or before the most Blessed Sacrament, and placing yourself in a particular manner in the presence of God, implore of Our Lord light and grace to prepare yourself worthily for the reception of this Sacrament. The prayers given here below may serve you as a guide and rule.

What I most particularly recommend is that you should not merely glance at them, or hastily run through them, as is often done with spiritual books, or with other vocal prayers, which, precisely because they are frequently repeated over, are recited by many persons carelessly and through custom. Read attentively, and let your heart feel all that is expressed in the acts and prayers which you are reciting, endeavoring to excite within your soul those affections of the will signified by the words. And if from time to time you stop to make a short but devout pause, you will find ample subject for meditation both in the Preparation and in the Thanksgiving.

Prayer before Beginning
The Examination of Conscience

BEHOLD at Thy feet, O my sweet Jesus, a new prodigal son, terrified at the sight of his sins, who can find no other remedy for them but to confess them at Thy sacred feet, and trust in the immensity of Thy mercy. Thou knowest me, O my Jesus: I am unhappily that ungrateful son who has so ill corresponded with all Thy love and tenderness, and has so shamefully outraged and offended Thee, the best of Fathers. I am no longer worthy to be called Thy child, but yet my poor heart cannot live at a distance from Thee. I should deserve, my sweet Jesus, to behold Thee now as my severe judge; but, most happily for me, I behold Thee hanging on the Cross, with Thy arms stretched forth to clasp me once more to thy loving Heart, and Thy Wounds are as so many mouths calling me to repentance, and tenderly whispering to my heart, *"Return to me, O My son, return and repent; doubt not My love for thee."* O my Crucified Jesus, complete then the work which Thy immense charity has begun; bestow upon me some small portion of that knowledge and sorrow which Thou hadst for my sins, when through horror at, and contrition for them, Thou didst sweat blood in the Garden, and fall almost fainting on the ground, that I might thereby comprehend their gravity and malice, and conceive a proper degree of sorrow for them! Enlighten my mind, and strengthen my memory, that I may remember all my sins, as also their number and attendant circumstances; inflame my will with an eternal hatred of sin, and with an ardent love of Thee, O my Crucified Love. O Mary, most sorrowful Mother, assist me now in this my great spiritual necessity. And thou, my holy Angel Guardian, lend me now thy special aid, that I may worthily prepare myself for Confession.

Having made this prayer, you should recollect yourself, and begin your examination with the utmost diligence and application of mind. Examine yourself particularly upon that passion to which you are most inclined, and that virtue against which you are most frequently tempted. Mark down in your memory the sins you find you have committed, their kind and number; and when you cannot exactly be certain of the number, at least remember for how long a time you continued to commit that sin, and as nearly as possible how often you committed it in the course of a week or month, that you may tell your confessor.

When you have finished your examination, before going to Confession you should excite yourself to contrition, and make a purpose of amendment; and as these acts are of the utmost importance, and, in fact, absolutely necessary, endeavor to make them, not in a mere cursory manner, but several times over, repeating the act of contrition as well as that of attrition,* for greater security, although either

---

*By contrition and attrition are meant perfect contrition and imperfect contrition, respectively. (See footnote on p. 285.) The traditional Act of Contrition includes both an act of

act, well made, is sufficient for forgiveness in Confession. Whether you make them out of your own head, or read them from a book, take care to accompany the words uttered by your lips with the inward feeling of your heart,** otherwise they will avail you nothing. That you may make these acts well, reflect seriously upon the motives which should excite you to them, and which I here propose to you in the form of short considerations.

Considerations and Motives to Excite in Our Souls a Lively Sorrow for Our Sins

One or more of these considerations may be read, according to the time and circumstances, and the disposition of the penitent.

1. *You have deserved Hell.* Consider, my soul, how great is the evil which thou hast committed by falling into sin. Thou hast deserved Hell. If God had struck thee dead when thou wert in a state of sin, where wouldst thou be now? That pleasure, that interest, that point of honor, or that revenge, has made thee a child of perdition. Oh, how many souls are burning in Hell for one single mortal sin! And how many hast thou committed? How often hast thou deserved Hell? How long wouldst thou already

imperfect contrition and an act of perfect contrition. (See p. 312). —*Publisher*, 2002.

**Contrition (perfect or imperfect) is essentially *an act of the will*, by which one chooses to regret and renounce his sins. An emotional *feeling* of sorrow, while good, is not required for contrition. —*Publisher*, 2002.

have been burning in Hell, if Divine mercy had not awaited thy repentance? Ungrateful soul, what is thy conduct with regard to so good a God? This: thou makest use of His very mercy to outrage Him. Ah, begin from this moment to bewail thy sins. Descend in spirit into Hell; look at those flames, those torments, and those devils awaiting thee. There thou wouldst now be weeping in despair, if thou hadst died in thy sin. There thou wilt weep for all eternity if thou diest in thy sin. My soul, how sayest thou?—what are now thy resolutions? With one tear of repentance thou mayest extinguish those flames, close up the abyss of Hell and gain Heaven. Oh, how much am I indebted to Thee, my God, for having waited for my repentance even until now, and for having saved me from Hell! How much do I owe Thy loving mercy? Behold, I yield. I detest my sins above every other evil, because by them I have deserved Hell and lost Heaven, but more, far more, because I have offended Thee, my God, my Sovereign and Infinite Good. Never more will I commit sin, O my God, never more.

2. *You have lost Heaven.* Consider, my soul, what an inestimable good thou hast lost by sin. Raise thy eyes to Heaven, contemplate that blessed country, where God, the Fountain of all happiness, is possessed forever. Before thou didst fall into sin, Heaven was thy home, thy inheritance, thy country, thy blessed abode. There was written thy name—there was to be thy place of eternal repose. But no sooner, unhappy soul, didst thou fall into sin, than thou didst forfeit all this happiness, and deserve every evil. Thy name was erased from the Book of Life. Thou didst become an enemy of God. Thy Saviour became a Judge, breathing vengeance. Thou didst cease to be a faithful child of Mary. Thou didst become the slave of Satan. Thou didst renounce thy right to eternal glory. Thou didst lose Heaven. Oh, how great, how inconceivable a loss! And that for the sake of a foolish pleasure, a shameful outburst of anger, or some momentary gratification! Rouse thyself, O my soul, there is yet time to remedy so many losses. By one tear, one sigh, one good Confession, God will be appeased. Yes, God will pardon thee, and render thee once more worthy of the glory thou hast lost. O Heaven, would that I had never lost thee! O sin, would that I had never committed thee! O my God, would that I had never offended Thee! Behold me at Thy feet, penitent and sorrowful. I wish I could efface the evil I have done. I wish I could wash it away in my own blood. I detest my hateful sins. I abhor my guilty pleasures. I renounce inordinate attachment to creatures. I bitterly bewail having lost a Paradise of delights, but far, far more do I weep and lament for having displeased a God so good, so amiable, so worthy of being loved. My Father and my God, allow me to be reconciled to Thee, now and forever; deprive me of life rather than let me live to offend Thee more. Let me love Thee, or die.

3. *You have crucified Jesus anew.* Behold, O my soul, the great evil thou hast done in committing sin. Look at Jesus on that Cross; look at His torn and mangled limbs; look at the streams of Blood flowing from His Wounds. All that is the work of thy sins. Thy evil thoughts have crowned His Head with sharp thorns. Thy immodesty has defiled His face with bruises and spittle. Thy impurity has cruelly scourged Him from head to foot. It is thou who hast inflicted all those wounds, mangled those hands, transfixed those feet, torn that innocent flesh by thy sins. It is thou who hast displayed such wanton cruelty against that adorable Body, sacrificing and drawing forth from it streams of Blood, without one thought of pity, where the gratification of thy unworthy passions was concerned. It is thou who hast drenched that Divine mouth with vinegar, by so many evil words, and so much licentious conversation. It is thou who hast afflicted and grieved that loving Heart by thy hatred, aversions, and rancor toward thy neighbor. It is thou who hast barbarously pierced that sacred Side, when thou didst give entrance into thy heart to that illicit love. It is thou who hast overwhelmed thy Lord with shame and ignominy by thy pride and vanity. It is thou who hast by thy execrable sins put thy Father, thy Creator, and thy God, to a cruel death. It is thou who hast trampled His adorable Blood underfoot each time that thou hast returned to thy sins. Read, cruel soul, read in the Wounds of thy Jesus, the greatness and malice of thy sins. Measure the enormity of thy crimes by the greatness of the torments and sufferings of thy loving Redeemer. My suffering Jesus! How, oh, how could I ever have had the heart thus cruelly to torture Thee? How was it that I did not fall down dead through alarm and horror at the sight of my own impiety? And what evil hast Thou done me, O my sweet Jesus, that I should treat Thee with such horrible inhumanity? Ah, hast thou ever ceased for a moment to love me and load me with blessings? Even on the Cross Thou didst pray for me, invite me to repentance, offer me pardon, and satisfy Divine justice for my sins at the price of Thy own precious life. My Crucified Redeemer, behold me humbled, penitent, and sorrowful at Thy feet; ah, do not cast that soul which cost Thee so dear into eternal flames! My sweet Jesus, receive me into Thy tender embraces, hide me in Thy opened side, press me to Thy loving Heart! I confess that it is I who am Thy crucifier, that it is I who have nailed Thee to the Cross, by my sins. I do not deserve pardon for such shameful impiety. But those Wounds speak for me, that Divine Blood pleads in my behalf, and they obtain mercy for a traitor who deserves it not. Mercy, O my Jesus, mercy and pardon! I detest all my sins from the very bottom of my heart; I hate and abhor them, because they have inflicted on Thee so many sufferings and so painful a death. Wash my soul in Thy Precious Blood, let my heart break with sorrow, and make me fully comprehend what mortal sin is—mortal sin, which has put to death the Son of God—that so I may never cease while I have life to bewail the great evil which I have done in committing it.

4. *You have offended God, the Sovereign Good.*
Consider, my soul, how, by committing sin, thou
hast offended, insulted, and maltreated thy Benefactor, thy Sovereign Good—thy God, the fountain
of love and infinite goodness. Tell me what evil has
thy God ever done thee? In what has He offended
thee? Answer me. Why hast thou grieved that loving Heart? Thy God created thee, adopted thee for
His child, and redeemed thee by His Blood; He has
so often fed thee with His most precious Body,
loaded thee with blessings, bestowed on thee so
many graces, and prepared Heaven for thy eternal
abode. Why hast thou betrayed so amiable a Benefactor? Why hast thou turned thy back upon the
best of Fathers? Is this, then, the gratitude, love
and fidelity thou dost owe thy God? Ah, my God! I
ought indeed to die from sheer grief at the thought
of my monstrous ingratitude. What! did I proudly
turn my back upon Thee, and didst Thou pursue
me, inviting, nay, even imploring me to return to
Thy arms? I hated Thee, and Thou didst love me! I
rebelliously offended Thee, and Thou, my loving
Father, didst continue loading me with benefits! I
refused to acknowledge Thee as my God. I wished
to hurry on to my own perdition, and Thou didst
preserve my life, offer me pardon, and breathe to
me in loving accents, *"Son, why dost thou fly from
Me? What evil have I done thee?"* My most beloved
God! How, oh, how could I have the heart to offend
so good a Father? How could I live so long at a distance from Thee, a rebel to Thee, and Thy enemy?
Great has been my misfortune, my God, in losing

Heaven and meriting Hell, but far greater evil have I done in displeasing Thee, the Sovereign, Infinite Good! I lament the evil I have done myself; but infinitely more do I lament the displeasure I have caused Thee, my God, who art worthy of all my love. Ah, would that I could cancel the evil I have done, at the expense of every drop of my blood! O God of compassion and of infinite goodness, since Thou dost so mercifully offer me pardon upon the sole condition of my repentance for having offended Thee, behold me prostrate at Thy feet; I repent with my whole heart and soul of all the offenses I have committed against Thee, my Father, my God, and my Sovereign Good! Now do I begin to love Thee with all my strength, above all else, O God of Love. I renounce every inordinate love, I renounce the world, the devil and sin, in order to love Thee above all things. Never more, O my Heavenly Father, never more will I renew my offenses against Thee, never more will I commit sin. I will ever bewail that unhappy moment in which I offended Thee, my Sovereign Good; do Thou grant that my tears of repentance may cancel my sins.

An Act of Contrition and Purpose of Amendment

O MY Crucified Lord, behold me prostrate at Thy feet with the deepest feelings of humility and confusion, acknowledging myself guilty of so many grievous offenses against Thee. Have mercy, O tender Father, have mercy upon this my soul, which Thou hast redeemed with Thy Precious Blood. Have mercy upon this Thy prodigal child, who now returns to Thee weeping and penitent. I acknowledge and confess, O my God, that I am guilty of innumerable faults, and of the malice pertaining to each one of them. I am guilty of having outraged Thy goodness. I have a thousand times deserved Hell, and should be already burning in its flames, had not Thy mercy waited for my repentance. I am deeply penitent, O my God, for having done so much evil to my soul by my shameful sins, but far more do I grieve, and does my heart reproach me, when I reflect that in sinning I have offended Thee, my Sovereign Good. Oh, how dreadful is it to behold my Jesus nailed to a Cross by my hands! O Jesus, have my sins then rendered Thee the Man of Sorrows? I see those sharp thorns which are the unhappy fruit of my proud and impure thoughts. I see those painful Wounds which my guilty pleasures have inflicted on Thy virginal Body. I see that Heart pierced through and through, in consequence of my sinful affections. Ah, my sweet Jesus, since Thy mercy has led me to Thy feet, let me here die of grief, let my soul be breathed forth in contrition for such shameful ingratitude! Yes, my Jesus, let this body of sin die, provided only my soul may live. I ask this favor of Thee, through that most Precious Blood which flows from Thy dying limbs—look at me, O my Jesus, prostrate at the foot of Thy Cross, and already sprinkled with Thy most Precious Blood. It is not I who speak to

Thee, my beloved Redeemer, but Thy Blood which calls loudly for pity, mercy and pardon, and implores for me the grace of an unbounded hatred for sin, and that I may die a thousand times rather than ever lose Thy grace again. O my God, O Father of mercies, look upon Thy Son, crucified and dying for my sake, to make satisfaction for my sins. In His Name, through the merits of His sacred Passion, of His scourging, of His crowning with thorns, of His Blood, and of His death, look at my sinful soul with eyes of compassion and mercy; give me a most sincere and burning contrition for my sins. I repent, O Lord, I repent of them all, and I am grieved above every other evil for having offended Thy infinite Goodness, Thou, my Sovereign Good, Thou, who art a Being of infinite perfection, the Fountain of all good, the Author of all good, the Perfection of all perfection, and infinitely worthy of being loved, obeyed, served, and honored. And I, miserable, vile creature as I am, instead of serving, honoring, obeying and loving Thee, have outraged, insulted and abandoned Thee; I have transgressed Thy most holy law to gratify the shameful caprices of my corrupted heart and perverse will. I would willingly die at Thy feet of grief for having offended Thee, my God and for having been by my sins the guilty cause of the death of Jesus. I am resolved, and firmly purpose, by the help of Thy grace, to die a thousand times rather than ever more offend Thee. Yes, O my God, I will fly sin, whatever it may cost me; I will avoid all occasions of sin; I will lead an entirely different life for the future; I will love Thee with my whole heart; I will die rather than offend Thee again. My sweetest Mother and Queen of Dolors, by those tears which thou didst shed at the foot of the Cross, obtain for me a most lively, sincere, pure sorrow for my sins, that, when I receive absolution from the minister of God, I may receive the abundant fruits of the Blood shed by thy Jesus for love of me. Do thou assist me that I may accuse myself of all my sins, detest them all, and thus recover the grace and friendship of my God.

RECOMMENDATIONS WITH REGARD TO CONFESSION

1. Having concluded your preparation for Confession, go to your confessor with the utmost humility and modesty, as though you were approaching Jesus Christ in person and confessing your sins to Him who sees your heart and will one day judge you. If you have some time to wait, persevere in devout silence and recollection, making repeated acts of contrition for your sins. Look upon yourself as a criminal loaded with chains, who has been already tried and convicted, and is now called upon to present himself before the Judge, who is also the very person he has injured and offended.

2. When you have entered the confessional, kneel down with the utmost reverence and humility, imagining yourself to be in the presence of Jesus Crucified, who wishes to hear from your own lips the sincere confession of all your sins, and provided you truly repent, is ready to pardon them and cleanse your soul in His most Precious Blood, through the medium of the sacramental absolution pronounced by His minister. Make the Sign of the Cross, and say with sincere contrition: "Bless me, Father, for I have sinned."

3. Then, with the greatest humility, in a clear intelligible voice, and slowly, not hurriedly, with your eyes cast down and your hands joined, say in the first place how long it is since your last Confession, and whether you have performed your Penance.

4. If you have any grievous [that is, mortal] sins to confess, accuse yourself of them in the first instance, explaining yourself clearly concerning their kind, number, circumstances, etc. Say whether you frequently fall into them, whether you are in the habit of committing any one of them; whether anything is to you a near occasion of sin; whether you have any sinful attachment, or are under any sinful promise. Say also if you have not fulfilled any important obligation. Tell your confessor everything with the utmost sincerity and clearness, both in order that he may prescribe proper remedies, and that you may not run the risk of making a bad Confession—a misfortune which might easily happen.

5. If you have no mortal sins of which to accuse yourself, confess the venial sins you have committed, and let your sorrow extend to all the sins of your past life. In order to secure contrition and a firm purpose of amendment, it will be as well for you in this case to accuse yourself of some really grievous sin of your past life, and this you may do in every Confession, for your greater humiliation, and to purify your soul more and more.

6. If you are really desirous of making good Confessions, imagine every Confession that you make to be your last, and that you are to be judged by God immediately after it. Think that your eternal salvation or damnation may depend upon that one Confession. Act so that when death really comes, your Confessions may be a source of consolation, not of remorse, to you. It is related of a Dominican friar, that when exhorted on his deathbed to make a good Confession, he replied, "For thirty-five years I have made each Confession as though it were to be my last." Imitate his example.

7. When you have accused yourself of all your sins, and have nothing more to say to your confessor, listen to the good advice he gives you with attention and humility. Accept the penance enjoined you with great submission, as also whatever else the minister of God may please to impose upon you.

8. When you are about to receive absolution, renew from your heart your act of contrition for your sins, firmly resolving never more to commit them. To excite in yourself feelings of more tender devotion and lively contrition, it is well to imagine that you are at the foot of the Cross of Jesus on Mount Calvary, and that when the priest absolves you, the Precious Blood of your Redeemer is flowing on your soul and cleansing all its stains. With your mind absorbed in these or similar pious reflections, receive sacramental absolution, making the Sign of the Cross.

9. On leaving the confessional, it is good to animate yourself with the liveliest feelings of joy and confidence that God has pardoned you your sins. Perform your penance as soon as possible, and thank Our Lord for the great blessing He has bestowed upon you.

Prayer to Be Said after Confession

O MY sweet Jesus, behold me, although most unworthy of Thy mercy, cleansed from the stains of my grievous sins, solely and entirely through the effects of Thy compassion. What claim had I to be restored to Thy friendship, which I had so frequently outraged? To Thy merits and Thy goodness am I indebted for so great a favor. O beloved Redeemer of my soul, how much do I owe Thee! To merit for me this favor, Thou, although perfectly innocent, didst shed every drop of Thy Blood, endure so many sufferings, submit to such cruel tortures, and finally even die upon a Cross!

And I, the unworthy author of so much evil, have made amends for my crimes by a single short act of contrition! Oh, mercies of my Jesus! And what thanks could ever be adequate to so great, so loving a favor? O most holy Mary, and you, blessed Angels and Saints of Heaven, assist me to thank my Lord for His great goodness! Do you obtain me grace never more to abandon Him, but to persevere in the resolutions I have made and here renew, never more to offend Him, but to love and serve Him until death. Grant, O my most sweet Jesus, grant that I may never again lose the fruit of Thy Precious Blood. May I die a thousand times rather than ever again commit a single mortal sin, and offend Thy infinite goodness. Whenever and by whatever death I die, permit not, O my loving Saviour, that my soul, which has cost Thee so dear, should be lost!

INSTRUCTIONS FOR AFTER CONFESSION

In order not to relapse into sin:

1. Reflect that the man who commits mortal sin again pronounces in his heart this iniquitous sentence: "The devil, to whose service I now return, is a better master than God, whose service I leave, after having tried it, had experience of its perfections, and tasted its sweetness." Can a greater degree of perfidy be conceived?

2. Reflect that the man who commits mortal sin forms in his heart a new Calvary, and raises thereon a new Cross, on which he is desirous of seeing Jesus die anew; he cries aloud that Jesus is to be crucified, and he takes arms in his hands with which to put Him to a cruel death. Oh, fearful impiety!

3. Consider what roads led you to a relapse into sin, after former Confessions, and close them up carefully, for if you leave them open you will speedily go astray as before. You will always find it far more easy to fly the occasions of sin than to avoid sin when frequenting its occasions. You have promised God in Confession to sin no more, but if you do not fly from the occasions of sin, you break your word, for you voluntarily expose yourself to a relapse. Oh, if penitents were to avoid all the occasions of sin, how far more faithful would they remain to their Lord, and how far more constantly would they persevere in the grace they had regained.

4. If you have hitherto relapsed into sin after Confession because you did not often recommend yourself to God, be most careful never again to neglect prayer. If you have fallen into sin because you neglected to meditate upon the Passion of Christ, make it a rule to reflect upon that sacred subject as often as possible. If you have sinned, owing to neglect of the Sacraments, promise Our Lord that you will frequent them; in short, let nothing appear to you too arduous. If you have committed sin because you did not have recourse to our blessed Lady as your dear Mother, never estrange yourself from her tender love and powerful protection; invoke her, have recourse to her in every temptation and danger; consecrate each day to her; beseech her to save you from sin, and most assuredly she will do so.

Act of Contrition*

O MY God, I am heartily sorry for having offended Thee, and I detest all my sins because I dread the loss of Heaven and the pains of Hell; but most of all because they offend Thee, my God, Who art all good and deserving of all my love. I firmly resolve, with the help of Thy grace, to confess my sins, to do penance, and to amend my life. Amen.

---

*Added by the Publisher, 2002. This is the Act of Contrition traditionally memorized by Catholics.

∽ EXERCISE 7 ∾

Practical Instructions
For Worthily Approaching
Holy Communion

THE Sacrament of the Holy Eucharist is that most adorable Sacrament instituted by Jesus Christ our Lord the night before His Passion and death, in which is contained, under the species of the bread and wine consecrated by the Priest, the true Body and Blood, Soul and Divinity of Jesus Christ, and he who eats thereof feeds on Jesus Christ Himself, and is nourished with the most holy Flesh and adorable Blood. Our Divine Redeemer Himself assures us of this when He says, "He that eateth my Flesh and drinketh my Blood abideth in me, and I in him." How sweet, and at the same time how stupendous a reflection it is, that God should so love us as to conceal Himself beneath the Sacramental species in order to become our food! But what an incomprehensible mystery of ingratitude it is, that we Christians should display indifference and coldness toward our God in the very Sacrament in which He gives us such efficacious proofs of the excess of His love for us!

Our Divine Saviour is absolutely independent of men, and yet He thinks nothing of remaining hidden to the end of time for their sakes in a Host, so much does He love and delight to be with the children of men. Men, on the other hand, cannot persevere in His service without the assistance of His grace, and yet appreciate but little the favor he does them in dwelling among them. But little do they love Him, but little do they value Him, but little do they care to unite themselves to Him, and receive Him in the adorable Sacrament, while He is burning with desire to enter their hearts!

Very many Christians through guilty negligence, many others through unwillingness to leave their sins, and many more through tepidity of spirit, approach but rarely to receive their Lord in the Sacrament of Holy Communion. To abstain from Communion because of imperfections is to refuse medicine and a doctor because you are ill. To abstain from Communion because you are not holy is to require that which properly is the effect of this Sacrament as a preparation for it, and thus never attain true sanctity. To abstain from Communion because you are living in sin is to determine never to rise from that state of perdition. If you have sufficient religious feeling to deter you from wishing to make an unworthy Communion, take courage, and have resolution sufficient to liberate yourself from what keeps you at a distance from the sacred Table. But this is precisely what terrifies lukewarm, careless Christians. Preparation is necessary, and preparation is troublesome

and unpleasant. It is necessary to deprive yourself of certain gratifications, to withdraw yourself
from certain occasions, to renounce certain vain
attire, to mortify your senses; in short, to
renounce sin, to which you are fondly attached—
this is what gives you pain; and in the meantime
you keep at a distance from this Sacrament of life
and grace, and hurry on in the path that leads to
eternal death. It is true that your faith should be
lively and your reverence profound in regard to
this great Sacrament; but instead of deciding on
this account to keep away from Communion, you
should resolve to reform your evil habits, amend
your life, and renounce sin, in order thus to render yourself less unworthy of approaching to
receive the Bread of Angels.

All the Saints have ever regarded the Sacrament of Holy Eucharist as the richest treasure of
the law of grace, and the source of all their
strength, their fervor, and their holiness. Dear
Christian, if you also are desirous that your soul
should partake of the unspeakable benefits which
this august Sacrament can bestow, if you need
strength to overcome the enemies of your salvation, if you wish for abundant graces to preserve
you from falling into sin, if you desire to be imbued
with fervor and courage to walk in the path of the
Commandments, often receive the Bread of
Angels. Look upon the time of Communion as the
most precious of your whole life, and let your soul
burn with an ardent desire to feed on this heavenly Bread. Remember, nevertheless, that he that

eateth unworthily, eateth to his own condemnation. Besides the fast from the previous midnight to the moment of Communion,* which you should most carefully observe, it is necessary that you should be in the grace of God, that is to say that your soul should be unburdened from any mortal sin, to which state you may attain, after having fallen, by means of a good Confession; otherwise you will commit a most horrible sacrilege. If you have venial sins only on your conscience, there is no obligation to confess them, but it would be better to do so; and it is a fault not to endeavor, as far as possible, to cleanse your soul from the smallest venial sin, both on account of the respect you owe the most holy Sacrament, and in order to derive greater benefit from it; therefore, if you cannot actually go to Confession, make at least an act of contrition, and beseech Jesus Christ to cleanse your soul with His Precious Blood.

But this is not sufficient preparation for so sacred an action, in order to perform it devoutly, and derive from it abundant fruits. You must fervently prepare your soul, animating your faith by pious reflections and meditations, considering with the utmost attention who the great Lord is whom you are about to receive in the Holy Communion, and making pious acts of adoration, hope, love, desire, humility, and repentance,

---

*This was a former discipline of the Latin Rite of the Church regarding the Communion fast. Since the late 1960's, a fast of only one hour is required, and water does not break the fast. —*Publisher*, 2002.

which I subjoin for your greater convenience.

Do not limit your preparation to those few moments which precede your Communion after you enter the church, but endeavor to keep it present to your mind the previous day, and in the evening before going to bed. And if you chance to awake in the night, let your mind be instantly occupied with this sweet thought: *I am to receive Communion. I am to receive into my breast Jesus Christ my Redeemer, my Father, and my God.*

Remember, above all, that the intention of Jesus Christ in instituting this most holy Sacrament, and in leaving us this most precious pledge of His love, was, that as often as the Divine Mysteries should be celebrated, or His most holy Body received in the Blessed Eucharist, so often should there be a special remembrance of Him, and of all that He had done and suffered for us. It is therefore very pleasing to God, when approaching the Sacred Table to receive Jesus in the Blessed Sacrament, to remember the sufferings, crucifixion, and death of this most loving Redeemer, and to bestow one thought at least upon that Divine Blood which He shed for you at the expense of so much suffering, and of which He has made you a most delicious banquet in the Holy Eucharist.

St. Charles, St. Philip Neri, St. Francis de Sales, and other Saints, advise all seculars [lay persons], of whatever state or condition, to approach the sacred Table once a week. Do you also follow this salutary counsel, when your confessor gives you leave,* and without necessity never depart from so excellent a custom, and your soul will surely derive great benefit from it. One means of persevering in the practice of frequent Communion is to propose to yourself some particular pious intention, to which you may direct a certain number of Communions, renewing your intention each time.

I here propose some for your consideration which may serve as a sweet and holy inducement to you to approach the holy Table so many times for each intention, until all the weeks of the year have passed away.

Pious Intentions for Communion

1. The love of God: That through this most holy Sacrament the soul may be more and more united to its God by the way of perfect love.

2. Devotion to the sacred Passion of Jesus Christ: That Our Lord, in the Blessed Sacrament, may impress upon our soul the memory of His bitter sufferings, and bestow upon it grace constantly and devoutly to think of them.

3. Devotion to the Blessed Virgin: To obtain tender filial affection and loving confidence in this

---

*This refers to a former discipline of the Church, before the instruction of Pope St. Pius X (1903-1914) urging frequent and even daily Communion for all Catholics who are in the state of grace, are observing the prescribed Communion fast, and have a right intention. —*Publisher*, 2002.

most amiable Queen, from Jesus, who bequeathed her to us from the Cross, to be our Mother.

4. Adoration of the Divine Majesty of God: Desiring and intending to acknowledge, adore and love It in Jesus Christ, and through Jesus Christ in the Blessed Sacrament, from whom God receives infinite honor and glory.

5. Desire to thank God for all the blessings received from His hand: And we cannot offer the Eternal Father anything more pleasing or dear to Him than His adorable Son in the Blessed Sacrament.

6. Satisfaction for our sins: Offering this Divine Victim, who is sacrificed for our salvation, and the price of His Precious Blood, in payment and expiation of all the offenses we have committed against God's Majesty.

7. Desire to obtain some particular favor from God, through the merits of Jesus in the Blessed Sacrament, either for ourselves or for our neighbors.

8. The cure of our own spiritual infirmities, in order that this Divine Physician, on coming into our soul, may heal and cure it, and infuse into it fresh strength and vigor, that so it may relapse no more.

9. Victory over temptations: That through the power and merits of Jesus Christ, who has by His death triumphed over the devil, we may be defended from his assaults, and preserved from his snares, and that by virtue of this Sacrament we may be strengthened to combat with valor.

10. Perseverance in God's grace: Fervently asking, through the merits and love of Jesus, for grace never to commit mortal sin, nor to displease the infinite goodness of God.

11. Desire to praise God in His Saints, and to honor their memory, offering our Communion to the most holy Trinity in thanksgiving for the favors bestowed upon them, and for the glory they enjoy. You should have this intention especially on their festival days.

12. On the festivals of the Blessed Virgin, you should go to Communion, in honor of the Queen of Saints, thanking Our Lord, in her name, for having made her His Mother, and for having endowed her with innumerable singular privileges.

13. Zeal for the salvation of poor sinners: Since there is nothing that can more efficaciously make intercession for them with the Eternal Father than that precious Blood which His most holy Son has shed for them.

14. Compassion for the sorrows of your neighbor: To obtain for all the needy, afflicted, and suffering, the grace of patience, comfort and consolation from Jesus Christ, who is the loving Father of all mankind.

15. An especial devotion toward Jesus Himself in the Blessed Sacrament, that our Divine Redeemer, who has been pleased to institute the most holy Sacrament of the Altar that so He may forever abide with us, may enkindle in our hearts, and in those of all mankind, a true love and sincere devotion toward Him and an earnest desire to receive Him frequently.

16. Desire to acquire the spirit of Christ, and to be entirely transformed into Him, that is to say, that by means of this Sacrament you may put on the spirit of Jesus Christ, and follow Him in His life and virtues, and thus become entirely His, for this should be the principal end of each of your Communions.

Having called to mind one or other of these pious intentions, and made an offering of your Communion to that end, you should place yourself with great recollection in the presence of God, and then, if you like, you can read the following Acts, as a preparation for the great action you are about to perform. Be careful not to go through them hurriedly and in a cursory manner, but read them more with your heart than with your eyes, and with great feeling and devotion. Pause whenever any expression excites in your heart especial feelings of piety and recollection. Your soul will not be so much benefited by reading many pages as by sincere compunction for your sins and tender love for Jesus Christ. If you act thus, the consequence will be that your heart will be well prepared and you will derive great fruit from your Communions.

ACTS BEFORE COMMUNION

An Act of Faith

MY MOST sweet Jesus, I believe with a firm and lively faith that in this adorable Sacrament are Thy Body and Blood, Thy Soul and Divinity. I believe that in this consecrated Host I shall receive that same Body which was formed in the pure womb of the Blessed Virgin Mary, which suffered so many pains and torments for love of me on a Cross, and which rose gloriously the third day from the dead. I believe that I shall receive that most holy Soul which is enriched with all the treasures of the Divinity—that I shall receive my God Himself. I believe that I shall receive Thee, O God, my Creator, Preserver, Redeemer, and Judge. Yes, I believe, O my God, but do Thou strengthen my faith, and animate it with deeper sentiments of adoration for Thy Divinity really present in the most Blessed Eucharist. Increase and enliven it not only in my heart, but also in the hearts of all the faithful, and grant that the light of faith may also illumine those who are unhappily sleeping in the darkness and shadows of death, heresy, and infidelity. My soul being thus prepared by faith, may a pious and tender remembrance of Thy Passion and Death, which Thou hast commanded me to renew whenever I approach to receive Thee in Thy most holy Sacrament, be awakened within me. Yes, my sweet Jesus, I beseech Thee, by all the love Thou didst manifest for me upon the Cross, to transform my heart into a new Calvary, sprinkled with Thy Blood, that so it may be worthy of Thy Divine presence.

Motives for an Act of Hope

What more canst thou require, my soul, now that God is coming to visit thee? And He is coming to enlighten, console, and enrich thee, to unite thy heart to His own, and to give thee a sure pledge of that glory which He has prepared for thee in Heaven. Delay not, therefore; open wide thy heart, have confidence, and know that thou shalt obtain in proportion to thy hope. Thy Jesus is all-powerful; there is nothing He cannot bestow upon thee, and it costs Him nothing to give thee whatever thou requirest. Thy Jesus is a Father who tenderly loves thee, and is desirous of giving thee everything thou canst desire. Thy Jesus is faithful, He has promised to hear thee, and has pledged His word that He will grant thy requests. Therefore, to receive all thou requirest, thou hast but to ask with earnest faith. Have confidence then, my soul, have confidence.

An Act of Hope

HOW many favors and mercies may I not hope to obtain from Thee, O my Jesus, hidden beneath the Sacramental veils, at the moment when Thou vouchsafest to come and dwell within me! How many favors may I not expect from Thy infinite goodness and power, now that I am about to receive Thee in the most holy Sacrament! If the mere remembrance of those Wounds with which Thy sacred Body, O my Jesus, was covered, and of that Blood which Thou didst shed for love of me, fills me with the hope of enjoying the fruits of Thy Passion and Death, what faith, what trust, what confidence must I not feel at knowing for certain that in a very short time that same most holy Flesh will be my food, and that same most precious Blood my drink! Yes, I hope, O my Jesus, that this Communion will sanctify my soul, cleanse it from every stain, deaden within it the fires of concupiscence, and fill it with all graces. I hope, O my Jesus, and on Thee do my hopes rest. I well know that I am absolutely unworthy of Thy mercies, I know that I have sinned many and many times; but I likewise know that Thou, my Crucified Jesus, art my Saviour; I know that Thou hast died on a Cross for me; I know that Thou art coming this morning to renew in the most holy Sacrament the sacrifice of Thy precious life, that my soul may live; I know that Thou art infinitely good and merciful, and in Thy infinite goodness and mercy do I place all my hopes, sure of never being confounded.

Motives for an Act of Charity

What more could a God do to gain thy love, O my soul? A God has been made man for thy sake, has died on a Cross for love of thee, has remained in the Blessed Sacrament to be thy food, and is ever ready to come to thee. Nay, more, with what infinite love does He invite thee to receive Him, and call upon thee to come to Him, almost as though He could not exist without thee. O sweet eagerness of charity! O excess of love in a God enamored of mortal man! A God is this morning about to bestow upon me a favor never granted to the Seraphim! And thou, my soul, dost thou not burn with love for a God who so tenderly loves thee.

An Act of Charity

MY MOST loving Jesus, can there be in this world a heart so hard and insensible, as not to be touched at the sight of the immense love Thou dost manifest in the Holy Eucharist, which is a perpetual memorial of Thy Passion and Death? Can I believe that Thou dost renew in this Sacrament, through excess of love, the sacrifice of Calvary—that Thou dost give me Thy own Flesh and Blood to be my food and drink, and my heart yet not be consumed in the flames of the most ardent love for Thee? Ah, my dear Jesus, my Love, God of my soul, my Sovereign Good, I love Thee with my whole heart. I love Thee with my whole soul, and with all my strength; I love Thee more than myself, I love Thee above all things. Oh, that I had innumerable hearts to love Thee, innumerable tongues to praise Thee, and innumerable lives to be devoted and consecrated to Thy love! Oh, that I were all love, that so I might love Thee, the sole object of my desires, my Beginning, my Last End, my God, the infinitely worthy Object of all my love, and thus make amends for those years in which I loved Thee not! Ah, my poor heart is filled with sorrow at the tender reproaches for my ingratitude and want of love, in which Thou dost address me from this consecrated Host, which contains Thy sacred Humanity, to the Wounds of which Thou dost point as proofs of Thy infinite love for me. But if I have not loved Thee, O my Jesus, during my past life, now at least do I begin to love Thee with my whole heart. I know that it is Thy Will that I should be entirely Thine, and that I should consecrate myself completely to Thy love; and, for my part, I do renounce every inordinate love in order to love Thee alone, my most amiable Jesus. Do Thou give me that burning charity and perfect love which Thou dost require of me. Draw me to Thee by the sweet chains of Thy many perfections; take possession of my poor heart, and unite it to Thy most loving Heart with the indissoluble band of everlasting charity. Thou, Thou alone, shalt henceforward live in my heart, or rather, my heart shall live but in Thine, and shall there die to all love that is not for Thee, my most loving Jesus.

Motives for an Act of Humility

My soul, the moment is approaching in which thou wilt receive the King of glory. Hast thou carefully reflected upon who God is, and who thou art? If thou wert a Seraphim burning with charity, or if thou wert possessed of the purity of the Angels, or of the holiness of all the Saints, yet wouldst thou not be worthy on that account even once to receive God. And wilt thou be worthy, being as thou art a poor wretched beggar, defiled with innumerable filthy stains, being, in short, a miserable sinner? Ah, humble thyself to the very dust, before the infinite, incomprehensible Majesty of Thy God.

An Act of Humility

AND who am I, who dare approach to receive the Immaculate Flesh of the adorable Incarnate Son of God? Who am I, in contrast with the splendor of Thy infinite sanctity, O my God? I am a vile atom, a despicable nonentity; this do I confess and declare, prostrate on the ground before Thee, O my God. I am a poor sinner, most unworthy to approach Thee, who art the Fountain of Sanctity. No, my Jesus, this heart is not worthy to receive Thee; this heart, which has been until now filled with earthly affections, guilty inclinations, evil passions, and hateful sins—this is not an abode suitable for Thee, the Holy of Holies! Thy infinite Majesty would be too far dishonored, O

Lord, by dwelling in so unclean a heart as mine. Seek elsewhere a clean heart, a pure heart, a loving heart, and Thou wilt find it in many holy persons, who have ever preserved unspotted the white robe of their innocence, or have wiped away every stain by tears of true repentance. I am filled with confusion at the sight of my unworthiness, and humbly confess that I am indeed utterly unworthy that thou shouldst debase Thy infinite Majesty so far as to come to visit me. I am not worthy that Thou shouldst even bestow a passing thought upon me, a wretched creature. And yet, O indescribable perfection of the love of Jesus! Thou dost invite me, urge me, to come to Thy Table, and even threaten me with Thy anger if I refuse to approach and receive Thee as my food. But knowest Thou, O my Jesus, knowest Thou how many times I have rebelled against Thee in the most shameful manner imaginable, and expelled Thee, my only true and legitimate Master, from my soul, to give place to my most cruel enemy and Thine—the devil and sin? And yet, after having been not once, but many times, thus unworthily treated by me, dost Thou forget, as it were, all my past rebellions, and thus lovingly return to take possession anew of my heart and bestow Thy whole self upon me? Ah, my sweet Jesus, what can I do in return for so much goodness? Can I refuse to reply to Thy call, drive Thee away from me, refuse to admit Thee into my poor heart? Far from it, O Lord. If I am not worthy to receive and love Thee, Thou art, nevertheless, worthy to be received and loved! I humbly beseech

Thee to vouchsafe to bestow upon my heart the dispositions with which it is Thy Will I should receive Thee. Cleanse my soul from all its stains in Thy Precious Blood, enrich it with Thy merits, adorn it with Thy virtues. O my Jesus, say but the word, and my soul will be sanctified, cleansed, purified, and less unworthy of Thee!

Motives for the Act of Contrition

Remember, O my soul, the ingratitude with which thou hast corresponded with the many graces and mercies shown thee by thy God. Remember how often thou hast trampled underfoot the precious Blood which Jesus shed for thee in His Passion, and has so frequently applied to thy soul by means of the holy Sacraments. Remember how often thou hast outraged thy God, who yet loved thee with all the tenderness of a Father. Oh, how bitterly shouldst thou bewail thy ingratitude and want of love! As often as thou hast committed sin, so often has thou crucified Jesus anew. Deplore thy impiety and weep for it at His feet.

Act of Contrition

O MY dear Jesus, by my sins I have mangled Thy sacred Flesh, nailed Thee to the Cross, wounded Thy side, and put Thee to a cruel death! I am not worthy to live, far less to receive Thee in this most Blessed Sacrament. I deserve the

heaviest punishments Thy wrath can inflict upon
me. But, O my Lord, how great is Thy goodness!
Ungrateful as I have been to Thee, grievously as I
have outraged Thee, Thou art yet ready to make
peace with me; and provided I repent of my sins,
Thou art willing to restore me to Thy grace, Thy
friendship, and Thy love. Oh, infinite goodness of
my God! I would willingly die of grief for having
offended so good a God, so loving a Father so merciful a Redeemer. I repent, O my Sovereign Good,
I repent of having displeased Thee; I detest all my
sins with all the powers of my soul above every
other evil, because they offend a God of infinite
goodness. I will rather die than ever more offend
Thee. O my Jesus, my Sovereign Lord, through
Thy precious Blood, through Thy Wounds, through
Thy Death, pardon my sins! Eternal Father, I do
not deserve pardon, after having committed such
grievous offenses against Thee; but Thy Jesus and
mine has merited it for me, and in His name do I
earnestly ask and firmly hope for it.

Motives for an Act of Desire

Behold, O my soul, the happy moment is
approaching in which thy sweet Jesus will come to
thee. Beholding the King of kings, the Lord of
lords, thy Father, thy Friend, and thy Spouse, thy
God Himself, about to enter thy heart. He comes,
His hands filled with the treasures of His grace
which He is desirous of showering upon thee.
Come, then, my soul, hasten to meet Him at least

by holy desires, and an earnest wish to be united to Him, and to feed upon His most sacred flesh. If thou couldst receive holy Communion but once in thy life how fervently wouldst thou not approach the sacred Table? And now that this God of infinite goodness is ever ready to enter thy heart, dost thou approach Him so coldly and carelessly? Dost thou approach to receive so great a God with so little desire? My soul, my soul, endeavor to awaken within thee an earnest desire to receive Jesus Christ. Sigh after this Sovereign Good, as the thirsty stag longs for the fountains of water. Call Him, invite Him, and desire His presence.

An Act of Desire

COME, O Divine Food, come, and nourish my soul! Come, Furnace of love, and inflame my heart. Come, O Heavenly Physician, and heal me. Come, O my Father, my Spouse, my Treasure, my Life, and my Sweet Consolation. Come, O Thou the sole Object of my desires, the sole End of all my wishes, my Jesus, hidden beneath the Sacramental veils. Come, for my soul desires and sighs after Thee, and is languishing to be united to Thee. Delay not, O my Jesus, but come to break asunder any worldly fetters which may still prevent my heart from giving itself to Thee without reserve. Dispose of me as Thou dost please, for from henceforward I am entirely Thine. Come, and with Thy nails fasten my heart to Thy Cross; with the lance wound it through and through with the most perfect charity; and with the thorns of Thy crown surround it as with an impregnable wall, that so it may withstand all the assaults of its enemies. Come, and be Thou all mine, as I desire to be all Thine. Come, and feed me with Thy immaculate Flesh, and thus destroy within me all craving for earthly goods. Come, and bestow upon me a share in that ardent charity which is an essential characteristic of Thy divine heart. Come, O Love of Loves, my beloved Jesus, come, and do not delay—*Veni Domine, noli tardare!*

An Act of Oblation

TO MAKE amends in some measure for my great unworthiness, I offer Thee, O my Jesus, the sanctity, love, and fervor with which those chosen souls who are the dearest to Thy Heart have ever received Thee, do receive Thee, or will receive Thee to the end of time.

I offer Thee all those perfect and fervent acts of love with which Mary, Thy most sweet and tender Mother, received Thee, not only at the moment of Thy Incarnation in her chaste womb, but also whenever she approached the sacred Table. I offer Thee her profound humility, her unspotted purity, her burning charity, and her most loving heart itself. I offer Thee that ineffable sanctity with which thou didst receive Thyself at the Last Supper; and, as a preparation for my Communion, I offer Thee all the sorrows, sufferings, and torments which Thou didst endure upon the Cross, and in virtue of which I hope that Thou wilt give me a share in those graces which Thou dost bestow upon those who worthily receive Thee.

I offer Thee this Communion by the hands of the Blessed Virgin, to honor, praise, and glorify the Holy Trinity by this action, which is the most sacred I can possibly perform. I offer it to Thee in memory of, and in thanksgiving for Thy most bitter Passion and Death for my salvation. I offer it to Thee in thanksgiving for all the benefits Thou hast prepared for me from all eternity, and bestowed upon me and upon all mankind. I offer it to Thee to obtain the grace of final perseverance, and the assistance needed for the salvation of my soul and the souls of all my relations, friends, benefactors, and enemies, and of all those who have recommended themselves to my prayers. I offer it to obtain the entire pardon of all my grievous offenses, and the conversion of poor sinners; and more especially do I offer it, O my sweet Jesus, for the conversion of my country to the True Faith and unity of the Holy Catholic Church. Finally, I offer it for the relief of the holy souls in Purgatory, especially those for whom I am more particularly bound to pray, for those who have been most devout to the Blessed Sacrament, to Thy sacred Passion, and to Thy blessed Mother, and, above all, for those who are especially dear to Thee, and whom Thou most particularly dost will should be helped.

(You may also offer your Communion for other ends, and particularly for the one to which you are specially directing your intention.)

Prayer to Our Blessed Lady

O MOST sweet Mother of God, and Immaculate Virgin Mary! I have ever besought thee to be my Protectress, and to assist me in all my necessities; I now beseech thee with the utmost fervor of my soul to conduct me thyself to the heavenly banquet. Do thou thyself present my Jesus to me, as thou didst present Him to the shepherds, to the wise men, and to holy Simeon. When I behold the hand of the priest about to place the adorable Host on my lips, I will imagine I behold thy Jesus and mine borne in thy arms. And if thou, O my dear Mother, will permit it, I will imagine that I receive Him from thy pure hands, that I may thus receive Him with greater reverence, greater devotion and greater fruit. Amen.

ADVICE FOR THE TIME OF COMMUNION, AND CONCERNING THANKSGIVING AFTER COMMUNION

Endeavor to spend the time intervening between the recital of the foregoing acts and the moment of Communion as piously as possible, exciting yourself more and more to feelings of faith and desire to receive your dear Lord in the Blessed Sacrament. Remain devoutly recollected, and remember that the benefit you derive from the reception of this most Blessed Sacrament will be proportioned to the piety of your preparation. Your immediate preparation for Communion should be made during the time of Mass. When the moment of Communion is arrived, and the priest says the *Domine non sum dignus* ["Lord, I am not worthy"], humbly bow down your head, modestly strike your breast, and renew your acts of contrition, humility and hope. Endeavor to excite yourself to feelings of holy joy and earnest desire to receive Jesus Christ the Bread of Angels. Go up to receive Communion with your whole soul inflamed with Divine love, with a modest and humble demeanor, your eyes cast down and your hands clasped; then modestly raise your head, open your mouth, and respect-fully advance your tongue, which is to be the first to touch the adorable Body of Jesus. Imagine that you receive the sacred Host from the hands of blessed Mary, or from those of Jesus Christ Him-self. Be careful not to fix your eyes on the face of the priest, or on any other object, or to recite vocal prayers at the moment of Communion, but let your heart alone pour itself forth in pious affections, unexpressed by the lips.

Remember that one single Communion well made would be sufficient to make you a saint, since you receive into your heart the Holy of Holies, or rather Holiness itself—Jesus Christ, who when on earth had but to touch a dead man on his way to the grave, and the dead man arose. A woman touched but the hem of His garment, and she was healed at the same moment. The virtue which then went forth from Jesus is by no means diminished now, neither is His power less, or His goodness exhausted. Besides, it is not merely the hem of the garment of Our Lord that you have the happiness to touch in the Holy Communion, but the very Body and Blood of Jesus Christ that you there receive and eat.

What wonders then should be worked, and what holy effects produced, in the man who has the happiness of communicating!

And yet very few miracles are worked nowadays by Our Lord in the Blessed Sacrament, and very few spiritual cures wrought in those who receive Him in the Holy Eucharist. Spiritual maladies are the same after Communion as before; the passions, defects, and weaknesses of the soul remain unaltered. The soul is as cold and languid after Communion as though it had not partaken of the heavenly banquet, and continues to be imperfect and indevout, nay, even perhaps more depraved, after innumerable Communions, than before. Such a reflection, which is unfortunately but too true, must terrify every man who has the slightest sense of religion; for, the case of that sick person on whom the strongest and most efficacious remedies have no effect is almost desperate.

But whence, then, can it be that the adorable Body and Blood of Jesus Christ in the Holy Eucharist bring no benefit, and are in fact almost entirely useless to so many Christians? Because they receive this Divine Sacrament without proper dispositions or preparation, and approach the sacred Table without devotion, with very little faith, with dissipated minds, through custom and, in short, as nothing more than a pious ceremony. Another reason is because they take but very little pains to thank their Divine Saviour when they have received Him, and do not profit by this most precious time to make known to Jesus all the wants of their soul, but immediately after communicating allow their minds to be distracted and drawn away to other objects. This is the opinion of St. Teresa.

Dear Christian, are you desirous that your Communions should sanctify you, and be sources of continual grace to your soul? If so, be not satisfied with making for each a preparation such as I have proposed to you above, but direct your utmost efforts to making truly devout and fervent thanksgiving to your Lord in the Blessed Sacrament, when you have received Him into your heart.

When you have received the sacred Host on your tongue, endeavor to swallow it as soon as possible, and then, with your eyes cast down, and your whole soul devoutly recollected, imagine that you are clasping the Child Jesus to your heart, or that you are kneeling at the feet of Jesus upon the Cross. Embrace Him closely and lovingly, and say to Him, with all the tenderness of your soul: *O my Jesus, I adore Thee, I love Thee, I thank Thee. I offer Thee my tongue, my mind, and my heart. I give Thee my memory, my understanding, my will, my thoughts, my affections, and my whole self. I beg Thee to accept this offering and this gift, and to give me grace to derive benefit from this Communion.*

After having made this or a similar prayer in your heart, retire on one side, in order to converse unrestrainedly with your sweet Jesus, and give free vent to your grateful affection for the God who is now present within you. Remember that it is a fault not to employ at least a quarter of an hour in returning thanks to Jesus Christ in the Blessed Sacrament, who remains corporeally present within you for that space of time, that is to say, until the sacramental species are entirely consumed. And if it is so highly recommendable for a person to be more than usually recollected during the whole of the day on which he receives Communion, how much more should he endeavor to employ the quarter of an hour immediately following Communion with the utmost piety and fervor! This is the time, says St. Teresa, in which you may think of all the affairs of your soul with God.

If you cannot otherwise employ half or a quarter of an hour with devotion and recollection of mind, you may slowly and attentively recite the following prayers, pondering deeply upon what you read, and making a slight pause whenever you feel yourself particularly moved to devotion and fervor.

DEVOUT ACTS TO BE MADE AFTER COMMUNION

An Act of Adoration

I ADORE Thee, O my God, my Creator, and my Redeemer, with the deepest respect and most profound reverence of which I am capable. Ah, if I could but adore, honor, and glorify Thee as Thou dost deserve! If I could only, even at the expense of my life, cause all creatures to know Thee and adore Thee!

I adore Thee, O most holy Soul of my Jesus, Who art here present. I beseech Thee to sanctify by Thy holy presence my soul, my memory, my understanding, and my will. I adore Thee, O most pure Body of my Lord; O most chaste Eyes of Jesus, sanctify my eyes; O most innocent Tongue of Jesus, purify my tongue; Immaculate Flesh of the Son of God, let Thy touch cleanse all my body. I adore Thee, O precious Blood, which was shed for my salvation. Wash me, impart fervor to my heart, and inebriate me with the love of Christ.

I adore Thee, O ineffable Divinity united to the Humanity of my Jesus, and since I am not capable of adoring Thee as Thou dost deserve, accept the adorations of all the Angels and Saints of Heaven. Accept the adorations of all the just souls who are at present, or will ever be on earth; but, above all, I beseech Thee to accept the adorations of blessed Mary, the Queen of Saints, and particularly those which she offered Thee every time she received Thee in Holy Communion. And to crown all these adorations, in which I here unite with all the powers of my poor soul, I offer to Thy infinite Majesty all those which the most holy Soul of Jesus has rendered and will continue to render to Thee for all eternity.

O my dear Lord, would that I could cause all my fellow creatures to receive Thee worthily every day, beneath the sacramental species, and every heart to be impressed, by virtue of this great Sacrament, with an everlasting remembrance of Thy Passion and Death. Do Thou, most loving Jesus, receive these very desires themselves as so many acts of profound adoration, which I intend to make continually, but especially during every moment of this happy day on which Thou hast vouchsafed to become the food of my soul.

An Act of Thanksgiving

MY GOD, how great is Thy condescension! Thy Sovereign Majesty to come in person to a vile worm of the earth, a wretched sinner! What gratitude do I not owe Thee, O my Jesus, for the infinitely precious gift Thou hast made me in bestowing Thyself upon me? Not satisfied with all the Blood thou hast shed for me, not satisfied with dying on a Cross for my salvation, Thou hast also concealed Thyself beneath the sacramental species for love of me, and hast come to dwell even in my poor heart. O ineffable goodness! O inconceivable love! O incomprehensible excess of charity in my Jesus! How can I ever return Thee sufficient thanks for so great, so loving a favor? I thank Thee with all the respect and reverential love of which my heart is capable for this greatest of all Thy gifts which Thou hast made me in giving me Thy whole self in this adorable Sacrament. And since I cannot by any possibility thank Thee as I ought, and as I should wish, for the immense favor of receiving Thee within me, I unite my thanksgivings with those which Thou, O my Jesus, didst render to thy Eternal Father, and with those offered Thee by Mary, Thy beloved Mother, who is also my Mother. I thank and bless Thee for the countless mercies which Thou hast bestowed upon my soul and body. I thank Thee for the love with which from all eternity Thou hast chosen me in preference to so many others who would have served Thee better than myself. I thank Thee for having created me for so noble a destiny as is that of loving Thee in this life, and enjoying Thee in the next. I thank Thee for having died on a Cross for my salvation, overwhelmed with sorrow and ignominy, and for having applied the fruit of Thy Passion to my soul by so many inspirations, by the frequent reception of the Sacraments, and by the inestimable gift of faith. I thank Thee for the patience with which Thou hast so long borne with my sins and ingratitude. I acknowledge my everlasting obligations to Thy Wounds and Blood, both for having so frequently received the pardon of my sins, and for having been delivered from the eternal fire of Hell. May the offering which I hereby make to

Thee, O my Jesus, of these great mercies which
Thou hast shown me, and of all Thy own infinite
perfections and Divine attributes, be accepted by
Thee as a thanksgiving proportioned to the greatness of Thy gifts. But I beseech Thee in particular
to accept the offering of Thy ardent charity, of
that charity which caused Thee to die for me, the
offering of Thy immaculate Flesh, agonizing
beneath a thousand torments for love of me in
Thy sacred Passion, and, finally, the offering of
that Precious Blood which Thou didst shed, even
to the last drop, for my redemption, and which
Thou hast vouchsafed this morning to give me to
drink, as a blessed pledge of a happy eternity
which I hope one day Thou wilt bestow upon me,
as the crowning piece of all Thy favors. Amen.

An Act of Petition

SINCE, O most loving Jesus, Thou hast been
pleased to enter my house and take up Thy
abode in my heart, can I doubt of Thy willingness
to grant me all the favors I ask of Thee? Can He
who has so freely given me Himself, refuse me His
gifts? It is impossible, dear Jesus, and therefore
do I feel firm confidence that I shall obtain everything from Thy goodness. I confess, O Lord, that I
deserve nothing; but the more unworthy I am of
Thy favors, so much the more wonderful will Thy
goodness appear in bestowing them on me.

I beg of Thee, then, O loving Redeemer of my
soul, to bestow upon me the full pardon and

remission of all my sins, which I most sincerely detest and abhor. And as regards the severe punishments I have deserved, I desire to gain all the indulgences that I can; and I beseech Thee in Thy infinite goodness to grant me grace to fulfill all the conditions attached to them. I implore and humbly beseech Thee, O most Precious Blood of my Jesus, which, in union with His Body, Soul and Divinity, I have this morning received, to cleanse my heart anew from every stain and defilement. O my Jesus, create in me a pure and clean heart, and bestow upon me a just and upright spirit! Fill my soul with all the gifts of the Holy Ghost, and adorn it with all virtues, but especially with humility, patience, meekness and a spirit of mortification. Detach my heart from all created objects, render it like unto Thine, and unite it forever to Thyself by the ties of perfect charity. Give me strength and courage to resist even unto death all temptations. I determine and promise to drive them away immediately and to avoid all occasions of sin, that so they may not come; but Thou knowest that I can do nothing of myself, therefore I implore Thy aid, and that the merits of Thy Blood may be applied to my soul.

I beseech Thee to impress upon my heart so strong a remembrance of Thy Passion and Death, and of the bitter sorrows of Mary, Thy dear Mother, who is my Mother also, that nothing may ever efface it, but that I may continually meditate upon it henceforward, that so, from this moment to the hour of my death, I may, as it were, live on

Calvary, at the foot of the Cross, in the company of our most holy Mother, the Queen of Sorrows.

I most humbly and most fervently implore Thee in Thy infinite mercy to deliver me once for all from the tyranny of my predominant passion, and of the sin into which I habitually fall. (*Here name what this passion, sin, or failing is.*)

I beg and beseech Thee also, my most sweet Jesus, to grant me such temporal blessings as Thou seest will be most conducive to Thy glory and the eternal salvation of my soul. I might very possibly ask for what would be less useful, or perhaps even hurtful to my soul: therefore I place myself absolutely in Thy hands, asking only for what Thou wilt; and I confide entirely in Thee, whose goodness equals Thy wisdom.

I humbly beseech Thee to add to all these favors the great and most precious gift of final perseverance, which will complete and crown all Thy other gifts.

O my Jesus, do thou ask it for me of Thy Eternal Father, show Him Thy Wounds, offer Thy precious Blood in my behalf, and then I am sure that my request will be heard, for Thou Thyself hast assured me that whatever I ask the Father in Thy name shall be given to me!

Lastly, I beseech Thee, O my Jesus, before Thou dost leave me, to give Thy blessing to my soul. I recommend it to Thee for the whole of my life and for the hour of my death. Every day, every hour, every instant brings me nearer to that most important moment. Defend me then from all temptations, give me grace to overcome them, and grant me the assistance of Thy dear Mother, the Blessed Virgin, who is my Mother also. And above all, permit not that in punishment of my sins, and in particular for my irreverence and indifference with regard to the blessed Sacrament, and for my careless, or perhaps, alas, even bad Communions, I should leave this world without having received the Last Sacraments in proper dispositions. Amen.

Here you may make to your Heavenly Guest any little prayer which your heart may dictate for your neighbor. Do not forget to pray for our holy Mother the Church, for the Pope, and for all superiors, whether spiritual or temporal. Beseech Our Lord to be mindful of the clergy, secular and regular, and to bestow upon them the true spirit of their holy vocation. Pray especially for your confessor. Pray for your relations, friends, and benefactors, and for the sick and agonizing, as also for all who are in tribulation and suffering. Pray for poor sinners, and beg of God, in His mercy, to convert and save them from Hell fire. Do not forget to pray for heretics and infidels, begging Our Lord to enlighten them and give them grace to embrace the True Faith; and pray particularly that your own country may be restored to the bosom of the True Church. "For the last fifty years," St. Paul of the Cross used to say, "I have prayed for the conversion of England, and I could not have helped doing so even had I wished, for the moment I began to pray, my thoughts would fly to that unhappy country. I also pray for it every morning when I say Mass." Imitate this blessed servant of God by praying for the same end every time you go to Communion.

An Act of Oblation

TOO great would be my ingratitude, O my Jesus, if when Thou hast given me Thy whole self in this Communion, I delayed for one moment giving myself entirely to Thee. I offer Thee, O my loving Jesus, and give Thee my entire liberty and my whole soul. I give Thee my understanding, in order that it may be sanctified by Thee, and may be employed day and night in the remembrance of Thy Passion and Death, and in the contemplation of Thy Divine perfections. I give Thee my memory, that I may ever remember the infinite mercies which Thou hast showered forth upon my poor soul. I give Thee my will, that by virtue of Thy holy love, it may be entirely transformed into Thine. I desire nothing but what Thou willest, and I reject all that displeases Thee. I give Thee my whole self to be sanctified, soul and body, and my intention in this offering is to make Thee an entire, irrevocable, eternal sacrifice of myself and of all that belongs to me.

I offer and consecrate to Thee this poor heart of mine, which earnestly desires to make amends for all the infidelity of my past life, by love proportioned to my sins. My sweet Jesus, detach my heart from all created objects, unite it perfectly to

Thine own, hide it in the precious Wound of Thy Side, and there impress upon it the memory of Thy painful Passion, and of the Dolors of Blessed Mary, Thy Mother, that so, by continual meditation upon such great mysteries, it may be consumed with a sorrow so deep as to make some amends for my sins, by loving contrition and earnest desire to correspond with Thine infinite charity.

I offer Thee all the senses of my body, particularly my eyes and tongue, and I beseech Thee not to permit that they should offend Thee any more. I offer Thee my thoughts, words, and works. I desire to offer all in union with the merits of Thy most holy Passion and Death, and in union with the merits of the Blessed Virgin, and of all the Saints of Heaven. I desire also to offer Thee all the good works that I have done or shall do during the whole course of my life, intending them all to be for Thy greater honor and glory, and of a preparation and thanksgiving for the most holy Sacrament. I offer Thee all the acts of adoration, love and thanksgiving, which Thou Thyself didst offer to Thy Eternal Father at the moment of the institution of the most holy Sacrament, as well as all those which Thou didst offer Him during the time of Thy abode upon earth, together with those offered by the Blessed Virgin, the holy Apostles, and all the Saints now in Heaven. May all these acts of thanksgiving supply for those which I cannot and know not how worthily to offer Thee, greatly as I desire it.

Praised and adored without ceasing be the most holy Sacrament of the Altar, and blessed forever be the pure and Immaculate Conception of the Blessed Virgin Mary. Amen.

INSTRUCTIONS FOR AFTER COMMUNION

1. Call to mind as frequently as possible during the day, that you have received Jesus, concealed beneath the sacramental veils, into the house of your soul. If all communicants would frequently call to mind during the course of the day of their Communion the following reflection—*"This morning Jesus Christ, the Son of God, vouchsafed to enter the house of my soul, and bestow His whole self upon me"*—what an infinitely greater degree of profit would be derived from Communion! What far greater patience in affliction, how far more anxiety to persevere in God's grace, and how incomparably more devotion would be seen in those who approach the heavenly banquet! If you are mindful of this practice, you will sanctify your own soul, and give good example to others, while at the same time the thought will be to you a continual incentive to lead a Christian life.

2. Often retire within yourself to renew your acts of adoration and thanksgiving to your dear Lord for the loving visit He has made you this morning, and endeavor to enkindle in your heart the flames of divine charity, by some fervent ejaculation to Jesus Christ. The warmth of devotion and of the love of God would not so soon die away in the soul were it more exercised, and Jesus would not have to complain of the coldness with which men love Him, did they think more frequently of the benefits He has bestowed on them, and of His love, displayed to an infinite degree in the most Blessed Sacrament, and they would thank Him with real heartfelt devotion.

3. Often renew the offering of your heart to Jesus in the most Blessed Sacrament. His design in bestowing His whole self upon you is to force you, as it were, to love Him, and give Him your whole heart, which He earnestly demands of you, in exchange for the infinite gift He has made you. Can you, then, be so ungrateful to Jesus, as on the very day when He comes to take possession of your heart, to refuse it to Him, in order to give it to the world and the devil! No! But as you have consecrated it to your sweet Lord in the Holy Communion, ratify and confirm your offering; and if the world, with its flatteries, vanities and false pleasures, seeks to re-enter your heart, protest and declare that you have bestowed it irrevocably upon Jesus. If the devil with his suggestions, or the flesh with its temptations, assail your heart with intent to regain possession of it, reply generously that you have given it to Jesus, and that to Jesus it shall belong forever. If all Christians acted thus after Communion, they would persevere in God's grace and not return to their sins.

4. Remember that your tongue was the first part of your body which had the happiness of receiving the Lord of Heaven and Earth, and of touching His most holy Body concealed beneath the appearance of the sacred bread. This thought, if duly reflected upon, will be sufficient to make you take the utmost care not to defile that tongue, which has been so honored and favored by Christ, with evil conversation or impure words. You should also call to mind this thought whenever you are tempted to address impatient, angry or offensive words to your neighbor, and I assure you that you will not then be likely to offend your Lord with the very tongue that has been sanctified by contact with His most sacred Flesh.

5. Make it a custom to visit the most holy Sacrament every day in some church; at least in the evening, in order to finish your day piously: and for that intention you must make a spiritual Communion, awakening within your soul an earnest desire of receiving your dear Lord in the Blessed Sacrament.

Jesus Christ remains in the holy Sacrament day and night, for love of us, earnestly desiring to communicate Himself to our souls, and shower forth His graces upon them; would it not then be a mark of the most fearful carelessness and ingratitude if Christians refused to visit, venerate, and adore Him at least once a day?

❧ EXERCISE 8 ❧

The Interior Life Rendered Easy to All Christians

THE Interior Life is a life of silence, recollection, prayer, detachment and separation from creatures, remembrance of the presence of God, and repose in God alone. Such was the life of Jesus Christ; such were the lives of the Saints; and such should be the life of every Christian. This life is a hidden source of sweetness, graces, virtues, and merits, and is a pledge of eternal bliss. It is unknown to the worldling, and despised by the carnal man; but he who is in possession of it knows its value and enjoys its sweetness with an eagerness that is never satiated.

Its Acts and Practices are:

1. To see God: that is to say, habitually to dwell and to perform all our actions in His presence.

2. To listen to God: that is, to be attentive to the interior motions of the grace which is drawing us ever nearer to God, and which sweetly speaks to our hearts, and to be faithful in following His divine inspirations.

3. To speak to God: that is, to converse habitually with Him, speaking to Him rather with the heart than with the lips, by frequent ejaculatory prayers, by pious reflections, and by the sweet repose of our heart upon His adorable Heart.

4. To do everything—prayer, work, study, recreation, etc.—by the impulse of the Spirit of God, solely to fulfill His holy Will, and for His greater honor and glory, without at all looking to ourselves, or acting with a desire of gratifying our own inclinations, or any other created being.

The Means of Attaining To the Interior Life

1. Great purity of conscience: that is, a great horror of every sin, imperfection, or infidelity; a great desire to preserve ourselves from every stain, and a great anxiety to purify ourselves from all defilement of sin.

2. Great purity of heart: that is, great detachment from all created objects, such as the riches, pleasures, and conveniences of life, relations and friends, reputation, the esteem of the world, spiritual consolations, health, and even life itself.

3. Great purity of spirit: that is, assiduous and

constant care to banish from the mind all useless thoughts and reflections concerning the past, present, or future, that so there may be nothing to prevent it from being sweetly occupied with God alone.

4. Great purity in our actions. We should take charge of such affairs only as our duty prescribes, repress all over-eager solicitude or over-anxious diligence, and perform every action quietly, peacefully and calmly, by the impulse of the Spirit of God, in His presence, and for His greater honor and glory. Before proceeding from one action to another, we should be most careful to pause and recollect ourselves for a moment, to renew our intention, and offer to God the action upon which we are about to enter.

5. A spirit of recollection and mortification: that is, we should separate ourselves as much as possible from creatures, in order to converse with God alone; we should not frequent places of profane and worldly amusements, nor enter into dissipated society and worldly assemblies; we should also keep a watch over our senses, and never allow ourselves one single useless look, or idle word, or the indulgence of vain curiosity.

6. Great modesty and simplicity in our dress, furniture, conversation, manners, carriage, and whole deportment.

7. Great bodily mortification. We should never allow ourselves any satisfaction which has not reference to some virtuous object; we should seek out and impose upon ourselves some penance in everything that we do, and mortify our senses in proportion to our fervor, with the approbation of our confessor.

8. Great care to regulate all our daily actions: the hour of rising, of going to bed, of working, of all other occupations, of prayer, of taking what food we may require, of our exercises of piety and charity, and, in short, of all our actions; we should punctually perform each at its own proper time, that so we may never act from mere natural impulse, but solely to obey the Will of God.

9. Great exactitude in the performance of all our exercises of piety, such as our prayer and meditation in the morning, our particular examination in the middle of the day upon some predominant fault, such as, for instance, dissipation of mind, or the too great liberty we have allowed our senses; or else upon some particular virtue, as, for instance, interior recollection, purity of intention, submission to the Divine Will, etc. We should be exact, towards evening, in saying the Rosary, reading some devout book, making our visit to the Blessed Sacrament, saying our prayers and making our meditation, reciting the *Angelus Domini* ["The Angelus"], and carefully saying grace before and after meals. We should also carefully avoid too great anxiety and dissipation of mind; we should beware of performing our actions from custom, and without reflection; and when we pray, we should not try to say many words, but to enter into the whole spirit of our prayer, and pause thoughtfully from time to time to listen in silence to the voice of God.

10. Great familiarity with God: doing everything in His presence, often speaking to Him in love and simplicity, telling Him of all that concerns us, and consulting Him with confidence in all that happens to us.

11. To neglect nothing that can serve to strengthen tender, affectionate piety in us, keep up devotion, and preserve a spirit of interior recollection; carefully to avoid all that can weaken devotion or cool our fervor, without however attaching ourselves too much to spiritual sweetnesses, and without making violent efforts to procure them.

12. Often to make our particular examination upon our own conduct, both interior and exterior. We should ever be upon our guard against our own heart and our own thoughts and affections, that they be not usurped by any creature, and we should keep a continual watch over our senses, thus more easily to remain habitually and modestly in God's holy presence.

13. Often to offer and consecrate our hearts to

God, renewing our sincere protestations that we will never more commit sin, nor do anything that can offend His supreme goodness.

14. To receive all from the loving hands of God, accepting everything that befalls us, whether agreeable or otherwise, willingly, and with humble resignation in the Divine Will.

EXERCISE 9

The Stations of the Cross, or The Way of the Cross

*Adapted for the Members of the
Confraternity of the Passion*

THE Devotion of the Way of the Cross, called also the Stations of the Cross, has been enriched by different Popes with all the indulgences which can be gained by personally visiting the holy places of Jerusalem.* These indulgences are applicable to the holy souls in Purgatory.

The conditions are: **1.** While visiting the *Via Crucis* (Way of the Cross), to meditate, as well as each one's capacity admits, upon the Passion of our Divine Redeemer; and **2.** To pass from one Station to another, so far as the number of people present will permit.

The Devotion may be practiced, either alone or publicly, wherever the Stations are duly erected.

When it is performed in public, as soon as the priest has recited the Act of Contrition, the people

---

*For current requirements for obtaining a plenary indulgence for making the Stations of the Cross, see p. 392. —*Publisher*, 2002.

should rise from their places, and coming up the middle of the church, follow him from one Station to another.

If the number present should happen to be too great to allow all to do this, those who cannot follow should rise after each Station, and turn round as well as they can towards the place at which the priest is. The form of the devotion here followed is taken principally from that of St. Leonard of Port-Maurice, as practiced in the Coliseum.

[Those who are "impeded" from making the Stations (for example, the sick) can gain the same indulgence if they spend at least one half an hour in pious reading and meditation on the Passion and Death of Our Lord Jesus Christ. (*Enchiridion of Indulgences*, 1969).]

Incline unto My Aid

V. *Deus in adjutorium meum intende.*

R. *Domine ad adjuvandum me festina.*

Gloria Patri, etc.

V. Incline unto my aid, O God.

R. O Lord, make haste to help me.

Glory be to the Father, etc.

Oremus

Actiones nostras quaesumus Domine, aspirando praeveni et adjuvando prosequere ut cuncta nostra oratio et operatio a te semper incipiat, et per te caepta finiatur, per Christum Dominum nostrum. Amen.

Let us pray.

Precede, we beseech Thee, O Lord, our actions with Thy holy inspirations, and carry them on with Thy gracious assistance, that all our prayers and works may begin from Thee, and by Thee be happily ended, through Christ Our Lord. Amen.

An Act of Contrition

To be said by the Priest, kneeling before the
High Altar, and repeated by all present.

O MY Jesus, most merciful Lord, because Thou art infinitely good and full of compassion, I love Thee above everything, and I grieve with all my heart for having offended Thee, the Supreme Good. I offer Thee this holy pilgrimage, in honor of that most sorrowful one which Thou didst perform for me, an unworthy sinner: and I make an intention of gaining the holy indulgences, in the hope of obtaining Thy mercy in this life and eternal glory in the next.

Here let each one make his intention for the application of the indulgences to be gained. The procession then moves to the first Station, singing as follows:

Stabat Mater dolorosa, *Juxta crucem lacrymosa,* *Dum pendebat Filius.*	At the Cross her station keeping, Stood the mournful Mother weeping, Close to Jesus to the last.

When many persons perform the Way of the Cross, one part may either sing or recite a verse of the Stabat Mater, *and the other repeat each time the following verse:*

Sancta Mater! istud agas, *Crucifixi fige plagas,* *Corde meo valide.*	Holy Mother! pierce me through: In my heart each wound renew, Of my Saviour crucified.

Station I

Jesus Is Condemned to Death

(All stand as the Station is announced.)

Genuflect while saying:

V. *Adoramus te, Christe, et benedicimus tibi;*
R. *Quia per sanctam crucem tuam redemisti mundum.*

We adore Thee, O Christ, and we bless Thee:
For, by Thy Holy Cross, Thou hast redeemed the world.

Stand as the priest reads:

Consider, O my soul, the wonderful submission of Jesus, our innocent Lord, in receiving so unjust a sentence; and remember that thy sins were the false witnesses, and thy blasphemies, backbitings, and evil-speaking the reason the impious judge pronounced it. Turn, therefore, to thy loving God, and say to Him with the heart rather than with only the lips:

Kneel:

AH, DEAR Jesus! How tender, beyond all utterance, is Thy love! For the sake of so unworthy a creature as I am, Thou hast suffered imprisonment, chains and scourges, and to crown all, hast been condemned to so shameful a death! Ah, surely this is enough to touch my heart, and make me detest all those sins of the tongue which have been the cause of it. Yes, I detest and bitterly repent of them; and all along this way of sorrows I will continue to lament and bewail them, while I repeat: My Jesus, mercy! My Jesus, mercy!

Pater noster . . .	Our Father* . . .
Ave Maria . . .	Hail Mary* . . .
Gloria Patri . . .	Glory be to the Father* . . .
V. Miserere nobis, Domine.	V. Lord, have mercy on us.
R. Miserere nobis.	R. Have mercy on us.

Cujus animam gementem,
Contristatem et dolentem,
Pertransivit gladius.

Through her heart, His sorrow sharing,
All His bitter anguish bearing,
Now at length the sword had passed.

---

*For *Our Father*, *Hail Mary* and *Glory Be*, see page 391.
—*Publisher*, 2002.

Station II

Jesus Is Laden with the Cross

(All stand as the Station is announced.)

Genuflect while saying:

V. *Adoramus te, Christe, et benedicimus tibi;*

R. *Quia per sanctam crucem tuam redemisti mundum.*

We adore Thee, O Christ, and we bless Thee:

For, by Thy Holy Cross, Thou hast redeemed the world.

Stand as the priest reads:

Consider how Jesus, our most gentle Lord, embraces the Cross, and see with what meekness He suffers the blows and insults of that vile rabble; whereas thou impatiently dost shrink from the slightest suffering! And yet dost thou not know, poor sinner, that without the Cross thou canst not enter Heaven? Weep for thy blindness, and turning to thy Lord, say to Him with sorrow of heart:

Kneel:

MY JESUS, this Cross should be mine, not Thine! Ah, most heavy Cross, prepared by my sins! O dear Saviour, give me fortitude to embrace all the crosses which my most grievous sins deserve! Grant that I may die embracing the holy Cross; and enable me to say again and again, with Thy beloved daughter St. Teresa, "To suffer or die! To suffer or die!"

Pater noster . . .	Our Father . . .
Ave Maria . . .	Hail Mary . . .
Gloria Patri . . .	Glory be to the Father . . .
V. Miserere nobis, Domine.	V. Lord, have mercy on us.
R. Miserere nobis.	R. Have mercy on us.

> *O quam tristis et afflicta*
> *Fuit illa benedicta*
> *Mater Unigeniti!*
>
> Oh, how sad and sore distressed
> Was that Mother, highly blest,
> Of the sole-begotten One!

Station III

Jesus Falls the First Time under the Weight of the Cross

(All stand as the Station is announced.)

Genuflect while saying:

V. *Adoramus te, Christe, et benedicimus tibi;*	We adore Thee, O Christ, and we bless Thee:
R. *Quia per sanctam crucem tuam redemisti mundum.*	For, by Thy Holy Cross, Thou hast redeemed the world.

Stand as the priest reads:

Consider how Jesus, our most afflicted Lord, weakened by the continual shedding of His Blood, fell the first time to the ground. Ah, see how those wretches overwhelm Him with blows, and kicks,

364

and stripes! And yet our most patient Lord opens not His lips, but suffers in silence, while thou in thy slightest troubles dost murmur and complain, or perhaps dost even rashly curse or blaspheme. Detest heartily this pride and rebellion, and say to thine afflicted Lord:

Kneel:

MOST beloved Redeemer, behold at Thy feet the greatest sinner in the world! Oh, how often have I fallen! How often have I plunged into an abyss of sin! Stretch out Thy sacred hand to raise me. Help me, O my Jesus, help me! Grant that during the remainder of my life I may never fall into mortal sin, so that when I come to die I may secure my eternal salvation.

Pater noster . . .	Our Father . . .
Ave Maria . . .	Hail Mary . . .
Gloria Patri . . .	Glory be to the Father . . .
V. Miserere nobis, Domine.	V. Lord, have mercy on us.
R. Miserere nobis..	R. Have mercy on us.

Quae moerebat et dolebat,
Pia mater dum videbat
Nati poenas incliti.

Christ above in torment hangs;
She beneath beholds the pangs
Of her dying, glorious Son.

Station IV

Jesus Meets His Most Holy Mother

(All stand as the Station is announced.)

Genuflect while saying:

V. *Adoramus te, Christe, et benedicimus tibi;*

We adore Thee, O Christ, and we bless Thee:

R. *Quia per sanctam crucem tuam redemisti mundum.*

For, by Thy Holy Cross, Thou hast redeemed the world.

Stand as the priest reads:

Alas, what sorrow pierced the Heart of Jesus! Alas, what anguish wounded the heart of Mary in this meeting! Mary, full of affliction, seems to say, "O ungrateful soul, what has my Jesus done to thee?" "What has my poor Mother done to thee?"

asks Jesus, in the midst of His sufferings. "Ah, forsake sin, which has caused our pain and sorrow!" What answer dost thou make, my soul? Oh, hardened though thou be, say thus to Him:

Kneel:

O DIVINE Son of Mary! O most holy Mother of my Jesus! Behold me at your feet, humbled and filled with compunction. I confess that I am the traitor who made by my sins that sword of sorrow which has pierced your most tender hearts. Ah, I sincerely repent of all my sins, and ask of you both mercy and pardon. Mercy, my Jesus, mercy! Ah, grant me such a measure of mercy that I may sin no more, but may meditate day and night on your pains and sorrows.

Pater noster . . .	Our Father . . .
Ave Maria . . .	Hail Mary . . .
Gloria Patri . . .	Glory be to the Father . . .
V. Miserere nobis, Domine.	V. Lord, have mercy on us.
R. Miserere nobis.	R. Have mercy on us.

Quis est homo qui non fleret,
Matrem Christi si videret,
In tanto supplicio?

Is there one who would not weep,
'Whelmed in miseries so deep,
Christ's dear Mother to behold?

Station V

Jesus Is Helped by the Cyrenean to Carry His Cross

(All stand as the Station is announced.)

Genuflect while saying:

V. *Adoramus te, Christe, et benedicimus tibi;*

R. *Quia per sanctam crucem tuam redemisti mundum.*

We adore Thee, O Christ, and we bless Thee:

For, by Thy Holy Cross, Thou hast redeemed the world.

Stand as the priest reads:

Consider that thou art the Cyrenean helping to carry the Cross of Christ against thy will, because thou art too much attached to the fleeting goods of this world. Rouse thyself once and for all, and

relieve thy God of so great a burden, accepting
with hearty good-will all the troubles which come
to thee from the hand of God, protesting thy willingness to receive them not only with patience,
but with lively gratitude.

Kneel:

O JESUS, my most beloved Lord! I thank Thee
for the many and favorable occasions which
Thou dost give me of suffering for Thee, and of
meriting for myself. Make me, I beseech Thee, O
my God, so to suffer patiently that which seems
evil in this life, that I may lay up a store of eternal goods in the next; and so to weep with Thee
here below, that I may be made worthy to reign
with Thee in Paradise.

Pater noster . . .	Our Father . . .
Ave Maria . . .	Hail Mary . . .
Gloria Patri . . .	Glory be to the Father . . .
V. Miserere nobis, Domine.	*V.* Lord, have mercy on us.
R. Miserere nobis.	*R.* Have mercy on us.

Quis non posset contristari,
Christi Matrem contemplari,
Dolentem cum Filio?

Can the human heart refrain
From partaking in her pain,
In that Mother's pain untold?

Station VI

Veronica Wipes the Face of Jesus

(All stand as the Station is announced.)

Genuflect while saying:

V. *Adoramus te, Christe, et benedicimus tibi;*

R. *Quia per sanctam crucem tuam redemisti mundum.*

We adore Thee, O Christ, and we bless Thee:

For, by Thy Holy Cross, Thou hast redeemed the world.

Stand as the priest reads:

Consider the likeness of Jesus, wan and suffering, imprinted on that cloth; and lovingly strive to form a lively representation of it in thy heart. Oh, happy wilt thou be, if thou dost live with Jesus engraven upon thy heart—and oh, blessed above measure, if with Jesus engraven upon thy heart thou dost die! Pray to thy Lord to be made worthy of so great a happiness.

Kneel:

O MY LORD, Who art so tormented, I beseech Thee, impress deeply on my heart the image of Thy most sacred countenance, that day and night I may think always of Thee, and with Thy most sorrowful Passion before my eyes, may ever bewail my most grievous sins. Ah, I protest that I desire to eat of this bread of sorrow until I come to die, and ever to detest my sins.

Pater noster . . .	Our Father . . .
Ave Maria . . .	Hail Mary . . .
Gloria Patri . . .	Glory be to the Father . . .
V. Miserere nobis, Domine.	V. Lord, have mercy on us.
R. Miserere nobis.	R. Have mercy on us.

Pro peccatis suae gentis,
Vidit Jesum in tormentis,
Et flagellis subditum.

Bruised, derided, cursed, defiled,
She beheld her tender Child
All with bloody scourges rent.

Station VII

Jesus Falls beneath His Cross the Second Time

(All stand as the Station is announced.)

Genuflect while saying:

V. *Adoramus te, Christe, et benedicimus tibi;*	We adore Thee, O Christ, and we bless Thee:
R. *Quia per sanctam crucem tuam redemisti mundum.*	For, by Thy Holy Cross, Thou hast redeemed the world.

Stand as the priest reads:

Consider thy Lord stretched on the earth, weighed down by His sorrows, trampled underfoot by His enemies, derided by the mulitude; and reflect that it was thy pride which made Him fall,

372

thy self-conceit which thus prostrated Him. Ah, for once bow down thy head, and with bitter contrition for thy past sins, resolve for the future to humble thyself beneath the feet of all, and say to thy sorrowful Lord:

Kneel:

O MY MOST Holy Redeemer, although I see Thee fallen, I acknowledge Thee at the same time to be the Almighty God, and beseech Thee to bring down all my proud thoughts, my ambition and self-esteem, that I may ever humbly and thus willingly embrace abjection and contempt, and thus by that deep and heartfelt humility which is so pleasing to Thee, raise Thee up from this sorrowful fall.

Pater noster . . .	Our Father . . .
Ave Maria . . .	Hail Mary . . .
Gloria Patri . . .	Glory be to the Father . . .
V. Miserere nobis, Domine.	V. Lord, have mercy on us.
R. Miserere nobis.	R. Have mercy on us.

Vidit suum dulcem natum
Moriendo desolatum,
Dum emisit spiritum.

For the sins of His own nation,
Saw Him hang in desolation,
Till His Spirit forth He sent.

Station VIII

Jesus Consoles the Women of Jerusalem

(All stand as the Station is announced.)

Genuflect while saying:

V. *Adoramus te, Christe, et benedicimus tibi;*	We adore Thee, O Christ, and we bless Thee:
R. *Quia per sanctam crucem tuam redemisti mundum.*	For, by Thy Holy Cross, Thou hast redeemed the world.

Stand as the priest reads:

Consider that thou hast a double cause to weep: both for Jesus who suffers so much for thee, and for thyself, who art so ungrateful that thou canst find no pleasure to thy liking without at the same time offending Him. Canst thou, at the sight of such sufferings, still remain unmoved? Ah, now that thou dost see what compassion Jesus shows for these poor women, take courage, and with sorrow and contrition say to Him:

Kneel:

O MY DEAREST Saviour, why is my heart not all steeped in tears of true repentance! I ask tears of Thee, my Jesus—tears of sorrow and compassion—that with tears in my eyes, and sorrow in my heart, I may deserve to obtain that pity which Thou didst show to those poor women. Ah, grant me this, my only consolation, that after being regarded by Thee with eyes of pity in this life, I may behold Thee in peace at the moment of my death.

Pater noster . . .	Our Father . . .
Ave Maria . . .	Hail Mary . . .
Gloria Patri . . .	Glory be to the Father . . .
V. Miserere nobis, Domine.	V. Lord, have mercy on us.
R. Miserere nobis.	R. Have mercy on us.

Eia Mater, fons amoris,
Me sentire vim doloris,
Fac ut tecum lugeam.

O thou Mother, fount of love!
Touch my spirit from above,
Make my heart with thine accord.

Station IX

Jesus Falls Beneath His Cross the Third Time

(All stand as the Station is announced.)

Genuflect while saying:

V. *Adoramus te, Christe, et benedicimus tibi;*

R. *Quia per sanctam crucem tuam redemisti mundum.*

We adore Thee, O Christ, and we bless Thee:

For, by Thy Holy Cross, Thou hast redeemed the world.

Stand as the priest reads:

Alas, how painful was this fall of Jesus! Behold, with what fury the most gentle Lamb is torn to pieces by raging wolves! See how they bruise and strike Him, and drag Him in the mire! Ah, accursed sin, which thus maltreated the Son of God! Surely the sight of a God thus oppressed, a God thus trampled underfoot, deserves thy tears. Oh, turn to Him in sorrow of heart, and say:

Kneel:

O MY GOD! Thou Who art Almighty, Thou Who with Thy finger alone dost sustain Heaven and earth; who is it that has made Thee fall thus miserably to the ground? Alas, it is I, by my sins and repeated relapses; and I have added torments to torments, by accumulating sin upon sin. But behold me now, contrite at Thy feet, most fully resolved never more to offend Thee. With tears and sighs I will repeat a hundred and a thousand times: Never more will I sin, O my God! Never, never more.

Pater noster . . .	Our Father . . .
Ave Maria . . .	Hail Mary . . .
Gloria Patri . . .	Glory be to the Father . . .
V. Miserere nobis, Domine.	V. Lord, have mercy on us.
R. Miserere nobis.	R. Have mercy on us.

Fac ut ardeat cor meum,
Fac amando Christum Deum,
Ut sibi complaceam.

Make me feel as thou hast felt,
Make my soul to glow and melt,
With the love of Christ my Lord.

Station X

Jesus Is Stripped of His Garments, And Is Given Gall to Drink

(All stand as the Station is announced.)

Genuflect while saying:

V. *Adoramus te, Christe, et benedicimus tibi;*	We adore Thee, O Christ, and we bless Thee:
R. *Quia per sanctam crucem tuam redemisti mundum.*	For, by Thy Holy Cross, Thou hast redeemed the world.

Stand as the priest reads:

Consider, O my soul, how Jesus, covered with bruises and wounds outwardly, was now inwardly tormented with a most loathsome draught of gall. See how, by His nakedness, He atones for thy want of modesty and thy vanity in dress; and by the bitterness which He tastes, for thy excesses in eating and drinking! Wilt thou not, then, be moved to pity? Oh, cast thyself at the feet of Jesus, and say to Him:

Kneel:

O MY MOST afflicted Lord, what a horrible contrast is this! Thou all blood, all wounds, all bitterness, and I all comfort, enjoyment, and sweetness. Ah, no, this is not as it should be! I beseech Thee, dearest Lord, make me change my life; and let the sweetness of this world become bitter to me, so that henceforth I may have no relish but for the sweet bitterness of Thy most holy Passion, and so may in the end enjoy with Thee the delights of Paradise.

Pater noster . . .	Our Father . . .
Ave Maria . . .	Hail Mary . . .
Gloria Patri . . .	Glory be to the Father . . .
V. Miserere nobis, Domine.	V. Lord, have mercy on us.
R. Miserere nobis.	R. Have mercy on us.

Sancta Mater! istud agas
Crucifixi fige plagas
Corde meo valide.

Holy Mother! pierce me through,
In my heart each wound renew
Of my Saviour crucified.

Station XI

Jesus Is Nailed to the Cross

(All stand as the Station is announced.)

Genuflect while saying:

V. *Adoramus te, Christe, et benedicimus tibi;*	We adore Thee, O Christ, and we bless Thee:
R. *Quia per sanctam crucem tuam redemisti mundum.*	For, by Thy Holy Cross, Thou hast redeemed the world.

Stand as the priest reads:

Consider the exceeding pain which Jesus, our good Lord, suffered when He felt the nails pierce and tear His veins, bones, nerves and flesh with unspeakable anguish. Art thou not melted into tenderness at the sight of so much pain, and the

380

recollection of thy many sins? Ah, give vent to thy sorrow, and say:

Kneel:

O JESUS, my most merciful Lord, crucified for my sake, subdue, utterly subdue, my hard heart with Thy holy fear and love; and since my sins were the cruel nails which pierced Thee, grant that now my sorrow may pierce and nail to the Cross all my ill-regulated passions; that so it may be my happy lot to live and die crucified with Thee on earth, that I may come to reign gloriously with Thee in Heaven.

Pater noster . . .	Our Father . . .
Ave Maria . . .	Hail Mary . . .
Gloria Patri . . .	Glory be to the Father . . .
V. Miserere nobis, Domine.	V. Lord, have mercy on us.
R. Miserere nobis.	R. Have mercy on us.

> *Tui nati vulnerati,*
> *Tam dignati pro me pati,*
> *Poenas mecum divide.*
>
> Let me share with thee His pain,
> Who for all my sins was slain,
> Who for me in torments died.

Station XII

Jesus Is Raised on the Cross, And Dies upon It

(All stand as the Station is announced.)

Genuflect while saying:

V. *Adoramus te, Christe, et benedicimus tibi;*

R. *Quia per sanctam crucem tuam redemisti mundum.*

We adore Thee, O Christ, and we bless Thee:

For, by Thy Holy Cross, Thou hast redeemed the world.

Stand as the priest reads:

Raise thine eyes and see Jesus, thy most dear Lord, hanging on the Cross fastened by three nails! Gaze on that divine face of Jesus dying! Mark how He prays for those who offend Him, gives Paradise

382

to him who asks it, leaves His Mother to the care of John, recommends His soul to His Heavenly Father, and, at length, bowing His head, dies.

Jesus then is dead—dead on the Cross for thee! And what art thou doing? Ah! Take care not to go hence without expressing thy sorrow and compunction; embrace the Cross of Jesus, and say to Him:

Kneel:

MY DEAREST Redeemer, I know and confess that my most grievous sins have been the merciless executioners who have taken away Thy life. I do not deserve to be pardoned, for I am the traitor who has crucified Thee! But oh, what consolation for me to hear Thee praying for those who crucified Thee! What shall I do for Thee, Who hast done so much for me? My Lord, I am ready and willing to pardon everyone who has offended me. Yes, my God, for love of Thee I pardon all, I wish well to all; and so I hope to hear Thee say to me, in my last moments: *"Hodie mecum eris in Paradiso"*—"Today shalt thou be with Me in Paradise."

Pater noster . . .	Our Father . . .
Ave Maria . . .	Hail Mary . . .
Gloria Patri . . .	Glory be to the Father . . .
V. Miserere nobis, Domine.	V. Lord, have mercy on us.
R. Miserere nobis.	R. Have mercy on us.
Fac me tecum pie flere,	Let me mingle tears with thee,
Crucifixo condolere,	Mourning Him who mourned for me,
Donec ego vixero.	All the days that I may live.

Station XIII

Jesus Is Taken down from the Cross

(All stand as the Station is announced.)

Genuflect while saying:

V. *Adoramus te, Christe, et benedicimus tibi;*

R. *Quia per sanctam crucem tuam redemisti mundum.*

We adore Thee, O Christ, and we bless Thee:

For, by Thy Holy Cross, Thou hast redeemed the world.

Stand as the priest reads:

Consider what a sword of sorrow pierced the heart of our disconsolate Lady, when she received her dead Son into her arms! Alas, at the sight of His wounds all the anguish of her most tender heart was renewed; but the sharpest sword which pierced her heart was sin—sin which deprived of life her dearest Son. Weep, then, for accursed sin; and mingling thy tears with those of the afflicted Virgin, say to her:

Kneel:

O QUEEN of Martyrs, when shall I be worthy to understand and sympathize with thy sorrows, by having them ever present in my heart? Ah, mighty Lady, grant that I may weep night and day for my sins, which have caused thee so much suffering; that so, weeping, loving, and hoping, I may die of pure sorrow for thy sake, to live forever with thee.

Pater noster . . .	Our Father . . .
Ave Maria . . .	Hail Mary . . .
Gloria Patri . . .	Glory be to the Father . . .
V. Miserere nobis, Domine.	V. Lord, have mercy on us.
R. Miserere nobis.	R. Have mercy on us.

Juxta crucem tecum stare,
Et me tibi sociare,
In planctu desidero.

By the Cross with thee to stay,
There with thee to weep and pray,
Is all I ask of thee to give.

Station XIV

Jesus Is Placed in the Holy Sepulchre

(All stand as the Station is announced.)

Genuflect while saying:

V. *Adoramus te, Christe, et benedicimus tibi;*

R. *Quia per sanctam crucem tuam redemisti mundum.*

We adore Thee, O Christ, and we bless Thee:

For, by Thy Holy Cross, Thou hast redeemed the world.

Stand as the priest reads:

Consider how great were the lamentations of John, Mary Magdalen, the other Marys and all the immediate followers of Christ, when He was enclosed in this Holy Sepulchre. But more than all, consider the desolation of Mary's afflicted heart, when she was parted altogether from her most loving Son. At the sight of their tears, conceive a just shame that thou hast shown so little sorrow and compassion in the course of this holy pilgrimage. Now at least rouse thyself; kiss the stone of the sacred tomb; try hard to leave thy heart within it; and with bitter sorrow pray thus to thy dead Lord:

Kneel:

O JESUS, my most compassionate Lord, Who, solely for love of me, hast chosen to accomplish this sorrowful journey, I adore Thee dead and enclosed in the Holy Sepulchre. I desire now to enclose Thee within my poor heart, that united to Thee, I may rise, after this holy exercise, to a new life; and by the gift of final perseverance, happily die in Thy grace. Oh, grant me, by the merits of Thy most holy Passion on which I have been meditating, that my last food at that last hour may be the most Divine Sacrament, my last words *Jesus* and *Mary*, and that my last sigh may be united with that with which Thou didst expire upon the Cross for me; that thus, with lively faith, firm hope, and burning love, I may die with Thee and for Thee, and come to reign with Thee forever and ever! Amen.

Pater noster . . .	Our Father . . .
Ave Maria . . .	Hail Mary . . .
Gloria Patri . . .	Glory be to the Father . . .
V. Miserere nobis, Domine.	V. Lord, have mercy on us.
R. Miserere nobis.	R. Have mercy on us.

Virgo virginum praeclara,
Mihi jam non sis amara,
Fac me tecum plangere.

Virgin of all virgins best!
Listen to my fond bequest,
Let me share thy grief
    divine.

Fac ut portem Christi
    mortem,
Passionis fac consortem,
Et plagas recolere.

Let me, to my latest breath,
In my body bear the death
Of that dying Son of thine.

Fac me plagis vulnerari,
Fac me cruce inebriari,
Et cruore Filii.

Wounded with His every
    wound,
Steep my soul till it hath
    swoon'd
In His very Blood away.

Flamis ne urar succensus,
Per te, Virgo, sim defensus,
In die judicii.

Be to me, O Virgin, nigh,
Lest in flames I burn and
    die,
In His awful judgment day.

Christe, cum sit hinc exire,
Da per Matrem me venire
Ad palmam victoriae.

Christ, when Thou shalt
    call me hence,
Be Thy Mother my defense,
Be Thy Cross my victory.

Quando corpus morietur,
Fac ut animae donetur
Paradisi gloria. Amen.

While my body here decays,
May my soul Thy
    goodness praise,
Safe in Paradise with Thee.
Amen.

Our Father, Hail Mary, *and* Glory Be, *according to the*
intentions of His Holiness.

V. *Christus factus est*
    obediens usque ad
    mortem.
R. *Mortem autem crucis.*

V. Christ was made for us
    obedient unto death.
R. Even to the death of the
    Cross.

Oremus.

Respice, quaesumus, Domine, super hanc familiam tuam, pro qua Dominus noster Jesus Christus non dubitavit manibus tradi nocentium et crucis subire tormentum. Qui vivis et regnas in saecula saeculorum. Amen.

Let us pray.

Look down, O Lord, we beseech Thee, upon this Thy family, for which our Lord Jesus Christ vouchsafed to be delivered into the hands of wicked men, and to suffer the torments of the Cross. Who livest and reignest forever and ever. Amen.

Oremus.

Deus in cujus passione, secundum Simeonis prophetiam, dulcissimam animam gloriosae Virginis et Matris Mariae doloris gladius pertransivit, concede propitius, ut qui transfixionem ejus et passionem venerando recolimus, gloriosis meritis et precibus omnium sanctorum, cruci fideliter adstantium, intercedentibus, passionis tuae affectum felicem consequamur. Qui vivis, et regnas per omnia saecula saeculorum. Amen.

Let us pray.

O God, at Whose death and Passion, according to the prophecy of Simeon, a sword of sorrow did pierce through the soul of Thy ever glorious and Virgin Mother Mary, mercifully grant that we, who devoutly celebrate her sorrows and sufferings, may, by the merits and prayers of all the Saints who stood faithfully beneath Thy Cross, obtain the blessed fruit of Thy Passion. Who lives and reigns, world without end. Amen.

A Visit to Our Lady of Sorrows

To be made before her altar or image, immediately after performing the Stations, or at any other time.

O MOST holy Mother, Queen of Sorrows, who didst follow thy beloved Son through all the Way of the Cross, and whose heart was pierced with a fresh sword of grief at all the Stations of that most sorrowful journey; obtain for us, we beseech thee, O most loving Mother, a perpetual remembrance of our blessed Saviour's Cross and death, and a true and tender devotion to all the mysteries of His most holy Passion; obtain for us the grace to hate sin, even as He hated it in the Agony in the Garden; to endure wrong and insult with all patience, as He endured them in the judgment hall; to be meek and humble in all our trials, as He was before His judges; to love our enemies even as He loved His murderers, and prayed for them upon the Cross; and to glorify God and do good to our neighbors, even as He did in every mystery of His sufferings. O Queen of Martyrs, who, by the dolors of thine Immaculate heart on Calvary, didst merit to share the Passion of our most dear Redeemer, obtain for us some portion of thy compassion, that, for the love of Jesus Crucified, we may be crucified to the world in this life; and in the life to come may, by His infinite merits and thy powerful intercession, reign with Him in glory everlasting. Amen.

Our Father

OUR FATHER, Who art in Heaven, hallowed be Thy Name. Thy kingdom come. Thy will be done on earth as it is in Heaven. Give us this day our daily bread, and forgive us our trespasses, as we forgive those who trespass against us. And lead us not into temptation, but deliver us from evil. Amen.

Hail Mary

HAIL MARY, full of grace, Lord is with thee; blessed art thou among women, and blessed is the fruit of thy womb, Jesus. Holy Mary, Mother of God, pray for us sinners, now and at the hour of our death. Amen.

Glory Be

GLORY BE to the Father, and to the Son, and to the Holy Spirit, as it was in the beginning, is now, and ever shall be, world without end. Amen.

Four Ways to Gain
A Plenary Indulgence*

A Catholic, being in the state of grace, can gain a *Plenary Indulgence* by many different prayers

---

*Added by the Publisher, 2002. Text from card entitled *How to Gain a Plenary Indulgence*, TAN, Imprimatur ✠ Most Rev. Thomas G. Doran, Bishop of Rockford, 1998.

and works of piety, but these four are worthy of special mention:

1. Making a visit to the Blessed Sacrament to adore It for at least one half hour.

2. Spending at least one half hour reading Sacred Scripture, as spiritual reading, with the veneration due to the Word of God.

3. Making the Way of the Cross. This includes walking from Station to Station. (At publicly held Stations, if this cannot be done in an orderly way, at least the leader must move from Station to Station.) No specific prayers are required, but devout meditation on the Passion and Death of Our Lord is required (not necessarily on the individual Stations).

4. Recitation of the Rosary (of at least 5 decades), with devout meditation on the Mysteries, in addition to the vocal recitation. It must be said in a church, family group, religious community or pious association.

Additional Requirements

In addition to performing the specified work, these three conditions are required:

1. Confession;
2. Holy Communion;
3. Prayer for the Holy Father's intentions. (One *Our Father* and one *Hail Mary* suffice.)

The three conditions may be fulfilled several days before or after the performance of the prescribed work; it is fitting, however, that Communion be received and the prayer for the intention of the Holy Father be recited on the same day the work is performed.

In addition, to gain a Plenary Indulgence, a person's mind and heart must be free from all attachment to sin, even venial sin.

If one tries to gain a Plenary Indulgence, but fails to fulfill all the requirements, the indulgence will be only partial. Only one Plenary Indulgence may be gained per day, except that, at "the moment of death," a person may gain a second Plenary Indulgence for *that* day.

What Is an Indulgence?

An Indulgence is the remission before God of the temporal punishment due to be suffered for sins that have already been forgiven. In granting Indulgences, the Church, as minister of the Redemption, authoritatively dispenses and applies the treasury of the satisfaction won by Christ and the Saints. The temporal punishment due for forgiven sins must be suffered either on earth or in Purgatory. A *Partial Indulgence* remits part of the temporal punishment due; a *Plenary Indulgence* remits all the temporal punishment due. Indulgences can always be offered for the Poor Souls in Purgatory, rather than for ourselves. If we generously offer indulgences for the Holy Souls in Purgatory, we may hope to obtain relief or release for many of them, in accord with God's holy Will. In gratitude, they may well obtain for us many great favors.

If you have enjoyed this book, consider making your next selection from among the following . . .